International Relations Theory for Twenty-First Century

International Relations (IR) theory has been the site of intense debate in recent years. A decade ago it was still possible to divide the field between three main perspectives – Realism, Liberalism and Marxism. Not only have these approaches evolved in new directions, they have been joined by a number of new 'isms' vying for attention, including feminism and constructivism.

International Relations Theory for the Twenty-First Century is the first comprehensive book to provide an overview of all the most important theories within international relations. Written by an international team of experts in the field, the book covers both traditional approaches, such as realism and liberal internationalism, as well as new developments such as constructivism, poststructuralism and postcolonialism.

The book's comprehensive coverage of IR theory makes it the ideal text for teachers and students who want an up-to-date survey of the rich variety of theoretical work and for readers with no prior exposure to the subject.

Martin Griffiths is Associate Professor in International Relations in the Department of International Business and Asian Studies at Griffith University, Brisbane.

International Relations Theory for the Twenty-First Century

An introduction

Edited by
Martin Griffiths

Routledge
Taylor & Francis Group

LONDON AND NEW YORK

First published 2007
by Routledge
2 Park Square, Milton Park, Abingdon, Oxon OX14 4RN

Simultaneously published in the USA and Canada
by Routledge
270 Madison Avenue, New York, NY 10016

Routledge is an imprint of the Taylor & Francis Group, an informa business

Typeset in Times New Roman by
Integra Software Services Pvt. Ltd, Pondicherry, India
Printed and bound in Great Britain by
TJ International Ltd, Padstow, Cornwall

British Library Cataloguing in Publication Data
A catalogue record for this book is available from the British Library

Library of Congress Cataloging in Publication Data
International relations theory for the twenty-first century : an introduction / edited
by Martin Griffiths.
   p.   cm.
Includes bibliographical references and index.
1. International relations—Philosophy.   I. Griffiths, Martin, 1961–
JZ1305.I5658 2007
327.101—dc22
2007011599

ISBN 10: 0–415–38075–8 (hbk)
ISBN 10: 0–415–38076–6 (pbk)
ISBN 10: 0–203–93903–4 (ebk)

ISBN 13: 978–0–415–38075–1 (hbk)
ISBN 13: 978–0–415–38076–8 (pbk)
ISBN 13: 978–0–203–93903–1 (ebk)

Contents

vi *Contents*

List of contributors

Rita Abrahamsen is Reader in the Department of International Politics, University of Wales, Aberystwyth.

Alex J. Bellamy is Professor in the School of Political Science and International Studies, University of Queensland.

Tom Conley is Senior Lecturer in the School of International Business and Asian Studies, Griffith University.

Jenny Edkins is Professor in the Department of International Politics, University of Wales, Aberystwyth.

Colin Elman is Associate Professor in the Department of Political Science, Arizona State University.

Cynthia Enloe is Research Professor of International Development and Women's Studies, Clark University.

Martin Griffiths is Associate Professor in the Department of International Business and Asian Studies, Griffith University.

Anthony J. Langlois is Senior Lecturer in the School of Political and International Studies, Flinders University.

Andrew Linklater is Woodrow Wilson Professor in the Department of International Politics, University of Wales, Aberystwyth.

John MacMillan is Senior Lecturer in the Department of Politics and History, Brunel University.

Andrew Bradley Phillips is Lecturer in the School of Political Science and International Studies, University of Queensland.

Heather Rae is Fellow in the Department of International Relations at the Australian National University.

Mark Rupert is Professor of Political Science in the Maxwell School of Citizenship and Public Affairs, Syracuse University.

Preface

This book has been three years in the making. A number of chapters began life as shorter entries in the *Routledge Encyclopedia of International Relations and Global Politics* (2005). As the editor of that volume, it struck me that they merited a wider audience. The *Encyclopedia* weighed in at nearly one thousand pages. This book is much more focused. It is written for students who have no prior experience with the broad subject of International Relations (IR) theory, and who may even be daunted by the word 'theory'. To be sure, the word is used in a bewildering variety of ways in the study of IR. It is applied to propositions and arguments at varying levels of abstraction, and debates over its most appropriate meaning have proceeded apace with little consensus achieved. If there is no agreement on how best to understand this term, let alone how best to engage in developing and criticizing the existing stock of IR theory, there is much greater consensus over the ways in which the term is used. Three in particular stand out.

First, for most scholars a theory is simply an explanation of an event or pattern of behavior in the 'real' world. This is otherwise known as *empirical* theory. A theory explains such patterns by elaborating on why they take place. In one (in)famous expression, a theory explains laws of behavior. According to this conception, theories are useful instruments. If we know why and how events relate to each other, we may then be able to intervene and perhaps change reality to suit our purposes. This conception of empirical theory rests on two important assumptions. First, there is a categorical distinction between theory and practice. The world consists of an apparently random collection of facts that need to be described and studied to discern how they are related. Theory and practice are linked by empirical propositions that summarize the degree to which certain facts are connected to other facts. Only when we have a large body of such propositions can we engage in the hard work of attempting to explain them. Second, theories are never true or false in any absolute sense. Whilst theories must always be tested against the evidence, they can only be replaced by better theories that are either more coherent or comprehensive in the scope of their explanatory power than their rivals. The sheer variety of empirical theory in the study of IR is very wide indeed. It is common to distinguish between *middle-range* theory and *grand* theory. For example, there is a big difference between a theory that tries to explain single events like the US invasion of Iraq in 2003, a theory that tries to account for the variation of patterns of war and peace among the great powers over the last two hundred years and a theory that attempts to explain why war itself takes place.

Second, it is common to come across the phrase *normative* theory. Unlike empirical theory, normative theory is concerned to elaborate the ethical standards used to judge international conduct. Today, there exists a large body of normative theory concerned with the use of force (just war theory) and distributive justice in IR. When is it right or appropriate to use military force? Is the present distribution of global wealth and income fair? These are the kinds of questions that normative theory seeks to answer.

Third, the term is sometimes used in a constitutive sense. Unlike empirical or normative theory, this use of the term is perhaps best expressed through other concepts such as *perspective*, *worldview* or *framework of analysis*. This book is primarily concerned with IR theory in this third sense. As I argue in the first chapter of the book, worldviews are fundamental lenses through which we interpret the main patterns of 'reality' that we then seek to explain, justify or criticize in a more formal sense via empirical and normative theories. The book then elaborates nine such worldviews or perspectives. The final three chapters are theoretically focussed analyses of particular issue-areas in contemporary IR, which assess the role of worldviews in shedding light on the process of state-making, the dynamics of globalization and the world economy, and in facilitating or impeding some of the key normative challenges of the twenty-first century. Each chapter concludes with a short section on further reading for those readers who wish to continue the journey.

Acknowledgments

An edited book always involves a number of debts. First, the book could not have been completed without the cooperation (and patience) of the contributors. To them I owe my greatest thanks. I am indebted also to Craig Fowlie at Routledge for his continuing support and patience as deadlines passed. A special mention is due to Robyn White and Natalie Pears for their invaluable assistance in preparing the manuscript. Finally, to Kylie and Jade; your love makes it all possible, always.

1 Worldviews and IR theory: Conquest or coexistence?

Martin Griffiths

Introduction

This book is an introduction to the diverse worldviews that underpin contemporary International Relations (IR) theory. In this chapter, I explore both the reasons for such diversity and two responses to it. The first response, conquest, opposes diversity and seeks to privilege one particular worldview. The second response, coexistence, is one that finds no good reason to privilege a particular worldview, and attributes a positive value to diversity and pluralism. The chapter proceeds as follows. First, I distinguish between two dimensions of a worldview and between worldviews and theories. Second, I provide a brief historical overview to account for the proliferation of worldviews in the field and the lack of consensus regarding the appropriate criteria for comparing and evaluating the merits of competing worldviews. Finally, I set out the main arguments associated with conquest and coexistence between competing worldviews.

Worldviews and theories in IR

A worldview is a broad interpretation of the world and an application of this view to the way in which we judge and evaluate activities and structures that shape the world. 'In simpler terms, our worldview is a view *of the world* and a view *for the world*' (Phillips and Brown 1991: 29). Worldviews have two interdependent dimensions. The first dimension is ontological. Worldviews contain fundamental assumptions and presuppositions about the constitutive nature of IR. Such assumptions or beliefs are our most fundamental thoughts about the nature of 'reality' in this particular domain or field of activity. As Dessler (1989: 445) points out, 'an ontology is a structured set of entities. It consists not only of certain designated kinds of things but also of connections or relations between them.' Worldviews do not reflect the world. Rather, they re-present it, not only constraining our vision but also enabling us to develop a language of concepts and terms that in turn make it possible to talk intelligibly about IR. As Gunnell (1987: 34) argues, worldviews 'are not instruments for understanding given objects. To describe, explain, or evaluate something is to appeal, at least implicitly, to an articulation of what kind of thing it is'. The second dimension of worldviews is evaluative, providing the basis for judging and prescribing institutional arrangements and principles of conduct with regard to or within the parameters of IR. The importance of the distinction, and the relationship between ontology and advocacy, has been noted by the philosopher Taylor (1971: 160) in the context of political theory.

On the one hand, they are distinct, in that taking a position on one does not force your hand on the other. On the other hand, they are not completely independent, in that the stand one takes on the ontological level can be part of the essential background of the view one advocates…taking an ontological position does not amount to advocating something; but at the same time, the ontological does help to define the options which it is meaningful to support by advocacy. This latter connection explains how ontological theses can be far from innocent.

Thus if one believes that IR take place in an environment that requires states to maximize their power relative to other states, it makes little sense to advocate cooperation among states if this requires them to act against their core interests. Similarly, if one believes that IR are structured in ways that *systematically* impede any attempt to moderate the inequities of global capitalism, then 'free trade' will be seen simply as a way to avoid focusing on the real problem.

'Worldviews' are not 'theories', although these terms are often conflated in the field of IR. For example, an empirical theory is an explanation of an event, or – more usually – of a pattern of events. Why did the United States invade Iraq in 2003? Why do wars take place? Why are some countries rich and others poor? To engage with such questions is to enter the world of IR theory. Worldviews shape the questions we ask, and provide some of the key interpretive concepts that are employed to build theories. But they are not identical. A worldview is a distinctive set of ideas and arguments about IR. Each worldview examined in this book embodies a set of concerns – for example, security, wealth, liberty, or social justice. It also includes a body of causal reasoning about how IR work, particularly in ways deemed relevant to explaining the identified concerns. Each worldview thus highlights certain types of issues, actors, goals, and types of relationships while ignoring or deemphasizing others. The first ten chapters of this book examine nine worldviews. Each chapter elaborates the fundamental assumptions of a particular worldview, as well as the main theoretical arguments that emerge from, and are consistent with, those assumptions and beliefs. There is nothing particularly significant about the number of worldviews discussed in this book, which aims simply to introduce readers to the diversity of approaches and perspectives in the field. Nonetheless, it is worth noting that the explicit recognition of such diversity has only emerged over the past decade or so (Dunne *et al.* 2007; Steans and Pettiford 2005). For much of the twentieth century, what Smith (1995: 7) calls a 'typology of the discipline…a way of pronouncing on what are the "key" debates and positions within it' not only silenced or marginalized particular worldviews, but also distorted those worldviews that were accepted as legitimate members of whatever typology was popular at a particular point in time. A good example of the distorting impact of typologies on the worldviews contained within them is the complex history of political realism, arguably the dominant worldview in IR theory, and the subject of the next chapter. Realism, like every worldview covered in this book, contains an identifiable set of core principles, but the realist worldview is itself an ideal-type, and it is important to recognize the limitations of trying to 'fix' the status of realism within a discipline whose very identity as a social science is constantly debated. An ideal-type is an abstract construct that extracts and reproduces the main elements in a diverse body of literature. As such, it is not a mirror image of that literature, and it is not obvious how best to engage in the process of extraction and reproduction. It depends on the kinds of problems being investigated, the research interests of those who engage in the process, and the context within which realism is contrasted to other competing approaches to the study of IR. That context is not itself static, nor is it uncontested.

To illustrate the problem, consider how realism manifests itself within three such contexts that have shaped 'great debates' in the study of IR. The first (popular in the interwar period) frames the study of IR in terms of a debate between realists and idealists. Not only did the realists themselves construct this debate in order to defeat their opponents, their use of the label 'idealism' as a black box concealed and marginalized important distinctions between scholars whose contribution to the study of IR has only been recovered years after the decline of 'realism/idealism' as a particular framing context in the study of IR (Schmidt 2002).

An equally problematic way to frame realism is to describe it as a 'paradigm', a term that became popular during the so-called 'third debate' in the study of IR in the 1970s and 1980s. The term 'paradigm' came to prominence in the philosophy of science in the late 1960s, mainly through the work of Kuhn (1970). Briefly, he argued that a paradigm consists of a set of fundamental assumptions about the subject matter of science. A paradigm, like a worldview, is both enabling and constraining. On the one hand, it helps to define what is important to study and so a paradigm is indispensable in simplifying reality by isolating certain factors and forces from a multitude of innumerable possibilities. On the other hand, a paradigm is constraining since it limits our perceptual field (what we 'see' as the most important actors and relationships in a particular field of study). In examining the history of science Kuhn argued that what he called *normal* science proceeded on the basis of particular paradigms, the truth of whose assumptions were taken for granted. A paradigm is therefore a mode of thinking within a field of inquiry that regulates scientific activity and sets the standards for research. A paradigm generates consensus, coherence, and unity among scholars. However, periods of normal science are punctuated by periods of crisis and *revolutionary* science as scientists confront problems (or *anomalies*) that cannot be solved within the terms of the dominant paradigm. A new period of normal science can only resume on the basis of a 'paradigm-shift' and the establishment of a new set of assumptions to account for anomalies that could not be accommodated within the assumptions of the old paradigm.

Although Kuhn had little to say about the social sciences, many scholars quickly seized upon his arguments in order to strengthen and clarify the historical, organizational, and sociological foundations of their own disciplines in the social sciences. Students of IR were no different in this regard. Lijphart (1974) was among the first to import the Kuhnian notion of a paradigm into IR. Writing in the early 1970s, he argued that the general pattern of development in IR theory paralleled Kuhn's version of theoretical progress in the natural sciences. He described the traditional paradigm in terms of state sovereignty and international anarchy. For Lijphart, realism had such a ubiquitous presence in the field that it qualified as a paradigm. It set out the key questions, determined the core concepts, methods, and issues, and shaped the direction of research.

There are, however, a number of problems in treating realism as a 'Kuhnian paradigm'. First, the term implies a greater homogeneity of thought within realism than is justified by a close reading of realist texts and authors. Second, as Waever (1996) has shown, the growth of knowledge in the study of IR has never followed the path that Kuhn elaborated in his historical reconstruction of the natural sciences. The term 'paradigm' is useful as a metaphor, but one should not exaggerate the degree to which paradigms in the study of IR develop in isolation from rival approaches to IR. Finally, as already noted, worldviews in IR do not stand in relation to practice as mere instruments to understand a given and unproblematic 'reality' whose anomalies can threaten to undermine theories and set us off in completely novel avenues of inquiry. In this field, the relationship between theory and practice in not contingent and instrumental. Instead, it is a conceptual and constitutive relation between belief and action. To put it bluntly, realism is true to the extent that it is believed to be true, particularly by policy-makers. Despite Waltz' protestation that 'the problem is not to say how to manage the world, including its great powers, but to say how the possibility that great powers will constructively manage international affairs varies as systems change' (Waltz 1979: 210), few realists have ever hidden their desire to influence the conduct of political leaders.

A third context in which to frame evaluations of realism is to identify its core beliefs not in terms of statements about anarchy, competition, and the ubiquity of violence, but in terms of political theory. Fundamentally, realism is 'a conservative approach to international relations ... that places a primacy on the maintenance of order and the preservation of tradition, and is sceptical about universalist claims or the possibilities for progress in the international system' (Welsh 2003: 174). In this context, realism is not to be understood (and thereby rendered potentially obsolescent) solely on its ability to generate testable empirical theories of IR, but as a manifestation of a venerable tradition of conservative thought. This way of framing realism has reemerged in recent years as the disciplinary borders (built in part by realists, one might add) between political theory and the study of IR have begun to collapse. If realism is understood in minimal terms as an approach that reminds us of the enduring patterns of power politics based on a historically contingent association of sovereignty, territory, and statehood in differentiating humanity politically, it can be argued that despite its deficiencies as a basis for testable theory, it is difficult to dismiss.

If, therefore, one should be wary of the ways in which IR has framed its debates in the past, and if the proliferation of worldviews in recent years is partly a consequence of the failure of any single disciplinary 'self-image' to generate sufficient consensus in the field about the relevant criteria for adjudicating between worldviews, are we left with a mere Babel of global voices? When the reader of this book comes to the end of Chapter 10, what then? On what basis is one worldview superior to the others? Must we even choose? And, if we must choose, is the conversation over? These questions dominate discussions of contemporary IR theory. Two broad responses are available, conquest or coexistence.

Conquest or coexistence?

The first response is self-evident. One worldview is right and the others are wrong. Or we could express it in more subtle terms: each of the worldviews discussed in this book may generate interesting insights, but one of them is far superior to the others. The reader could surely be forgiven for thinking that this response is intended by each of the contributors to the following nine chapters. Whatever problems they acknowledge with the particular worldview under discussion, it is the worldview that the contributor most identifies with and most deeply understands. And, indeed, it is not difficult to find numerous attempts to defend a particular worldview by attempting to demolish its competitors. Often, such 'demolition derbies' make for entertaining reading, but they usually generate more heat than light. As Holsti remarks (2001: 86), 'uncivil wars among scholars, like those within states, tend to be long, nasty and brutish'. A plurality of worldviews is simply a fact in the study of IR. There are three main reasons for this.

First, the subject matter of IR is simply vast. War, demographic change, state-making, global warming, unequal development, nationalism, the 'war on terror', international organization, shifts in power between the United States and China – the central issue or problem that should dominate the research agenda in this field is by no means clear. It is worth recalling that IR – as an autonomous field of study in political science – is a twentieth-century invention that began on the margins of the broader study of politics. As Armstrong (1995: 362) observes, it developed as a distinct discipline both as a response to events like the two World Wars and the Cold War and because there were certain phenomena – war, diplomacy, strategy, international law, the balance of power, the numerous ramifications of sovereignty – that were inadequately, or not at all, treated elsewhere in the social sciences.

If the problem of war was the chief justification for a separate discipline of IR, generating a hierarchy of issues for the discipline to study, that is no longer the case in the twenty-first century. Today, a whole host of issues compete for our attention, and it could be argued that one reason for the proliferation of worldviews is the proliferation of issues that each worldview seeks to privilege. Thus for realists, war between states remains the central problem. For liberal internationalists, the unequal distribution of political freedom for individuals is the problem. For Marxists, the central issue is the injustice of global capitalism and the stratification of class on a global scale. For critical theorists, it is the needless suffering caused not just by capitalism but also by other dynamics of modernity at the global level. Constructivists focus less on substantive issues than the broader problem of how changes in states' identities and interests can shift the culture of IR from one of conflict to one of cooperation. Members of the 'English School' broadly united by a shared concern with the history, dynamics, and future of something called 'international society'. Feminists are inspired by the ideal of gender equality, and outraged by the global consequences of what they regard as the gendered character of the modern sovereign state. Poststructuralists are interested in the processes and practices that make it possible to even conceive of the domain of 'international relations' as a distinct field of political practice. Finally, postcolonial theorists are interested in the stories, identities, and forms of political emancipation available to the marginalized members of the global South. What single worldview could possibly encompass all of the above?

If the profusion of different foci is part of the explanation for a diversity of perspectives, just as important is the absence of an epistemological consensus to adjudicate between rival worldviews. The first explanation is only partly true. Whilst different worldviews certainly can be differentiated on the basis of the political issues that preoccupy their adherents, this does not imply that they can happily coexist. For example, one simply cannot be a feminist as well as a realist, which is one reason why feminist literature is particularly concerned to critique realist literature and, although less in evidence since realists have rarely bothered to respond to feminist provocations, vice versa. An equally important part of the explanation lies in the decline of 'positivism' in IR theory, and the rise of 'post-positivism'. What is positivism, and what is its relationship to competing worldviews? To answer this question, it is important to distinguish between epistemology and methodology. The term 'epistemology' comes from the Greek word *epistêmê*, meaning knowledge. In simple terms, epistemology is the philosophy of knowledge or of how we come to know. Methodology is also concerned with how we come to know, but is much more practical in nature. Methodology is focused on the specific ways that we can use to try to understand our world. Epistemology and methodology are intimately related: the former involves the philosophy of how we come to know the world and the latter involves the practice.

Positivism is a philosophical movement characterized by an emphasis upon science and scientific method as the only sources of knowledge, a sharp distinction between the realms of fact and value, and a strong hostility toward religion and traditional philosophy. Positivists believe that there are only two sources of knowledge (as opposed to opinion): logical reasoning and empirical experience. A statement is meaningful if and only if it can be proved true or false, at least in principle, by means of the experience. This assertion is called the 'verifiability principle'. The meaning of a statement is its method of verification; we know the meaning of a statement if we know the conditions under which the statement is true or false. In its broadest sense, positivism is a position that holds that the goal of knowledge is simply to describe the phenomena that we experience. The purpose of science is to stick to what we can observe and measure. Knowledge of anything beyond that, a positivist would hold, is impossible. Since we cannot directly observe emotions or thoughts (although we may be able to measure some of their physical and physiological accompaniments), these are not legitimate topics for scientific study. In a positivist view of the world, science is seen as the way to get at truth, to understand the world well enough so that we might even predict and control it. The world and the universe are deterministic. They operate by laws of cause and effect that we can discern if we apply the unique approach of the scientific method. Science is largely a mechanistic or mechanical affair. We use deductive reasoning to postulate theories that we can test. Based on the results of our studies, we may learn that our theory does not fit the facts well and so we need to revise our theory to better predict reality. The positivist believes in empiricism, the idea that observation and measurement is the core of science. In turn, the key approach of the scientific method is the experiment, the attempt to discern laws of behavior. Consequently, the merits of any particular worldview rest primarily on the superiority of its theories over rival theories. Epistemology trumps ontology. The logic of discovery (the mysterious process by which one adopts a particular worldview) is far less important than the logic of justification (the allegedly transparent process of testing rival theories on the basis of their internal coherence and the correspondence of their causal hypotheses with empirical data).

Without delving into the voluminous literature on the strengths and weaknesses of positivism in IR, it is worth noting the main elements of postpositivist critiques of the attempt to adjudicate between worldviews by appealing to alleged logic of science. Indeed, the only shared characteristic among those who call themselves 'post-positivists' in the study of IR is a rejection of one or more aspects of positivism. The main problem lies in its rigid dichotomy between theory and practice, and between facts and values. It posits practice as an unproblematic and theoretically untainted realm of observable behavior, which can be classified, measured, and divided up into 'variables'. The role of theory is then to discover the direction and strength of their relationship, explaining the latter in terms of antecedent conditions plus laws of behavior. In turn, practice becomes the arbiter of theoretical competition, the source of support, or falsification for empirical hypotheses derived from (deduction) or giving rise to (induction) theory. Theories are mere instruments. According to postpositivists, the domain of IR is not independent of our ideas about it, even at the level of description and observation. As Sterling-Folker (2006: 5) argues, 'IR theory is a set of templates or prepackaged analytical structures for the multiple ways in which an event or activity … might be categorized, explained or understood. These templates may be laid over the details of the event itself, allowing one to organize the details in such a way that the larger pattern is revealed and recognized within and through the event.'

Perhaps of more importance is the postpositivist argument that our subject matter is not independent of the intersubjective understandings, intentions, and conduct of the actors whose 'behavior' we are seeking to make sense of. Conduct and behavior are not the same things. As Nardin (1985: 2) points out, conduct should be understood 'as an activity of thinking agents (the quality of whose thought may be excellent or poor) responding to an understood (or misunderstood) situation, in accordance with (or violation of) various practices, rules, or maxims of conduct'. Since these practices and rules are themselves informed by worldviews regarding the content and scope of appropriate conduct, the positivist attempt to drive an epistemological wedge between ontology and advocacy (and between empirical and normative theory) is of dubious validity. Whereas positivism requires us to radically distinguish between the language of theory and practice, in which the meaning of theoretical concepts is fixed by stipulation, deductively linked to empirical hypotheses via operationalization, postpositivists endorse a more hermeneutic methodology. So, for example, they would argue that a concept as seemingly simple as 'a great power' can never be defined exclusively by reference to observable and measurable material indices. Its meaning is infused with normative significance, endowing the states so defined with particular rights and duties *vis-à-vis* other states. Identifying a class of states with such a status is an inherently problematic and ambiguous exercise. Similarly, the concept of the balance of power cannot be shorn of its ambiguity by operational stipulation without distorting its meaning and role in diplomatic history. In short, as Banks (1984: 4) has argued, understanding IR 'is not a matter of hunting down immutable laws. It is an exploration of the manner in which some political ideas have become political facts, whereas others have not ... to seek understanding, therefore, is to take part in a debate about competing ideas'.

Finally, in addition to the complexity of our subject matter and the lack of epistemological consensus in the field, there are powerful institutional forces in academia sustaining the diversity of worldviews. These include academics with a professional interest in the perpetuation of their preferred approach, specialized journals and publishers that cater to the defense and elaboration of a specific worldview, and even academic departments in which senior scholars seek to appoint and promote colleagues sympathetic to their particular worldview. Paradoxically, however, the proliferation of worldviews and research 'outputs' from the field is not matched by a widespread acknowledgment within it of the most appropriate intellectual authorities and frameworks of analysis. IR is a notorious importer of gurus, ideas, concepts, and theories from beyond its poorly regulated borders. These factors mutually reinforce metatheoretical diversity, pushing worldviews into self-contained ghettos. Conquest is difficult when the targets have a remarkable capacity to reinvent themselves and to absorb, deflect, or simply ignore criticism. As Ashley (1991: 38) observes in the case of realism, 'if challenging realism is itself a normal activity, already accommodated within the discipline's official self-representations, then how serious can the challenges be? Perennially challenged, it also seems to be perennially affirmed as the central [worldview] to be challenged'. In this book, each of the worldviews under examination exhibits a high degree of internal heterogeneity, making it difficult if not impossible for potential conquerors to kill off their victim(s). 'You just don't understand' is the title of a well-known article by one of the leading feminist IR scholars in the United States (Tickner 1997: 611). To which a realist could well reply, 'neither do you'. For example, when some feminists attack realists, their understanding of realism is informed by feminist texts on realism rather than a direct engagement with realist texts (Lee Koo 2002). Thus diversity can easily lead to mutual incomprehension and a lack of mutual engagement between adherents of competing worldviews. Increasingly, books such as this one are edited, not written by a single author.

In defense of diversity (up to a point)

If the analysis so far suggests that formidable obstacles stand in the way of IR ever becoming an 'enterprise association' (Oakeshott 1962), fortunately we are not confronted with, on the one hand, having to choose a particular worldview without any plausible rationale or, on the other, having to live with a dialogue of the deaf. To avoid such a choice, however, we have to develop a worldview on worldviews, as it were. And perhaps the best way to do that is to place inverted commas around the disarmingly simple word, 'we'. The critical theorist Cox (1981: 128) famously wrote that 'theory is always *for* someone and *for* some purpose'. He was arguing that behind the positivist veneer of neutrality, IR theory was constituted by its authors' implicit audience (policy-makers, the oppressed, women) and larger purpose (stability, peace, or justice). He neglected to take a more radical starting point. Theory is always *by* someone as well as for someone. Despite the hyper-reflexivity of contemporary IR theory, there has been little attention paid to the process by which 'we' become enmeshed in and supporters of a particular worldview. There is a widespread acknowledgment that discovery and justification are linked somehow. We need to make this link explicit at the outset.

According to Ricks (2006: 127), the failure of the United States in Iraq stems from a prior flaw, its collective failure to recognize the difficulties involved in trying to answer a fundamental question, 'who are we, and what are we ultimately trying to do here?' The question is a good one, and not just for US policy-makers but for all of 'us'. The reason 'we' need inverted commas at the outset is because our identity or subjectivity is a tragic one, and IR is a domain of activity where the collective consequences of our tragic situation are potentially the most devastating. Over the past decade, a growing number of scholars in political theory and IR have suggested that notions of 'the divided self' and tragedy are our most appropriate starting points for exploring IR through IR theory. This 'worldview on worldviews' provides a basis for evaluating the latter by considering how well they recognize and facilitate the transformation of the situations that generate tragedy. As Frost (2003: 487) explains, 'tragedy reveals how each of the practices within which we are constituted as actors of a certain kind imposes on us a set of ethical imperatives. It shows how it often happens that these come to clash with one another. It shows how we as actors can be torn apart by this kind of ethical clash within, as it were, our own plural, contradictory, and conflictual ethical universe.'

The institutional form of the sovereign nation-state is a key contributory factor to our tragic condition. The world of humanity – climbing inexorably to over ten billion people in the next fifty years or so – is politically divided among sovereign states. War is an ever-present background possibility among states that coexist in a condition of anarchy (even if, as the constructivists believe, that condition is a variable, not a constant). There is no world government, although elements of 'governance' in the form of international organizations and sustained patterns of cooperation no doubt moderate the extreme image of IR as a jungle. In this environment, political authority is dispersed along territorial lines whose paths no global rational actor would design or endorse. It is therefore difficult to coordinate global action to deal with global problems that do not respect territorial borders. As human beings, we may be upset by images of starvation, barbaric cruelty, and injustice that bombard us nightly on our television screens. It may strike 'us' as arbitrary that we enjoy the privileges of peace and prosperity while other human beings suffer simply because they happen to have been born in Somalia or Iraq rather than Australia or Canada or the United States. Modernity, among other things, is an ethos of reason and a belief in the growth of reason to control our environment so that it fulfills human purposes and contributes to the sum of our collective well-being. Suffering, of course, does not correlate with territorial boundaries, but the political capacity to respond to it usually does. Our cosmopolitan moral sentiments are constantly frustrated by our particularistic political identity as citizens and as nationalists. We enjoy the fruits of political community as rights-bearing citizens within the state. In contrast, our obligations to humanity are thin (Walzer 1994), a pale reflection of natural law. Within the form of the state, historical progress is conceived along a temporal dimension, whereas the arbitrary spatial division of IR guarantees some degree of power politics among states. Within the state, the universal rights of citizenship are, in principle, available to 'all', yet that same universality depends crucially on the ability of the state to exclude outsiders (Walker 1993). And so it goes, on and on. This is our existential and historical condition, and the fate of the territorial state is central to that condition. In the final three chapters of the book, therefore, we descend from some of the lofty heights of IR theory explored in the first ten chapters, and consider the centrality of the state from three angles, state-making, states, and economic globalization, and the role of the state in contemporary normative IR theory. A central theme that emerges from these three chapters is the increasing 'disaggregation' of the state form in IR (Sørensen 2004), and how that transformation exacerbates the existential tragedy of IR. While students of IR have always recognized a hierarchy of state formations, their contemporary manifestation is bewildering in its complexity and lack of susceptibility to purposive guidance. The student of IR theory is thus confronted with a dual task, to assess the adequacy of each worldview to shed light on the ontological tragedy of the enduring human condition, and to assess its prescriptive or evaluative dimension in light of the changing state of the state.

Conclusion

Worldviews are necessary. They frame the domain of IR and provide the conceptual language and fundamental assumptions (both ontological and evaluative) on the basis of which specific phenomena and patterned relationships are explained *via* theory. Contemporary IR theory exhibits a wide variety of competing worldviews. To be sure, they are not all mutually exclusive. Productive conversations can take, and have taken, place between realists and liberals over the dynamics of cooperation among states and the conditions for regime maintenance in a variety of issue areas. Critical theory emerged from Marxism. Whilst it is presented here as a distinctive worldview, feminism is a multidimensional worldview in which liberals, radicals, and poststructuralists engage in dialogue with one another. Similarly, there is much overlap between Marxism, critical theory, and postcolonialism. 'The English School' is distinctive in that its members explicitly recognize a legitimate plurality of 'traditions of international thought'. It is not difficult to find further areas of actual and potential overlap. Nonetheless, as I have argued in this introductory chapter, neither conquest nor complete convergence between worldviews is likely in the foreseeable future. IR theory in the twenty-first century is therefore inextricably pluralistic. This situation is a cause neither for alarm nor for celebration in the name of diversity for the sake of it. I have suggested that a worldview on worldviews, or perspective on perspectives, is necessary in order to assess the merits of alternative worldviews. An appropriate starting point, I believe, is to recognize IR as an extreme manifestation of human tragedy. The question then becomes, to what extent does each worldview provide us with important insights into the dynamics of tragedy and empower us, if not to overcome it, at least to ameliorate its effects? This book is an introduction to the diverse ways in which IR theory can assist 'us' in answering this central question.

Further reading

Dunne, T., Kurki, M., and Smith, S. (eds) (2007) *International Relations Theories: Discipline and Diversity*, Oxford: Oxford University Press.

Steans, J. and Pettiford, L. (2005) *Introduction to International Relations: Perspectives and Themes*, Harlow: Pearson.

Sterling-Folker, J. (ed.) (2006) *Making Sense of International Relations Theory*, Boulder, CO: Lynne Rienner.

2   Realism

Colin Elman

Introduction

Often described as the dominant worldview in the study of International Relations (IR) (Forde 1992: 373), political realism has been implicated in every major debate in IR over the last 50 years. In describing and appraising the realist worldview, it is customary to differentiate realism from other worldviews and to separate realist theories into distinct subgroups. In this chapter, I first describe the contested antiquarian and classical roots of realism, before moving on to describe six varieties of twentieth-century realist scholarship. Despite their differences, they largely share the view that the character of relations among states has not fundamentally altered. Where there is change, it tends to occur in repetitive patterns. State behavior is driven by leaders' flawed human nature or by the preemptive unpleasantness mandated by an anarchic international system. Selfish human appetites for power, or the need to accumulate the wherewithal to be secure in a self-help world, explain the seemingly endless succession of wars and conquest. Accordingly, most realists take a pessimistic and prudential view of IR (Elman 2001).

The roots of the realist worldview

Realists regard themselves as heirs to an extended intellectual tradition (Waltz 2002: 198). It is customary to trace realism back to antiquity, with claims that its arguments can be found in important works from Greece, Rome, India, and China. Smith (1986) and other surveyors, for example, suggest that Thucydides' history of *The Peloponnesian War* illustrates realism's skepticism for the restraining effects of morality. Thucydides (Strassler 1996: 416) notes in a speech attributed to the Athenians in the Melian dialogue that 'right, as the world goes, is only in question between equals in power, while the strong do what they can and the weak suffer what they must'. Realists also argue that Thucydides (Strassler 1996: 49) explains Greek city-states' behavior by their power relations, famously observing that '[t]he growth of the power of Athens, and the alarm which this inspired in Sparta, made war inevitable'.

Realist arguments can also be found in Kautilya's *Arthashastra* from India, which, Seabury (1965: 7) argues, 'is concerned with the survival and aggrandizement of the state' and 'clearly instructs . . . in the principles of a balance of power system'. Haslam (2002: 14) similarly notes that 'Kautilya focuses on the position of the potential conqueror who always aims to enhance his power at the expense of the rest.'

Realists also claim Niccolo Machiavelli (1469–1527) among their number (Carr 1946: 63–4). Starting from a deeply pessimistic view of human nature, Machiavelli argues for strong and efficient rulers for whom power and security are the major concerns. Unlike individuals, such rulers are not bound by individual morality: 'any action that can be regarded as important for the survival of the state carries with it a built-in justification' (Smith 1986: 12). Realists also identify with Thomas Hobbes (1588–1679) and his notion of a 'state of nature' where the absence of overriding authority allows human appetites to be pursued without restraint – individuals engage in constant conflict, with their lives being concomitantly 'solitary, poor, nasty, brutish and short' (Hobbes 1962: 100).

Political realism's prolonged existence gives it a distinct advantage over relatively youthful liberal alternatives. It is important, therefore, to note that realist interpretations of antiquarian writings are often contested. Garst (1989), for example, argues that Thucydides' history cannot be read as an analogue of modern realism. Similarly, Butterfield (1966: 132–3) argues that Hume is mistaken in his interpretation of Polybius' account of Hiero and that 'the idea of the balance of power . . . did not exist in the ancient world'. Regardless of one's views on the longevity of realist thinking, however, there is more consensus that the millennia-long record of intergroup conflict seems to support realism's pessimistic worldview. While realism's interpretation of particular episodes has been disputed, even its critics (Wendt 2000) acknowledge that humankind has, in most times and in most places, lived down to realism's very low expectations.

This chapter distinguishes between two main variants of realism – classical realism and neorealism – and four flavors of contemporary realism: 'rise and fall', neoclassical, defensive structural, and offensive structural realism. While this ordering is not intended to suggest a strict temporal or intellectual succession, classical realism is usually held to be the first of the twentieth-century realist research programs.

Classical realism

Twentieth-century classical realism is generally dated from 1939 and the publication of Edward Hallett Carr's *The 20 Year's Crisis*. Classical realists are usually characterized as responding to the then-dominant liberal approaches to international politics (Donnelly 1995: 179) although some scholars (Kahler 1997: 24) disagree on how widespread liberalism was during the interwar years. In addition to Carr, work by Shuman (1933), Nicolson (1939), Niebuhr (1940), Schwarzenberger (1941), Wight (1946), Morgenthau (1948), Kennan (1951), and Butterfield (1953) formed part of the realist canon. It was, however, Morgenthau's *Politics Among Nations: The Struggle for Power and Peace*, which became the undisputed standard bearer for political realism, going through six editions between 1948 and 1985.

According to classical realism, because the desire for more power is rooted in the flawed nature of humanity, states are continuously engaged in a struggle to increase their capabilities. The absence of the international equivalent of a state's government is a permissive condition that gives human appetites free reign. In short, classical realism explains conflictual behavior by human failings. Particular wars are explained, for example, by aggressive statesmen or by domestic political systems that give greedy parochial groups the opportunity to pursue self-serving expansionist foreign policies. For classical realists international politics can be characterized as evil: bad things happen because the people making foreign policy are sometimes bad (Spirtas 1996: 387–400).

Although not employing the formal mathematical modeling found in contemporary rational choice theory, classical realism posits that state behavior can be understood as having rational foundations. As Morgenthau (2005[1948]: 5) notes,

> [W]e put ourselves in the position of a statesman who must meet a certain problem of foreign policy under certain circumstances and we ask ourselves what the rational alternatives are from which a statesman may choose who must meet this problem under these circumstances (presuming always that he acts in a rational manner), and which of these rational alternatives this particular statesman is likely to choose. It is the testing of this rational hypothesis against the actual facts and their consequences that gives theoretical meaning to the facts of international politics.

State strategies are understood as having been decided rationally, after taking costs and benefits of different possible courses of action into account. The 1960s saw classical realism coming under increasing scrutiny. Scholars who disagreed with Morgenthau and other classical realists on substantive grounds studied their work to find inconsistencies and contradictions. In addition, advocates of new behavioral and quantitative methodologies questioned the value of the traditional approach to inquiry. The 1970s saw the pendulum swing further against realism, with work (Keohane and Nye 1977) focusing on interdependence, and nonstate actors finding new prominence and popularity (Elman 2003).

Neorealism: Waltz's theory of international politics

The realist worldview was revived and revised with the publication of Kenneth Waltz's 1979 *Theory of International Politics*, which replaced Morgenthau's *Politics Among Nations* as the standard bearer for realists. Waltz argues that systems are composed of a structure and their interacting units. Political structures have three elements: an ordering principle (anarchic or hierarchical), the character of the units (functionally alike or differentiated), and the distribution of capabilities (Waltz 1979: 88–99). Waltz argues that two elements of the structure of the international system are constants: the lack of an overarching authority means that its ordering principle is anarchy, and the principle of self-help means that all of the units remain functionally alike. Accordingly, the only structural variable is the distribution of capabilities, with the main distinction falling between multipolar and bipolar systems.

One difference between classical realism and neorealism is their contrasting views on the source and content of states' preferences. In contrast to classical realism, neorealism excludes the internal makeup of different states. As Rasler and Thompson (2001: 47) note, Morgenthau's seminal statement of classical realism' relied on the assumption that leaders of states are motivated by their lust for power. Waltz's theory, by contrast, omits leader's motivations and state characteristics as causal variables for international outcomes, except for the minimal assumption that states seek to survive.

In addition, whereas classical realism suggested that state strategies are selected rationally, Waltz is more agnostic. According to Waltz, state behavior can be a product of the competition among states, either because they calculate how to act to their best advantage or because those that do not exhibit such behavior are selected out of the system. Alternatively, states' behavior can be a product of socialization: states can decide to follow norms because they calculate it to their advantage or because the norms become internalized. Since Waltz's theory provides such a minimal account of state preferences, it makes only indeterminate behavioral predictions, and Waltz is correspondingly reluctant to make foreign policy predictions. He nevertheless suggests that systemic processes will consistently produce convergent international outcomes. IR are characterized by a disheartening consistency; the same depressingly familiar things recur over time. This repetitiveness endures despite considerable differences in internal domestic political arrangements, both through time and through space. Waltz's purpose is to explain why similarly structured international systems all seem to be characterized by similar outcomes, even though their units (i.e. member states) have different domestic political arrangements and particular parochial histories. Waltz concludes that it must be something peculiar to, and pervasive in, IR that accounts for these commonalities. He therefore excludes as 'reductionist' all but the thinnest of assumptions about the units that make up the system – they must, at a minimum, seek their own survival.

By ignoring unit-level variables, Waltz aims to identify the persistent effects of the international system. Jervis (1997: 7) observes that '[w]e are dealing with a system when (a) a set of units or elements is interconnected so that changes in some elements or their relations produce changes in other parts of the system; and (b) the entire system exhibits properties and behaviors that are different from those parts.' Because systems are generative, the international political system is characterized by complex nonlinear relationships and unintended consequences. Outcomes are influenced by something more than simply the aggregation of individual states' behaviors, with a tendency toward unintended and ironic outcomes. As a result, there is a gap between what states want and what states get. Consequently, unlike classical realists, neorealists see international politics as tragic, rather than as being driven by the aggressive behavior of revisionist states (Spirtas 1996: 387–400). The international political outcomes that Waltz predicts include that multipolar systems will be less stable than bipolar systems; that interdependence will be lower in bipolarity than multipolarity; and that regardless of unit behavior, hegemony by any single state is unlikely or even impossible.

Waltz's *Theory of International Politics* proved to be a remarkably influential volume, generating new debates and giving new impetus to existing ones. For example, the book began a debate over whether states' concerns over relative gains impeded cooperation and added momentum to the question of whether bipolar or multipolar international systems were more war-prone. Partly because of its popularity, and partly because of its own 'take-no-prisoners' criticism of competing theories, Waltz's *Theory of International Politics* became a prominent target. As time went by, detractors (e.g., the contributors to Robert Keohane's 1986 edited volume *Neorealism and its Critics*) chipped away at the book's dominance. Nonrealist work, in particular neoliberal institutionalism and investigations of the democratic peace, became more popular (Keohane and Martin 2003; Ray 2003). Realism's decline in the 1990s was amplified by international events. The closing years of the twentieth century seemed to provide strong support for alternative approaches. The Soviet Union's voluntary retrenchment and subsequent demise; the continuation of Western European integration in the absence of American–Soviet competition; the wave of democratization and economic liberalization throughout the former Soviet Union, Eastern Europe, and the developing world; and the improbability of war between the great powers all made realism seem outdated (Jervis 2002). It appeared that liberal or constructivist theories could better appreciate and explain the changes taking place in the international arena. Not surprisingly, the post-9/11 era seems much more challenging and it comes as no revelation that political realism is regarded as being better suited to address threats to national security. It is, however, ironic that its renaissance is at least partly owed to transnational terrorist networks motivated by religious extremism, actors, and appetites that lie well outside realism's traditional ambit.

Varieties of contemporary realism

There are at least four strands of political realism today: rise and fall realism, neoclassical realism, defensive structural realism, and offensive structural realism. All four strands take the view that international relations are characterized by an endless and inescapable succession of wars and conquest. The four groupings can be differentiated by the fundamental constitutive and heuristic assumptions that their respective theories share. Briefly, the approaches differ on the sources of state preferences – the mix of human desire for power and/or the need to accumulate the wherewithal to be secure in a self-help world – while agreeing that rational calculation is the microfoundation that translates those preferences into behavior.

'Rise and fall' realism

Rise and fall realism sees the rules and practices of the international system as being determined by the wishes of the leading (i.e. most powerful) state. Since considerable benefit accrues to the leader, other great powers seek this pole position. Rise and fall realism explains how states first rise to and then fall from this leading position, and the consequences of that trajectory for foreign policies. In particular, the approach is concerned with the onset of great power wars that often mark the transition from one leader to the next. The microfoundation that explains this behavior is rational choice. Given a narrowing of the gap between the first- and the second-ranked states, the leader will calculate the need for preventive action. Failing that, the challenger will opt for a war to displace the current leader.

Perhaps the best (and best-known) work in the rise and fall tradition is Robert Gilpin's *War and Change in World Politics*. Gilpin (1981: 7) suggests that 'the fundamental nature of IR has not changed over the millennia. International relations continue to be a recurring struggle for wealth and power among independent actors in a state of anarchy.' Domestic and international developments lead to states growing at different rates, and as states rise and fall relative to one another, conflict ensues. States choose to engage in conflict because they calculate that the benefits of doing so exceed its costs. In particular, because the international system is created by and for the leading power in the system, changes in power lead to conflict over system leadership. Gilpin suggests that these dynamics have always applied to relations among states, and hence his framework is applicable to a wide swathe of human history.

Organski's (1968) power transition theory also argues that differential rates of growth cause wars over system leadership. However, because he argues that it is the timing of industrialization that causes states to rise and fall *vis-à-vis* one another, his theory applies to a much narrower time frame than Giplin's, bracketed by the first and last great power to industrialize. Organski argues that states go through three stages: potential power, where an agrarian state has yet to industrialize; transitional growth in power, where a state modernizes both politically and economically and enjoys a substantial increase in growth rates; and finally power maturity, where a state is industrialized. Because states go through the second stage at different times, it follows that their relative power position changes.

When states that are dissatisfied with the current status quo gain on the system leader, war is likely to ensue. Consequently, peace is most likely when current system leaders enjoy a substantial lead over other states. According to DiCicco and Levy (1999: 680), 'three generations of scholars have self-consciously identified with this research program and continue to refine the theory and test it empirically'. These have partly been aimed at testing Organski's original insight, and partly at extending the theory's domain. For example, Lemke (1995, 1996) applies power transition theory to dyads other than those involving states directly contesting for system leadership. Kim (1991, 1992, 1996, 2002) amends power transition theory to allow alliances, and not just internal growth rates, to be counted. The most prominent incarnation of rise and fall realism is Copeland's (2001) dynamic differentials theory, which suggests that major wars are typically initiated by dominant military powers that fear significant decline. Copeland's theory also incorporates structural realist arguments, however, since he sees the main virtue of power as ensuring survival, rather than allowing the arrangement of international affairs to suit the dominant state's interests.

Neoclassical realism

In part responding to what were perceived as the antireductionist excesses of neorealism (Snyder 1991: 19), neoclassical realism suggests that what states do depends in large part on domestically derived preferences. For example, Schweller (1993: 76–7, 84; 1994: 92–9) insists that acknowledging and including different state motivations best serve realism. As Rasler and Thompson (2001: 47) note, neoclassical realists stress a wider range of revisionist motives than classical realism's earlier reliance on human nature: 'things happen in world politics because some actors – thanks to domestic structure and institutions, ideology, and ambitions – practice disruptive and predatory strategies'. One prominent version of neoclassical realism is Schweller's (1993, 1994, 1996, 1998) 'balance of interests' theory, which develops a typology based on whether states are primarily motivated by, and the extent of, their fear and greed. Thus, states rationally decide foreign policies depending on a combination of power and interests.

In addition to emphasizing the distinction between status quo and revisionist states, neoclassical realists also focus on the domestic 'transmission belt' connecting resource endowments and power (Schweller 2006: 6). Neoclassical realists agree that material capabilities and the distribution of power are the starting points for an analysis of international outcomes. They insist, however, that state characteristics and leaders' views of how power should be used intervene between structural constraints and behavior. Accordingly, they also investigate domestic political features, such as the abilities of foreign policy-makers to extract resources for the pursuit of foreign policy goals. For example, Schweller (2006: 6) argues that

> states assess and adapt to changes in their external environment partly as a result of their peculiar domestic structures and political situations. More specifically, complex domestic political processes act as transmission belts that channel, mediate, and (re)direct policy outputs in response to external forces (primarily changes in relative power). Hence states often react differently to similar systemic pressures and opportunities, and their responses may be less motivated by systemic level factors than domestic ones.

Most realist theories predict that states will balance against threatening competitors, either by building their own arms or by forming alliances. However, Schweller argues that a review of the historical record reveals that states often 'under balance'. That is, they balance inefficiently in response to dangerous and unappeasable aggressors, when effective balancing was needed to deter or defeat those threats. Schweller locates his explanation for underbalancing at the domestic level of analysis. The more fragmented and diverse a state's various elite and societal groups, the less we can expect it to respond appropriately to external strategic pressures.

Defensive structural realism

Defensive structural realism developed, but is distinct, from neorealism (Glaser 2003; Waltz 2002). Defensive structural realism shares neorealism's minimal assumptions about state motivations. Like neorealism, defensive structural realism suggests that states seek security in an anarchic international system – the main threat to their well-being comes from other states (Glaser 2003; Waltz 2002). There are three main differences between neorealism and defensive structural realism. First, whereas neorealism allows for multiple microfoundations to explain state behavior, defensive structural realism relies solely on rational choice. Second, defensive structural realism adds the offense–defense balance as a variable. This is a composite variable combining a variety of different factors that make conquest harder or easier. Defensive structural realists argue that prevailing technologies or geographical circumstances often favor the defense, seized resources do not cumulate easily with those already possessed by the metropole, dominoes do not fall, and power is difficult to project at a distance. Accordingly, in a world in which conquest is hard it may not take too much balancing to offset revisionist behavior. Third, combining rationality and an offense–defense balance that favors the defense, defensive structural realists predict that states should support the status quo. Expansion is rarely structurally mandated, and balancing is the appropriate response to threatening concentrations of power. In contrast to neorealism, this is a dyadic, not automatic, balance of power theory – linear, not systemic, causation operates. Rationalism and an offense–defense balance that favors the defense means that states balance, and balances result.

Perhaps the best-known variant of defensive structural realism is Waltz's (1987, 1988, 1991, 1992a,b, 1996, 2000) 'balance of threat' theory. According to Waltz (1987: x), 'in anarchy, states form alliances to protect themselves. Their conduct is determined by the threats they perceive and the power of others is merely one element in their calculations.' Waltz (2000: 201) suggests that states estimate threats posed by other states by their relative power, proximity, intentions, and the offense–defense balance. The resulting dyadic balancing explains the absence of hegemony in the system:

> Together, these four factors explain why potential hegemons like Napoleonic France, Wilhelmine Germany, and Nazi Germany eventually faced overwhelming coalitions: each of these states was a great power lying in close proximity to others, and each combined large offensive capabilities with extremely aggressive aims.

Because balancing is pervasive, Waltz (1987: 27) concludes that revisionist and aggressive behavior is self-defeating, and 'status quo states can take a relatively sanguine view of threats . . . [i]n a balancing world, policies that convey restraint and benevolence are best'.

One difficult problem for defensive structural realism is that the research program is better suited to investigating structurally constrained responses to revisionism, rather than where that expansionist behavior comes from. To explain how conflict arises in the first place, defensive structural realists must appeal to either domestic level factors (which are outside their theory), or argue that extreme security dilemma dynamics make states behave as if they were revisionists. Herz (1950: 157) was an early exponent of the concept of the security dilemma, arguing that defensive actions and capabilities are often misinterpreted as being aggressive. Steps taken by states seeking to preserve the status quo are ambiguous and are often indistinguishable from preparations for taking the offense. 'Threatened' states respond, leading to a spiraling of mutual aggression that all would have preferred to avoid. This is IR as tragedy, not evil: bad things happen because states are placed in difficult situations.

Defensive structural realism has some difficulty in relying on security dilemma dynamics to explain war. It is not easy to see how, in the absence of pervasive domestic level pathologies, revisionist behavior can be innocently initiated in a world characterized by status quo states, defense-dominance and balancing. Because increments in capabilities can be easily countered, defensive structural realism suggests that a state's attempt to make itself more secure by increasing its power is ultimately futile. This is consistent with Wolfers (1962: 158–9) reading of the security dilemma, that states threatened by new, potentially offensive capabilities respond with measures of their own, leaving the first state in as precarious a position, if not worse off, than before. Hence, defensive realists suggest that states should seek an 'appropriate' amount of power. If states do seek hegemony, it is due to domestically generated preferences; seeking superior power is not a rational response to external systemic pressures.

Offensive structural realism

Offensive structural realists disagree with the defensive structural realist prescription that states look for only an 'appropriate' amount of power. The flagship statement, Mearsheimer's (2001) *The Tragedy of Great Power Politics*, argues that states face an uncertain international environment in which any state might use its power to harm another. Under such circumstances, relative capabilities are of overriding importance, and security requires acquiring as much power compared to other states as possible (Labs 1997). The stopping power of water means that the most a state can hope for is to be a regional hegemon, and for there to be no other regional hegemons elsewhere in the world.

Mearsheimer's theory makes five assumptions: the international system is anarchic; great powers inherently possess some offensive military capability, and accordingly can damage each other; states can never be certain about other states' intentions; survival is the primary goal of great powers; and great powers are rational actors. From these assumptions, Mearsheimer deduces that great powers fear each other, that they can rely only on themselves for their security, and that the best strategy for states to ensure their survival is maximization of relative power. In contrast to defensive structural realists, who suggest that states look for only an 'appropriate' amount of power (Glaser 1994/1995, 1997; Van Evera 1999), Mearsheimer argues that security requires acquiring as much power relative to other states as possible. Mearsheimer argues that increasing capabilities can improve a state's security without triggering a countervailing response. Careful timing by revisionists, buck-passing by potential targets, and information asymmetries all allow the would-be hegemon to succeed. Power maximization is not necessarily self-defeating, and hence states can rationally aim for regional hegemony.

Although states will take any increment of power that they can get away with, Mearsheimer (2001: 37) does not predict that states are 'mindless aggressors so bent on gaining power that they charge headlong into losing wars or pursue Pyrrhic victories'. States are sophisticated relative power maximizers that try 'to figure out when to raise and when to fold' (Mearsheimer 2001: 40). Expanding against weakness or indecision, pulling back when faced by strength and determination, a sophisticated power maximizer reaches regional hegemony by using a combination of brains and brawn.

Mearsheimer argues that ultimate safety comes only from being the most powerful state in the system. However, the 'stopping power of water' makes such global hegemony all but impossible, except through attaining an implausible nuclear superiority. The second best, and much more likely, objective is to achieve regional hegemony, the dominance of the area in which the great power is located. Finally, even in the absence of either type of hegemony, states try to maximize both their wealth and their military capabilities for fighting land battles (Mearsheimer 2001: 143–5). In order to gain resources, states resort to war, blackmail, baiting states into waging war on each other while standing aside, and engaging competitors in long and costly conflicts. When acting to forestall other states' expansion, a great power can either try to inveigle a third party into coping with the threat (i.e. buck-pass) or balance against the threat themselves (Mearsheimer 2001: 156–62). While buck-passing is often preferred as the lower-cost strategy, balancing becomes more likely, *ceteris paribus*, the more proximate the menacing state and the greater its relative capabilities.

In addition to moving Mearsheimer's focus to the regional level, the introduction of the 'stopping power' of water also leads to his making different predictions of state behavior depending on where it is located. While the theory applies to great powers in general, Mearsheimer distinguishes between different kinds: continental and island great powers, and regional hegemons. A continental great power will seek regional hegemony but, when it is unable to achieve this dominance, such a state will still maximize its relative power to the extent possible. An insular state, 'the only great power on a large body of land that is surrounded on all sides by water' (Mearsheimer 2001: 126), will balance against the rising states rather than try to be a regional hegemon itself. Accordingly, states such as the United Kingdom act as offshore balancers, intervening only when a continental power is near to achieving primacy (Mearsheimer 2001: 126–8, 261–4). The third kind of great power in Mearsheimer's theory is a regional hegemon such as the United States. A regional hegemon is a status quo state that will seek to defend the current favorable distribution of capabilities.

Mearsheimer's theory provides a structural explanation of great power war, suggesting that 'the main causes . . . are located in the architecture of the international system. What matters most is the number of great powers and how much power each [great power] controls' (Mearsheimer 2001: 337). Great power wars are least likely in bipolarity, where the system only contains two great powers because there are fewer potential conflict dyads: imbalances of power are much less likely and miscalculations leading to failures of deterrence are less common. While multipolarity is, in general, more war-prone than bipolarity, some multipolar power configurations are more dangerous than others. Great power wars are most likely when multipolar systems are unbalanced; that is, when there is a marked difference in capabilities between the first and the second states in the system such that the most powerful possesses the means to bid for hegemony. Mearsheimer hypothesizes that the three possible system architectures range from unbalanced multipolarity's war-proneness to bipolarity's peacefulness, with balanced multipolarity falling somewhere in between (Mearsheimer 2001: 337–46).

Conclusion

This chapter has reviewed six variants of realism: classical realism, neorealism, 'rise and fall' realism, neoclassical realism, defensive structural realism, and offensive structural realism. As the discussion has shown, realism is a multifaceted and durable tradition of inquiry in IR, with an extraordinary facility for adaptation. The divergence among the components of the realist tradition has at least two significant consequences.

First, while the research programs have some common characteristics with each other, none make wholly overlapping arguments or predictions. Although it is possible to support some general remarks about the realist worldview (e.g., the observations about realism's continuity and pessimism in the introduction to this chapter), one should otherwise be leery of statements that begin with the words 'realism says . . . ' or 'realism predicts . . . '. Different realist theories say and predict different things. They will also have very different implications when considered as the basis for prescriptive policy. For example, the best that offensive structural realism has to offer the world is an armed and watchful peace anchored in mutual deterrence, punctuated by wars triggered by structurally driven revisionism when a state calculates it can gain at another's advantage. In contrast, the best that defensive structural realism has to offer is a community of status quo states who have successfully managed to signal their peaceful intentions and/or refrained from obtaining ambiguously offensive capabilities.

Second, realism's capacity for change opens the tradition to some criticisms. For example, realists have recently been scolded for making self-serving adjustments to their theories to avoid contradiction by empirical anomalies. Vasquez (1997) argues that balance of power theory – as described and defended by Waltz (1979), Waltz (1987), Christensen and Snyder (1990), Schweller (1994), and Elman and Elman (1995) – is degenerative when judged by Lakatos' (1970) criteria for evaluating scientific progress. Vasquez suggests that balance of power theory is empirically inaccurate, but that succeeding versions of the theory have become progressively looser to allow it to accommodate disconfirming evidence. A related critique was launched by Legro and Moravcsik (1999), who argue that recent realists subsume arguments that are more usually associated with competing liberal or constructivist approaches. The result, they argue, is that realist theories have become less determinate, coherent, and distinctive. It should be noted that the critiques sparked vigorous responses from realist scholars, who argue that the detractors are mistaken in their descriptions of the tradition and in their application of metatheoretic criteria. For example, Vasquez's article set off a forceful debate in a 1997 forum in the *American Political Science Review* and motivated a follow-on volume (Vasquez and Elman 2003). Similarly, Legro and Moravcsik's essay provoked vigorous rebuttals, noting in particular their restrictive overarching definition of realism (Feaver *et al.* 2000). Realists regard their worldview's continuing fecundity as a strength, not a weakness. Thus those who are anticipating that realism will soon become obsolete are likely to be in for a long wait to see their expectations fulfilled.

Further reading

Donnelly, J. (2000) *Realism and International Relations*, Cambridge: Cambridge University Press.
Mearsheimer, J. (2001) *The Tragedy of Great Power Politics*, New York: WW. Norton.
Waltz, K. (1979) *Theory of International Politics*, Reading, MA: Addison-Wesley.

3 Liberal internationalism

John MacMillan

Underlying liberal internationalism – the projection of liberal thought and political principles to the international realm – is the assumption that one can apply reason to extend the possibilities for individual and collective self-rule, or freedom. Liberal internationalism emerged as a coherent worldview in the Enlightenment and reached its height as a systematic statement of international reform with Woodrow Wilson's Fourteen Points, intended to form the basis of the post-World War I peace. Liberals tended to believe that the outbreak of World War I had vindicated their critique of the prevailing system of International Relations (IR) and sought to establish a liberal peace marked by open diplomacy, the right of self-determination, free trade, disarmament, the peaceful settlement of disputes, and the establishment of an international security organization in the form of the League of Nations. The role of the League would be to resolve differences between states, guarantee their political independence and territorial integrity, and address a range of other contemporary international questions such as the position of labor and minorities. However, hopes for a reformed world, already badly damaged by the punitive Versailles Peace Treaty (1919), were shattered with the militarization and expansionism of Italy, Germany, and Japan in the 1930s, culminating in World War II. These events and the rapid onset of the Cold War after 1945 generated a number of influential realist critiques that were widely (if not necessarily fairly) perceived as devastating to liberal internationalism, both as an intellectual construct and as a guide to the practical conduct of IR. Since the 1980s, however, liberal internationalism has attracted renewed interest both on empirical and on normative grounds, and it may be that IR is moving toward a position in which it can provide a more satisfactory account of liberal internationalism's legacy, potentialities, and limitations.

Liberal assumptions and historical overview

Liberal internationalism reflects the broader liberal tradition of which it is part in that it comprises several political/philosophical strands, has emerged in a number of diverse national and historical contexts, has evolved over time in response to changing domestic and international conditions, and rests upon a body of elastic concepts that invite the exercise of judgment and interpretation in order to draw out their political and policy conclusions. When considered in these terms, liberalism is better understood not as providing a blueprint for thinking about IR or foreign policy, but rather as a cluster or matrix of underlying values, principles, and purposes that provide a guide and framework through which one can think flexibly about IR, albeit within certain normative parameters.

Despite this apparent indeterminacy, however, it is possible to identify a conceptual core within the worldview. Historically, its central normative and critical concerns have been to expand the capacity for collective self-rule and address the perennial problems of the abuse of power and illegitimate violence. Conceptually, one finds at the center of liberal internationalism an insistence upon the moral primacy of the individual and a tradition of political and philosophical interest in the conditions of individual freedom, or autonomy. When taken in conjunction with liberalism's egalitarian assumption of the moral equality of individuals, one can appreciate why liberals have advocated republics, constitutional monarchies, or what in contemporary terms are often referred to as 'liberal democratic' political systems. These are regarded as offering a rational means of facilitating the greatest collective domain of freedom for equal individuals through being bound by the principles of the accountability of power, political representation through an independent legislature and the rule of law, and the enjoyment of human rights. When the universal liberal assumption that the human species possesses a certain moral unity is also taken into account, one has the bases of the cosmopolitan sentiments that pervade liberalism. Two areas in which this universalism plays out politically are in the tension between liberalism and the Westphalian notion of state sovereignty, and in underpinning the cosmopolitan doctrine of human rights.

Within liberalism persons are not only the subject of moral discourse, but also regarded as key agents of historical and political change. But what conception of the individual do liberals hold? Whilst accounts vary, Kant's qualified endorsement of the human character (marked by self-interest and a desire for self-preservation yet also possessing the capacity for moral thought, reason, and human sympathy) avoids the extremes of either naivety or cynicism. This conceptualization is consistent with the traditional liberal emphasis upon education, individual, and collective responsibility for action, and the notion of enlightened self-interest as the best hope for individual and collective progress.

During the nineteenth century, liberals tended to concentrate primarily upon the achievement and consolidation of domestic political gains, but there was nevertheless an international dimension to their project. This pertained to the international requirements of the development of liberal politics at home and to the question of the legitimacy of intervention to assist liberal movements abroad. One finds in this period a largely uncritical faith in the universal benefits of free trade, self-determination (at least for Europeans), and the peaceful arbitration of disputes. The notion that a market-based realm of unhindered trans-societal relations would be beneficial, for civilization was implicit in Richard Cobden's (1804–1865) famous dictum 'as little intercourse as possible between Governments, as much connection as possible between the nations of the world'. However, this belief in the operation of providence or some other form of preordained or natural moral progression of human history could not survive the turmoil of the twentieth century. Whilst many liberals attributed World War I as much if not more to a systemic failure than to wilful design, the expansionism and raw brutality of the 1930s and the collapse of free trade presented a clear and unambiguous rebuttal of the optimistic assumptions of nineteenth-century liberalism.

It was also in this period that Carr published his influential critique of liberalism, *The 20 Years Crisis* (1946). Whilst several of Carr's specific points present virtual caricatures of the liberal tradition, one of its key arguments, that liberalism's claim to present universal values and identify universal goods were the unwitting reflection of particular national and class interests, remains pertinent. It is ironic, however, that Carr's work, often thought of as an astute commentary upon the character of political life, itself misjudged the requirements of security policy, for Carr himself advocated the appeasement of Hitler whereas the early application of some form of collective resistance, as advocated by many liberals and socialists, might have averted the Nazi leader's expansionism.

Following World War II, mainstream liberalism became increasingly absorbed with the question of the Soviet threat and rallied round the policy of containment as a way to prevent the spread of state socialist or communist regimes. A combination of military, political, economic, and ideological measures were employed, but with the expectation that ultimately state socialism would fail due to internal inefficiencies and domestic unpopularity. The containment doctrine came under criticism, however, from liberals on both the Left and the Right. On the left, containment was criticized for the pervasive militarization of foreign policy and support of authoritarian regimes with appalling human rights records, so long as they were anticommunist. On the right, despite the initial retreat from the 'rollback' in the 1950s, containment was often regarded as too moderate a doctrine and, particularly in the Reagan years, greater efforts were made to provide military aid for movements resisting communism in the Middle East, Central Asia, Central America, and elsewhere.

In the late 1980s, however, the implosion of the Soviet system was widely hailed by mainstream liberals as a vindication of containment, whilst the Right claimed that it vindicated Reagan's military buildup. The contingent nature of this latter claim has become more apparent since the end of the Cold War as disaffected and repressed social forces within authoritarian states allied with or formerly supported by the United States have emerged as hostile to the Cold War victors. Whilst the problem is not new – witness the Iranian Islamic Revolution of 1979 against the pro-American regime of the Shah – the rise of anti-American Islamic militancy in Saudi Arabia and the protracted issue of Iraq have created major new security problems for the United States. All three of these cases raise the question of the long-term wisdom of supporting authoritarian regimes and failing to conduct one's foreign policy in accordance with liberal principles and values, even when there may seem to be short-term or instrumental reasons for doing so.

This question of liberal foreign policy is but one aspect of the major debate with realism over the nature of IR and the possibilities for their reform. The liberal emphasis upon the determining power of factors at the state level – such as the spread of liberal democratic regimes – and the ability of states to refashion their national interests through the development of commerce has received fresh interest in recent years following the end of the Cold War as well as empirical support from the democratic peace research program. Before discussing liberalism's contribution to international affairs in more detail it is sobering to consider the scale of the task a reformist ideology such as liberalism faces as it is required to operate effectively across four distinct but properly interrelated dimensions: the critical, the normative, the political, and the administrative or managerial.

Liberalism's critical spirit was first directed to the bastions of privilege and tradition under the *ancien regime*, but for those at the progressive edge of the tradition the responsibility to continue to scrutinize political institutions and practices and the underlying terms and horizons of politics remains incumbent. Once liberalism fails to address itself to contemporary claims of justice and abuses of power it is prone to become the doctrine of the privileged and increasingly conservative or elitist in character. Liberalism's normative dimension has been manifest in the presentation of powerful and attractive claims such as self-determination and human and minority rights and the development of moral discourses on questions such as distributive and environmental justice and the challenge globalization presents to state-based conceptions of democracy. But, if liberalism fails to generate inspiring normative and political visions or fails to abide by those it does present, then it becomes open to charges of complacency, double standards, or hypocrisy and may generate disillusionment and cynicism, thereby squandering this valuable moral-political resource.

As a practical as well as a theoretical project a further dimension of the liberal project has been to develop a politics through which to achieve its goals. Central to this dimension is a significant liberal societal base composed of political parties and/or civil society organizations that are in positions of power or influence. One example of such a coalition is that mustered by Roosevelt to underpin the New Deal in the 1930s, comprising leaders of ethnic and minority groups, reform-oriented pressure groups, and civil society organizations (including the vanguard of the intelligentsia), as well as the organized interests of labor and the local party machines. Without a strong societal base, liberalism faces political marginalization or irrelevance.

Finally, the maintenance of liberal gains and achievements requires managerial and administrative competence to avoid liberal institutions and programs becoming inefficient and wasteful. This issue is particularly problematic at the international level given that anarchy has often been thought to generate disincentives to effective collective action and cooperation. To this end, liberals have tended to rely upon hegemonic leadership and/or international regimes through which to improve information and communication, stabilize expectations about the future, and develop trust between parties (Keohane 1984).

To satisfactorily attain any of these critical, normative, political, and administrative dimensions individually, let alone collectively, is clearly a major task. Yet given that they are necessarily interdependent, there ought ideally to be some holistic vision that informs developments within each dimension.

The historical development of liberal internationalism

Whilst the philosophical roots of liberalism are often located in the Judaeo-Christian traditions, it is in the eighteenth-century European Enlightenment that one first finds a systematic statement of liberal internationalism. Liberals tended to regard IR as a function of domestic politics and from this premise they identified a range of international practices, most centrally war itself, as the external buttresses of the *ancien regime*'s hierarchical domestic political order. The French *philosophes* in particular developed the fundamentals of what was to become the classic liberal and radical critique of the Westphalian international system. Politics, they argued, should concentrate primarily on developing and perfecting the domestic realm rather than satisfying the pursuit of glory overseas. Under the *ancien regime*, diplomacy was conducted in secret in order to serve the personal intrigues and ambitions of rulers rather than the interests of the people at large; treaties were regarded as temporary armistices; and the balance of power an inherently unstable system was prone to shocks and conflicts.

The promise of contemporary liberal internationalists was to supersede this 'war system' through responsible government, commerce, and ultimately the rule of law, with the rising European bourgeoisie and its intellectuals as the harbingers of the new age of reason. Whilst most liberals regarded war and the use of force as legitimate in certain circumstances, it was generally regarded as a failure of reason and an impediment to the liberal vision of political life. When it did occur it was typically regarded as a product of the bellicosity of despots or monarchical rulers, the consequence of faulty or unjust domestic political arrangements, or else the result of poor communication or of misunderstanding between parties. It is, however, the link between war and injustice that provides the most enduring and theoretically interesting insight into the analysis of war and violence. The importance that liberals have attached to the problem of war is apparent when one considers the central place it has occupied across a range of key areas that liberals have sought to reform in accordance with their normative and political concerns. These include civil–military relations, international political economy, and self-determination, as well as the emphasis that liberals have put upon such themes as the international rule of law, arbitration, and disarmament. Underpinning this major theme in liberal thought has been the view that war and preparation for war corrodes liberal domestic political structures and impedes the pursuit of liberty. This restraining influence sits in tension, however, with the argument that force might sometimes be legitimate for liberal political reasons such as collective security or the protection of human rights as well as the traditional right of self-defence.

Civil–military relations

A fundamental issue for emerging constitutionalist and liberal movements has been the need to provide for defense against foreign threats whilst at the same time avoiding the creation of a military force that threatens civilian rule and liberal politics domestically. Among the methods historically devised in Europe and North America have been legislative control of the military and its funding and reliance upon civilian militias alongside or instead of a professional military.

However, increased military specialization, industrialization, the experience of total war, and most of all the onset of the Cold War and the development of nuclear weaponry so radically transformed the conduct of warfare that military authority became increasingly removed from society and concentrated in the hands of military professionals and the executive branch of government. The rise of the 'imperial presidency' and the proliferation of executive agencies in the United States is the clearest example of this trend, with the emergence of a 'military industrial complex' during the Cold War indicative of the broader militarization of society in this period (Schlesinger 1974).

Following the end of the Cold War, whilst there was an initial decrease in military expenditure in the United States and the reassertion of Congressional influence, the trend toward greater cultural militarization apparent in the glamor of hi-tech and 'smart' weaponry, and encouraged by state agencies and the entertainment industry, receives remarkably little critical attention in mainstream liberal thought. Since 2001, this cultural fetishization of the military has been superseded by the more overt geostrategic militarism of the Bush administration.

Political economy

Liberal political economy emerged as a critique of mercantilism, which was a doctrine that sought to harness economic activity to the pursuit of state power. Mercantilism assumed the level of wealth in the world to be fixed, and encouraged the 'beggar thy neighbour' policies of maximizing exports and minimizing imports. By contrast, liberal thinkers such as Adam Smith, reflecting the views of earlier writers such as the French *physiocrats* and the Scot, David Hume (1711–1776), argued that the purpose of economic activity should be to increase overall levels of wealth and that increased division of labor and specialization could achieve this end. An invisible hand that made it self-regulating, Smith argued, guided the market. Accordingly, state intervention would lead to distortions and inefficiencies. In this *laissez faire* vision, the state's role was to be confined to the protection of society from external threats and the provision of certain public goods. Externally, free trade would increase the absolute wealth of all parties, and foster bonds of interdependence and peace between peoples. Indeed, this perceived progressive cosmopolitan role has been one of the principle reasons why free trade became for many liberals a fundamental article of faith.

However, the equity of free trade as an international doctrine was challenged by some observers in later industrializing states such as imperial Germany and the United States who argued that it favored the most advanced national economies and that some measure of state protection was required in order to allow their economies to catch up. Similarly, the success of the East Asian economies in the 1980s required strong and efficient state apparatuses, which were (in varying degrees) able to negotiate the terms of engagement with neoliberal economic forces.

The doctrine of *laissez faire* was also to become increasingly challenged as left-liberals in the late nineteenth century increasingly advocated greater public regulation of the economy in order to balance the claims of economic liberty with those of equality and social justice. 'New Liberals' identified growing tensions between democracy and capitalism and argued that the state should play a more active role in the development of 'positive freedom', understood as developing the social and economic conditions whereby persons were able to properly exercise and enjoy the formal rights and freedoms liberalism offered. This break with classical liberalism laid the foundations for the Keynesian economic doctrines that were to form the economic bases of the social democratic programs that became the orthodoxy in many liberal states from 1945 until the late 1970s. Indeed, this split between 'classical' and 'welfare' (or 'social') liberals constitutes one of the most fundamental dividing lines within the liberal tradition and carries with it important international implications. Central to the original 'New Liberal' critique was the argument that growing levels of domestic inequality were generating their own injustices, and that these were finding expression internationally in terms of trends toward autarky, greater militarism, imperialism, and conflict.

Keynes himself, in *The Economic Consequences of the Peace* (1919), warned that, given prewar levels of interdependence, the recovery of the German economy was a necessary prerequisite of a broader European recovery and of continental stability. One finds in Keynes' critique of the Versailles settlement a vindication of Norman Angell's argument in *The Great Illusion* (1913) that the extent of the international division of labor and the credit-dependent structure of modern wealth meant that conquest was no longer rational as a means through which states could expand their wealth. Keynes also criticized *laissez faire* and, for a brief period during the Depression, even argued for greater economic nationalism in order that political communities might pursue their respective political ends (such as full employment) without facing a 'flight of capital' from the national economy. Liberal thinkers, then, have been willing to reevaluate liberalism's doctrinal elements in light of changing political circumstances and considerations of justice.

The interwar collapse of the European economies and the rise of political extremism brought a greater recognition among political leaders of the need for public regulation of the international economy and of the need to pursue a benign rather than a punitive peace after World War II. Under US leadership, the Bretton Woods institutions and the General Agreement on Tariffs and Trade (GATT) established a relatively open and nondiscriminatory international trading and financial order. Politically, probably the greatest success of this period was to have successfully managed the peaceful integration of the defeated powers into the reconstructed international order. West Germany and Japan were led to accept the desirability of a democratic domestic political system, which for the liberal victors was a condition of their future peacefulness, and encouraged to participate in an open international economy that they were able to recognize as an avenue that would allow their dynamic economies to grow and prosper through nonmilitary means.

This aspect of liberal political economy pertaining to the management of relations between advanced economies has received considerable academic attention through the literature on interdependence, regimes, and institutions and is generally regarded as the mainstream liberal research agenda in the academic study of IR. As noted above, central to this agenda is an engagement with realism in order to demonstrate that even under conditions of anarchy it is rational for self-interested state actors to develop patterns of cooperation. This research agenda has been criticized, however, for its proximity to the key concerns of US foreign policy, particularly the possibilities of maintaining a favorable trading and financial order following the decline of US hegemony in the 1970s and 1980s. The problem, however, is less the nature of the research program (as argued above, the 'managerial' is a legitimate and important aspect of the liberal project, particularly given contemporary trends toward unilateralism and protectionism in the United States), but rather that the managerial dimension has become the predominant strand of academic inquiry at the same time that it has tended to disconnect from the other dimensions, notably the critical and the normative.

Scholars such as Richardson (2001) criticize the neoliberal insistence upon the virtue and necessity of the unregulated market that has emerged since the late 1970s and which has been promoted by the World Bank and the IMF and governments of states such as the United States and the United Kingdom. A liberal alternative to this is a development-centered approach along the lines advocated by the United Nations Development Program (UNDP). The changing political climate is reflected in the neglect among key policy makers of the work of scholars such as Beitz (1979), who has argued that under conditions of interdependence there are moral obligations upon the North to pursue redistributive policies toward the South, and Shue (1980), who has insisted upon the North's obligation to provide the basic right to subsistence toward those in need.

National self-determination

Implicit in the liberal pursuit of individual and collective freedom or autonomy is the right to self-government. During the French Revolution this principle was combined with nationalism to generate the principle of national self-determination, which legitimated the right of a people or nation to their own self-governing sovereign state. It is, however, important to disentangle this pairing in order to appreciate the evolution of liberal thought on the topic. In the nineteenth century, liberals were generally sympathetic to the independence struggles of the Greeks, Hungarians, Poles, and Italians. However, following the unification of Germany under Bismarck between 1860 and 1871 by 'blood and iron', it became increasingly apparent that nationalism could develop in nonliberal forms suited more to the development of states and empires as centralized power units rather than as republics engaged in the pursuit of liberal freedom. There developed, then, tensions between nationalism as the claim to maintain an exclusive territorial, political, and moral domain, and the liberal ideal of self-determination, concerned with the right and ability of a people to establish political control over the forces and decision-making processes that determine their social and political fates, compatible with the right and ability of others to do the same.

Following World War I, the problematic aspects of national self-determination became further apparent when applied to the multicultural regions of Central and Eastern Europe. Increasingly, liberal notions of self-determination came to require modifications or limitations upon the principle and practice of sovereignty. This has led liberal internationalism in the direction of support for minority rights, federalism, and the establishment of the partially postsovereign institutions of the European Union: the European Coal and Steel Community and the European Economic Community. One current effort to reimagine the question of self-government under conditions of globalization is the project of 'cosmopolitan democracy' (Held 1995). The challenge this project faces is to devise ways in which centers of power and decision-making can be influenced by and answerable to those groups they affect, despite the disjuncture between the (global) territorial scale of economic/political relations and the juridical/political division of the world into states.

Residual dilemmas of intervention and imperialism

The questions of whether to intervene to assist movements for national independence or to relieve violations of human rights or human suffering have generated legitimate differences of opinion within the liberal tradition. Most liberals have tended to fall somewhere between absolute noninterventionism and pro-interventionism. Immanuel Kant (1724–1804), for example, was a strong noninterventionist but did sanction the right of forced constitutional change against regimes that were persistent and serious violators of international law. John Stuart Mill (1806–1873), following the suppression of the liberal revolutions in 1848, came to sanction a right of counterintervention in cases where a foreign power had intervened to suppress liberal forces.

As discussed further below, the residual nature of questions of intervention is apparent in the prominence of this issue since the end of the Cold War. Whereas debate in the 1990s tended to focus on the question of intervention for humanitarian purposes, since 2001 and the emergence of the 'war on terror' attention has shifted to questions of preemptive and preventive intervention on security grounds. Two other areas in which liberalism shaped the recent international agenda, however, are the development of international law and the promotion of the idea of good governance.

The development of the international as a law governed realm has long been an aspiration for liberals and, accordingly, the rediscovery of the legal responsibility of individuals for war crimes and crimes against humanity as developed at Nuremberg after World War II is at face value a positive development. However, the institutional machinery – the UN tribunals for former Yugoslavia and Rwanda and the more ambitious Permanent International Criminal Court – remain in their infancy. Further, the lack of legal rights afforded to detainees at Camp Delta at Guantanamo Bay by the United States discredits the wider turn to law in the international system through demonstrating the selectivity of the attachment to due process.

The conventional liberal attention to the internal character of states has become manifest recently in the requirement for 'good governance' by states in transition or in the under-developed regions of the world and is often a condition of aid and loan transfers by Western donors and financial institutions. 'Good governance' has found support on both the right and the left of the tradition but does remain controversial. For right-liberals it has been a way of imposing greater external leverage and scrutiny upon governments and developing a hospitable environment for foreign capital. For left-liberals it has offered a richer approach to development than strategies that focus solely on neoliberal economic reform through recognizing the interdependent and mutually reinforcing nature of such political goods as human rights, development, the rule of law and peace, and a way of developing local civil society and democratic, participatory politics. The intrusive nature of this agenda does, however, raise the question of whether and to what extent 'governance' represents a new form of imperialism.

Historically, whilst many liberals such as Adam Smith, Kant, Cobden, and Bright were critics of colonialism, others such as John Stuart Mill went as far as to sanction despotism as a legitimate mode of government for 'uncivilized' non-Europeans. Whilst imperialism came increasingly to be perceived as illegitimate as the colonized claimed for themselves the 'universal' right of self-determination that the Europeans enjoyed, the broader issue of the widespread liberal presumption of moral superiority remains. The issue is particularly pointed given the relative power advantage liberals have to act on this premise and is discussed at greater length below. To conclude this section, liberalism has constructed the modern states system as a framework of interplay and tension between the Westphalian values of state sovereignty and liberalism's own internationalist and cosmopolitan ambitions, even if in its origin the reform of the international realm was often regarded primarily as a means of enabling the constitutional–institutional and social development of politics at the domestic level. The philosophical pursuit of individual and collective freedom had wide-ranging political implications across such areas as civil–military relations, political economy, the bases of state legitimacy and national self-determination, and for the rise of international organizations and the modern development of 'humanity' as a moral category. Liberalism's most significant achievements lie in the efforts to develop politics in accordance with the perceived requirements of justice and to develop ways through which states can move beyond the realist representation of IR as a war-bound realm with strictly limited potential for cooperation. Among its weaknesses, however, are a problematic association with capitalism, a presumption of moral superiority and inclination toward imperialism, and an inconsistent level of engagement with international affairs and issues. The next section of this chapter is concerned with the future of liberal internationalism.

Liberal internationalism in the twenty-first century

The starting point for this analysis of contemporary liberal internationalism – by which in practice is meant left-liberal and social-democratic internationalism – is the need to recognise that the project has become derailed. Despite its historical record discussed above, liberal internationalism has struggled to resolve tensions in the policy, political, and structural realms and faces an underlying crisis of belief in the intellectual and normative realms. Until this deeper crisis is satisfactorily addressed it is unlikely that liberal internationalism will reemerge as a major political force. Indeed, the future of liberal internationalism depends to a considerable extent upon whether the tensions and problems of contemporary liberal internationalism serve to fatally undermine the central project of combining individual and collective freedom or whether this crisis can be utilized as a regenerative experience from which a new globalism can emerge.

Clearly, this prognosis differs markedly from the upbeat mood of many liberals in the second half of the 1980s as the Cold War thawed. For many liberals it was the democratic internationalism of (the communist!) Mikhail Gorbachev that defined the spirit of the age. Gorbachev's 'New Political Thinking' – comprising greater political openness, economic reform, retreat from empire, and a revised conception of East–West relations in accordance with a model of 'common security' – dovetailed with the widespread demonstration of 'people power' to force the collapse of state-socialist regimes in Central and Eastern Europe and ultimately in the Soviet Union itself. The euphoria of the period is indicated by the reception afforded to Fukuyama's (1989) essay 'the End of History?' which argued that the combination of liberal democracy and free-market capitalism signified the teleological culmination of humanity's political evolution. Such (liberal) hopes were reflected in President George H.W. Bush's proclamation of a 'New World Order' in the wake of the Persian Gulf War of 1990–1991 and the Clinton administration's policy of 'democratic enlargement'. It is fair to say, however, that the scale of the liberal internationalist 'vision' among elite groups in the early 1990s was much narrower than that held by their predecessors in 1918 and 1945. Bush's 'New World Order' was first and foremost a symbolic rationalization of American leadership rather than an effort to endow international law and institutions with greater autonomy and power. Further, the conservative neoliberal turn in political economy continued to exert a powerful grip upon policy makers and set the structural context within which dominant notions of human rights, democratization, and global governance could operate.

The lack of substance in the 'New World Order' was soon exposed as a series of specific, complex, and urgent challenges emerged. Intrastate violence, ethnic conflict, and humanitarian emergencies in Northern Iraq, Somalia, Bosnia, and Rwanda pushed the question of 'humanitarian intervention' to the forefront of the policy agenda. However, the Western response exposed muddled thinking and a lack of resolve that in turn undermined its claims to moral and political authority. The Somalia debacle in which US troops were withdrawn after the loss of 19 Rangers in 1993 effectively foreclosed the prospect of intervention to prevent or halt the genocide in Rwanda the following year in which up to 800,000 people were killed. In Bosnia, Western policy was marked by confusion and indecision and a distinct lack of policy harmonization between actors. When NATO launched tactical airstrikes in March 1995, for example, the Serbs were able to seize 370 UN peacekeepers and their equipment as hostages. Yet it was the failure of the United Nations to protect its own 'safe havens', most infamously at Srebenica resulting in the genocide of over 7,000 Muslim males, which provides the darkest illustration of the dangers of poorly conceived interventionism. That the political and operational difficulties liberals face when using force for nondefensive purposes are residual was illustrated again in the 1999 Kosovan War. The lack of explicit UN authorization left it an illegal – but arguably legitimate – war, whilst the aerial bombing strategy that was responsible for civilian deaths but required due to the political sensitivities within democracies to the loss of their own citizens, even professional soldiers, highlights the standing contradiction between humanitarian aims and military means.

Whilst there have been efforts to develop the conceptual implications and clarify the principles and possibilities of humanitarian intervention – most notably the report of the International Commission on Intervention and State Sovereignty (2001) on the 'Responsibility to Protect' – these cannot change the fact that in many democracies the fundamental desirability and wisdom of such interventions remain contested and the political will inconsistent. The question of military intervention forces differences and uncertainties over national identity to the surface like no other, for it cannot but be discussed except with reference to the nature of a state's national interest and international role and thereby often stirs and intensifies deep divisions in national political cultures.

This absence of a domestic political consensus upon questions of intervention highlights a wider, general problem for liberal internationalism. That is, liberal-minded governments and administrations are often unable to make medium- to long-term commitments to internationalist institutions or programs as they themselves may be voted out of office and replaced by rivals with a narrower vision of the national interest. Indeed, as Clinton himself discovered, in domestic political systems marked by the separation of powers and a hostile

Congress, administrations may be prevented from pursuing an internationalist policy even during their term of office. This difficulty in pledging medium- to long-term commitment is itself a major obstacle to the credibility of liberal internationalism as a political force and highlights the residual paradox of requiring such commitment to develop international institutions yet needing effective institutions to ensure such commitment.

Indeed, international institutions are increasingly vital for international liberalism, yet a residual concern throughout the 1990s was the severe under-resourcing of existing institutions and, particularly after the issue became a pawn in US domestic politics, restrictions on the development of new institutions that might challenge US sovereignty and power. That the UN system relies upon state contributions enables powerful states to exert political leverage through withholding contributions. But in any case the sums involved are relatively small given the challenges the organization faces. 'The startling fact is that [in the year following President H.W. Bush's call for a New World Order] the sum of the U.N. regular budget and peacekeeping costs for 1992, was less than the cost of two Stealth bombers, or the combined cost of operating New York City's Fire and Police Departments for one year' (Ogata 1993: 2). Under-resourcing, however, is not confined only to finances as the current arrangements continue to fall well short of that envisaged by the founders of the United Nations as indicated, for example, by Article 43 of the UN Charter in which members 'undertake to make available to the Security Council . . . armed forces, assistance and facilities . . . necessary for the purpose of maintaining international peace and security'.

That liberal internationalism is faced, then, with an unstable and often weak political base, a host of internal tensions, and severe under-resourcing denotes a hardly propitious set of circumstances. What these factors highlight, however, is the severe underdevelopment of an effective and equitable system of global governance. Whilst there was significant interest in this question in the 1990s and the publication of such major reports on the subject as those by the Commission on Global Governance (1995) and World Order Models Project (Falk 1995), it remained underdeveloped and has more recently been displaced by the 'war on terror'. However, the scale and intensity of contemporary globalization means that the need for the regulation of transnational interactions, cooperation on a range of global issues, and the development of deeper levels of normative and cultural understanding is certain to increase. As the inherent limits and contradictions of the current ideological and militarized approach to IR become more apparent, there is likely to be greater receptivity in the international public realm to creative and innovative approaches to addressing both specific problems and the general nature of world order.

This does not, however, mean that liberal internationalism should (or indeed can) expect to operate as it has in the past: grounded in an ethnocentric mode of thought that justifies universal moral and political claims from within its own particular philosophical discourse. The power of the antifoundationalist critique in political philosophy has highlighted the problematic and unsatisfactory tendency dominant within liberalism to project transcultural norms from a particular liberal standpoint. Recent postmodernist critiques resonate with the tradition of skepticism within liberalism itself, such as to heighten sensitivity to the limits of one's own knowledge and the contingency of truth claims in general. Moreover, at the political level, such ethnocentrism is readily prone to silence and exclude others and to misunderstand and misrepresent their identities and interests, generating in turn alienation, resentment, and resistance. It is this connection between an ethnocentric universalism and power that keeps sensitivity to imperialism at the forefront of liberalism's critical reflections.

With this in mind there is a strong case for contemporary liberals and democrats to substantively and symbolically de-link aspirations toward 'progressive politics' from 'liberal internationalism' as a historically and culturally specific project. Whilst for some this may hardly be startling, it remains for many a radical proposition and one that has barely filtered through into mainstream political discourse. A key element of such a disposition ought to be greater sensitivity to the historical legacy of liberal particularism in relation to the non-Western world, and indeed to the wider legacy of Western domination with which liberalism has the ambivalent relationship of not only part-critic (through certain of its normative discourses) but also part-complice (through its close association with capitalism, justifications for imperialism, and willingness to rely on the West's power advantage to advance its own normative and political agendas).

At the normative level, liberals would do well to seek to ground a new globalism in the principle of the equality of peoples and civilizations. Key priorities are the need for better intercivilizational understanding, not least between the West and the Islamic world, and at the material level the question of underdevelopment – by far the greatest cause of human suffering. There is, however, no reason why liberals should not continue to advocate human rights and democracy as core values, but at the same time they should realize that they cannot claim a monopoly on the right to formulate and interpret the content of human rights, and that other traditions may be able to achieve a number of aims of human rights and other 'goods' through a different discourse. Human rights do, however, already carry with them a good measure of international legitimation through their standing in international law, and the 1993 Vienna Declaration confirmed the principle of universality whilst noting also the significance of national, religious, historical, and cultural differences. The radical potential of democracy is even more marked, and *contra* Fukuyama, it is quite likely that alternatives to the secular, free-market model will emerge.

There are also good political arguments for a new form of globalism. Mainstream foreign policy debate in the United States is divided not over the question of American leadership, but over the question of whether this be unilateral or multilateral in character. That the latter in practice places greater emphasis upon 'soft-power' dovetails with traditional liberal internationalist approaches (Nye 2004). However, in the wider world the contemporary militarization of US foreign policy has stiffened resistance to American leadership *per se*, whilst paradoxically also highlighting the limits of American power. The challenges to American leadership that have emerged in Latin America, Central Asia, and most notably in the Middle East and Gulf regions mark not only the limits of American power, but also the demise of the West's ability to set the cultural, normative, and ideological standards in and for an increasingly globalized world.

Indeed, there are reasonably strong indicators that international politics is becoming marked by a new pluralism and that the end of the Cold War may in fact have marked the zenith of Western power rather than its triumph. The rise of China and various local theatres of resistance to Western power and contemporary neoliberal globalization, coupled with the depletion of the fossil fuel resources that have been vital for capitalist production in the twentieth century, may force a significant rebalancing of world politics that forces major social and cultural change as nature and politics combine to erode the ability of the West to maintain its massively disproportionate access to and consumption of the planet's resources. Given liberalism's own ambivalent relationship to the West as a unit of power, this carries with it both threats and opportunities. In any case, the present militarization of foreign policy may itself be read as a response to fears of the decline of Western power, but as a response it is itself unsustainable and bound to fail. Whilst it may make sense in terms of certain class and sectional interests, it is detrimental and dangerous to the interests of the West as a whole.

Yet, as noted above, globality – of a sort – is the twenty-first-century condition and one requiring greater levels of equity and understanding than are possible under the conditions of ideological militarization that have characterized the first years of the new century. This, however, is a challenge not only for liberals but also for the global community at large. Moreover, the scale of the challenge is of the first order, for globalization – the growth of a world economy, the extent of global communication and information networks, and the proliferation of multiethnic communities – marks the endgame for the Westphalian system, both as an analytical model and as defining a political reality. That this raises serious questions over the meaning of statehood in the twenty-first century presents fundamental challenges to the key political concepts at the heart of liberalism that have traditionally been thought of in the context of the sovereign state: 'nation', 'citizenship', 'democracy', and 'accountability'. Until these concepts are given fresh substance appropriate to the global age there is the standing danger that populations will turn to reactionary conservative or fundamentalist political answers as traditional representations of politics become increasingly inadequate to address the political, social, and cultural issues of the age.

In the foreign policy domain, liberals and fellow reformists and activists can play a role in developing a sustained critique of the ideological and militarized turn and by advancing a bold and ambitious vision of an alternative foreign policy and global order, pursued through persuasion and politics. One may be looking at a ten to twenty years' time frame in which intellectuals, policy entrepreneurs, activists, and civil society organizations forge a series of global networks and coalitions that can undergird a global coalition. That such a call has a clear ring of the civil society discourse of the 1990s is to recognize that the vitality and dynamism of that decade, if ultimately disappointed, offers lessons upon which to build. The human security and human development agendas in particular – plus the innovative coalitions between a wide range of state, institutional, and nonstate actors that characterized, for example, the campaigns against landmines and for the development of a Permanent International Criminal Court – mark the kernel of a globalist coalition and alternative 'bloc' of social forces to that presently sustaining the elite-driven, militarized geoeconomic order.

There is also a growing body of ideas and technical 'know-how' to enhance the possibility of the 'international community' generating its own resources for the purposes of peacekeeping, development, humanitarian work, and disease eradication. Whether this be a tax on foreign exchange transfers or the market-based measures advocated by the UNDP's recent report on 'new public financing' (Kaul and Conceição 2006), there is a common theme that those who benefit from the global commons should contribute directly toward the maintenance costs of the international order (and where appropriate to the costs of its reform).

Strategically, it is important for liberals to bear in mind two key insights that ought to guide and underpin liberal contributions to a new globalism. The first is the fundamental incompatibility of liberalism with war and militarism. Tocqueville's observation that 'no protracted war can fail to endanger the freedom of a democratic country' remains salient. The increase of state power, corrosion of civil liberties, and militarization of politics reaffirm Tocqueville's view that 'if [war] does not lead to despotism by sudden violence, it prepares men for it more gently by their habits' and detracts from the important issues contemporary liberal societies have to address, such as multiculturalism, education, gender equality, employment opportunities and welfare provision, and climate change, not to mention the wider challenges that globalization presents for conceptualizations of democracy that remain rooted in the notion of the sovereign state. Indeed, it is notable that the European Union, one of liberalism's most significant if far from perfect achievements, has been conspicuous by its attention to the socioeconomic and constitutional–institutional bases of political order. This nonmilitary approach has underpinned the vital role it has played in stabilizing the political transition of many postcommunist countries in Europe in recent years, as it earlier did with the transitions of Greece, Spain, and Portugal from periods of authoritarian rule.

The second insight is that justice is an essential requirement for a stable and a deep peace. This theme runs throughout the work of many of the early liberals and has continued to inform analyses of the causes of war and violence as the tradition has evolved. Whilst the basic insight itself is straightforward, it does present significant challenges for the political imagination at the theoretical level, particularly when the global age requires justice between as well as within ethical traditions. At the same time, however, there are often situations in which the requirements of justice and the fact that this is a political rather than a theoretical problem are relatively clear. It is a point worth making that success or progress across a fairly small number of major problems, in conjunction with a more proactive approach to developing the institutions of global governance, could produce a very significant change in the direction of contemporary world politics and to the further development of the global realm as a civil sphere bound by norms and ultimately by law.

Conclusion

This chapter has argued that liberal internationalism lacks sufficient influence within Western societies and suffers from problems of credibility and legitimacy beyond them. It faces challenges across all four of the critical, normative, political, and administrative dimensions. In the twenty-first century, liberal internationalism must reevaluate the philosophical bases for its own knowledge claims and the procedural requirements for legitimate action at the international level as important steps in liberalism's evolution as a global rather than a Western project. Clearly this presents a major task of the first order, but not one that is impossible. In any case, it is not one that liberals should undertake by themselves.

Further reading

Howard, M. (1981) *War and the Liberal Conscience*, Oxford: Oxford University Press.
Mandelbaum, M. (2004) *The Ideas that Conquered the World: Peace, Democracy and Free Markets in the Twenty-First Century*, New York: Public Affairs.
Richardson, J.L. (2001) *Contending Liberalisms in World Politics*, Boulder, CO: Lynne Rienner.

4 Marxism

Mark Rupert

Introduction

Deeply enmeshed in intellectual and political projects spanning well over a century and much of the world, Marxism – the tradition of 'practical-critical activity' founded by Karl Marx – defies reduction to any simple doctrine or single political position. Its breadth and diversity is illustrated by the sheer mass of Leszek Kolakowski's multivolume survey *Main Currents of Marxism* (2005), a schematic overview of historical and actually existing Marxisms. Nevertheless, it is possible to understand this constellation of intellectual and political positions as constituting variants of historical materialism (the core of the Marxist worldview) insofar as they are animated by a critique of capitalism, understood as a particular historical form of organization of human social life, rather than a natural or necessary expression of some innate and invariant human nature. Without pretending to speak for the whole of Marxism, this chapter will present a particular interpretation of historical materialism and its relevance for global politics.

Contrary to simplistic caricatures which retain in some quarters a measure of academic currency, historical materialism has focused its attention upon capitalism as a material way of life, an ensemble of social relations which has never been coterminous with 'the economy' as we know it in the modern world, nor with the so-called 'domestic' sphere putatively contained within the boundaries of the sovereign state. Marxism has much to say about historically evolving structures and practices which have crossed national boundaries and linked the domestic and the international, the economic and the political – much to say, in short, about the social production of global politics. Historical materialism suggests that states and systems of interstate and transnational power relations are embedded in and (re-)produced through systems of relations that encompass (among other things) the social organization of production. The latter is itself structured according to relations of class (and, many contemporary Marxists acknowledge, by race and gender as well as other relations of domination), and is an object of contestation among social classes, state managers, and other historically situated political agents. Thus politics is not confined to the formally public sphere of the modern state, but permeates the economic sphere as well: just as the state and interstate politics can profoundly shape economic and social life, so the politics of the economy can have enormous implications – not generally recognized within the terms of liberal worldviews – for the historical form taken by particular states and world orders constructed among states. The point here, it must be emphasized, is not to reconstruct global politics on the basis of an economistic reductionism in which all causality is seen as emanating from an already constituted, foundational economic sphere (a sort of universal independent variable), but rather to argue something very nearly the opposite – that politics and political struggle are essential aspects of the processes by which all social structures are (re-)produced, and hence that the analytical separation of political from economic life – as well as domestic and international aspects of these – represents a false dichotomy which obscures much of potential political importance.

Historical materialism

Historical materialism begins from the premise that humans become what they are in large part because of the social forms through which they organize their material reproduction, a process that is at once both natural and social. Human social beings continually (re-)produce the conditions of their existence through socially organized productive activity that, because we are human and not animals, necessarily involves thinking, speaking, planning, and organizing together. Through this process, the material world, social relations and ideas, and human beings themselves are continuously reproduced or transformed. Thus, to paraphrase Marx, people make their own history and in the process determine what it means to be human in a particular sociohistorical context. However, they cannot just make themselves anew, from scratch, in any way they please (Marx 2000: 329). Rather, historically situated social agents – whose actions are enabled and constrained by the social relations and self-understandings which constitute their identities – inherit particular social forms from preceding generations and proceed to (re-) produce, alter, or transform the social world in which they find themselves situated. Marx distinguishes the process-oriented view characteristic of historical materialism from other ways of understanding social life: 'As soon as this active life-process is described, history ceases to be a collection of dead facts as it is with the empiricists ... or an imagined activity of imagined subjects, as with the idealists' (Marx 2000: 181). No longer need we understand the world as a collection of apparently objective facts mutely confronting and constraining us, nor it is the only alternative to imagine our world and ourselves as the creation of some mystical superhuman subject; rather the material-social world as it exists for us may be understood as a human social product, and since we are ourselves integral to that world, we are – potentially – capable of social self-determination in and through our socially organized productive activity. Under historical circumstances of capitalism, our inability collectively to determine the social organization of our productive activity, the kind of society we will live in, and the kinds of people we will become is for Marx an index of our unfreedom. In the guise of private property, '[m]an's own deed becomes an alien power opposed to him, which enslaves him instead of being controlled by him' (Marx 2000: 185).

The critique of capitalist social life

Capitalism, as Marx represents it, is not a seamless web of oppression, but rather a contradictory life of 'dual freedom'.

> For the transformation of money into capital ... the owner of money must find the free worker available on the commodity-market; and this worker must be free in the double sense that as a free individual he can dispose of his labour-power as his own commodity, and that, on the other hand, he has no other commodity for sale, i.e. he is free of all the objects needed for the realization of his labour-power.
>
> (Marx 1977: 272, 874)

The class relations of capitalism imply not only that, unlike the slave in bondage or the feudal serf tied to the lord's estate, the worker is free to sell his or her own labor; but also that the worker *must* do so insofar as he or she has no other means of access to the necessary means of production, which capitalism has rendered as the exclusive private property of an owning class. On such a dialectical Marxian view, capitalism entails liberation from the relations of direct politico–economic dominance characteristic of feudalism and other precapitalist forms, and hence presents real possibilities for individual liberty and 'political emancipation' within the parameters of republican forms of state, recognition of civil liberties, equality before the law, and so on (Marx 2000: 54–64). But capitalism simultaneously limits the historically real emancipatory possibilities it brings into being by (re-)subjecting these same individuals to the compulsions of market dependence and the disabling effects of an ideology which represents social life itself as a series of contracts and commodity exchanges among self-interested individuals (rather than as a process of collective self-determination by a community of producers). These dialectics of freedom and unfreedom, the powers they generate and resistances they engender, have produced families of capitalist historical structures that are fraught with tension and possibilities for change. Whether any such possibilities are realized, and in what particular ways, depend upon open-ended political struggles in which the class-based power relations of capitalism will necessarily be implicated.

One of the enduring insights of Marxian theory is that the seemingly apolitical capitalist market is permeated by structured relations of social power (especially class-based power) deeply consequential for political life and, indeed, for the (re-)production of social life as a whole. These class-based powers may be ideologically masked in liberal representations of a naturalized and privatized economy separate from the formally political sphere of the state. Representing these social powers as if they were natural or apolitical – individual rights associated with the ownership of private property – they may be rendered democratically unaccountable. The operation of this economy (and the implicit social powers residing within it) may then be represented as something approaching a universal social good, the engine of economic growth, and a generalized prosperity.

The critical leverage of a Marxian critique of capitalism is generated by its explicit focus on the social power relations that inhere in, yet are obscured by, the structures and practices of capitalist production and exchange. Under historical conditions of capitalism, social relations are mediated by things – commodities. Although the social division of labor under capitalism has brought together and collectively empowered human producers as never before, capitalism simultaneously divides and disables them by representing their social relations as naturalized relations of exchange between privately owned things – the famous 'fetishism of commodities' (Marx 1977: 163–77, 1003–6, 1020–5, 1052–5). To the extent that social relations are subsumed into a world of putatively independent objects – 'things' – communities of human producers are correspondingly disempowered.

> The social world of capitalism appears as something we inhabit . . . rather than some of the ways we are, and it is this estrangement of the real content of social life that grounds the abstractions which come to stand in for it: modernity's representations . . . of both society and self.
>
> (Sayer 1991: 88)

Inhabitants of the capitalist market, the subjects of capitalist modernity, are represented to themselves as abstract (i.e. atomistic) individuals who, as such, are largely unable to discern – much less communally to govern – the social division of labor in which they are embedded. The social division of labor takes on the appearance of objectivity, an uncontrollable force of nature, the mystical market whose price signals and compulsions individuals neglect at our peril. Concomitantly, capitalism's fetishism and reification serve to mystify social power relations by making power appear as a property of things that may be possessed (or not) by abstract individuals.

The implications for democracy are deeply ironic. For even as capitalism realizes 'political emancipation' through the development of the liberal republic in which citizens are formally equal, it effectively reifies, privatizes, and de-politicizes class-based social powers (by associating them with ownership of 'private property') and thereby evacuates from the purview of political democracy much of the substance of social life, vitiating democracy's promise of social self-determination.

Capitalism and class power

Behind these mystifications, capitalist social relations generate the possibility of asymmetrical social powers distributed according to class. Socially necessary means of production are constituted as private property, exclusively owned by one class of people. The other class, whose exclusion from ownership of social means of production is integral to the latter's constitution as private property, are then compelled to sell that which they do own – labor-power, their capacity for productive activity – in order to gain access to those means of production and hence, through the wage, their own means of survival. As consumer of labor-power, the capitalist may control the actual activity of labor – the labor process – and appropriate its product, which is then subsumed into capital itself as part of the process of accumulation. As a consequence of their position within the social organization of production, then, capitalists may exercise two kinds of social power.

As *employers*, capitalists and their managerial agents attempt to assert control over the transformation of labor-power – the abstract, commodified capacity for labor – into actual labor. Driven by the imperatives of competitive accumulation, they seek to maximize the output of workers in relation to wages paid for labor-power, and may lengthen the workday or transform the labor process itself in order to do so. This latter tendency was instantiated in struggles surrounding the Fordist workplace regimes associated with mass production industry. Displacing predominantly craft-based production in which skilled laborers exercised substantial control over their conditions of work, Fordist production entailed an intensified industrial division of labor; increased mechanization and coordination of large-scale manufacturing processes (e.g. sequential machining operations and converging assembly lines) to achieve a steady flow of production; a shift toward the use of less-skilled labor performing, *ad infinitum*, tasks minutely specified by management; and the potential for heightened capitalist control over the pace and intensity of work. At the core of the Fordist reorganization of production, then, was the construction of new relations of power in the workplace; to the extent that these relations of power could become established parameters of the work process, capital would reap the gains of manifold increases in output per hour of waged labor. The promise of massive increases in productivity led to the widespread imitation and adaptation of Ford's basic model of production through the industrial core of the US economy and in other industrial capitalist countries.

The social institutions of Fordist mass production began to emerge in the United States early in the twentieth century and were at the center of a decade-long process of social struggle that extended into the immediate post-1945 era. Cold War ideology played a crucial role in the political stabilization of Fordist institutions in the United States, providing the common ground on which de-radicalized industrial labor unions could be incorporated as junior partners in a coalition of globally oriented social forces which worked together to rebuild the 'free world' along liberal capitalist lines and to resist the encroachment of a presumed Communist menace globally and at home. Institutionalized Fordism, in turn, enabled the United States to contribute almost half of the total world industrial production in the immediate postwar years, and thus provided the economic dynamism necessary to spark reconstruction of the major capitalist countries after 1945, and to support the emergence of both the consumer society and the military–industrial complex in the postwar United States (Rupert 1995).

The second social identity through which capitalists are socially empowered is as *investors*. Deciding when, where, and how to invest is a prerogative attendant on ownership of private property in the means of production. As owner-investors, capitalists routinely make decisions which directly determine the social allocation of labor and resources – the pace of aggregate economic activity and the shape of the social division of labor. Further, insofar as governments in capitalist social systems must rely upon private investors to generate economic growth, tax revenues, and the popular legitimacy which is often associated with a growing economy, governments face a structural imperative to secure the conditions of successful capital accumulation and the stability of the capitalist system as a whole. If government fails to create a 'business friendly' climate attractive to private investors, or pursues policies that appear to threaten conditions of profitability, capitalists may decline to invest or send their capital elsewhere. Thus, even if they refrained from direct manipulation of public policy through the painfully familiar process of buying political influence with campaign contributions and lobbyists, the class-based powers of capitalist owner-investors nonetheless indirectly limit the scope of public policy through the constraint of 'business confidence' and the implicit threat of 'capital strike' or transnational capital flight.

These social powers have been amplified in recent decades by processes associated with globalization. In increasingly globalized financial markets, astonishing volumes of foreign exchange trading and speculative international investment now dwarf the currency reserves of governments and can readily swamp, or leave high and dry, the financial markets of particular nations. Responding to short-term differences in perceived conditions of profitability and variations in business confidence between one place and another, as well as speculative guesses about future market fluctuations, these enormous flows are highly volatile. Massive amounts can be shifted from one currency (or assets denominated in one currency) to another literally at the speed of light *via* the computer modems and fiber optic cables that link the world's financial markets and enable 'round the clock' trading. These changes have been consequential, for the new historical structures embody an enhancement of the social powers of capital, and especially finance capital, which can effectively preempt expansionary macro-economic policies aimed at increasing employment or wage levels. This disciplinary power has the effect of prioritizing the interests of investors, who are as a class effectively able to hold entire states/societies hostage.

Insofar as the social powers of capital are effectively privatized – associated with private ownership and exchange of property among legally equal individuals in an apparently de-politicized economic sphere – they are ideologically mystified and democratically unaccountable. Antidemocratic and disabling as they might be, however, these class-based powers are neither uncontestable in principle nor uncontested in fact. Like all relations of social power, capitalist power relations are reciprocal, constituting a 'dialectic of power' subject to ongoing contestation, renegotiation, and restructuring. The reproduction of these powers is always problematic, and must be politically secured on an ongoing basis in particular contexts. Successful reproduction of class power is hardly assured.

However, the process of challenging these powers may be significantly more complex than more fundamentalist versions of Marxism have been prepared to contemplate. Class powers must be actualized in various concrete sites of social production where class is articulated with other socially meaningful identities resident and effective in those historical circumstances. Capitalist power over waged labor has been historically articulated with gendered and raced forms of power: separation of workplace from residence and the construction of ideologies of feminized domesticity rationalizing unpaid labor; ideologies of white supremacy rationalizing racial segregation and inequality; gendered and raced divisions of labor; and so forth. Indeed, these relations of race and gender have had important effects on class formation. This implies that in concrete contexts, class cannot be effectively determining without itself being determined. However, this is not to say, in some pluralist sense, that class is only one of a number of possible social identities all of which are equally contingent. Insofar as productive interaction with the natural world remains a necessary condition of all human social life (as Marx maintained), I would suggest that understandings of social power relations which abstract from the social organization of production must be radically incomplete. To the extent that capitalism and its putatively private relations of power organize crucial parts of social life on a transnational scale, the struggles surrounding these relations and their various articulations in sites around the world merit serious study as part of the question of global power and resistance.

Gramsci: Capitalism, ideology, hegemony

If Marx left us with incisive theorizations of capitalism, its core structures and constitutive tensions, it was the Italian political theorist and communist leader Gramsci (1971) who contributed to the historical materialist tradition a conceptual vocabulary with which to enable processes of transformative politics. Marx suggested that socialist transformation might emerge out of the confluence of capitalism's endemic crisis tendencies, the polarization of its class structure, and the intensified exploitation of the proletariat, and, most importantly, the emergence of the latter as a collective agent through the realization of its socially productive power, heretofore developed in distorted and self-limiting form under the conditions of concentrated capitalist production. Gramsci accepted in broad outline Marx's analysis of the structure and dynamics of capitalism, but was unwilling to embrace the more mechanical and economistic interpretations of Marx circulating in the international socialist movement. Contrary to vulgar Marxist dogma, progressive social change would not automatically follow in train behind economic developments, but must instead be produced by historically situated social agents whose actions are enabled and constrained by their social self-understandings. Thus, for Gramsci, popular 'common sense' becomes a critical terrain of political struggle. His theorization of 'hegemony' as a social politics of ideological struggle – which he called a 'war of position' to distinguish it from a Bolshevik strategy of frontal assault on the state – contributed to the historical materialist project of de-reifying capitalist social relations (including narrowly state-based conceptions of politics) and constructing an alternative – more enabling, participatory, intrinsically democratic – social order out of the historical conditions of capitalism.

Popular common sense could become a ground of struggle because it is an amalgam of historically effective ideologies, scientific doctrines, and social mythologies. Gramsci understood popular common sense not to be monolithic or univocal, nor was hegemony an unproblematically dominant ideology that simply shut out all alternative visions or political projects. Rather, common sense was understood to be fragmentary and contradictory, open to multiple interpretations and potentially supportive of very different kinds of social visions and political projects. And hegemony was understood as the unstable product of a continuous process of struggle, 'war of position', 'reciprocal siege'. Gramsci's political project thus entailed addressing the popular common sense operative in particular times and places, making explicit the tensions and contradictions within it as well as the sociopolitical implications of these, in order to enable critical social analysis and transformative political practice.

Beginning with the seminal work of Cox (1981), Gramscian concepts have been deployed by scholars of world politics (not all of whom would be at home with the label 'Marxist') seeking to counter the predominant intellectual climate of state-centric atomism and its deeply conservative implications. Drawing on the relational and process-oriented conceptual underpinnings of historical materialism, Cox stressed the historical construction of various forms of state in the nexus between social forces (classes, social movements, and other collective social agents) on the one hand, and world orders on the other. He stressed that this relational nexus necessarily involves economic, political, and cultural aspects, all of which are bound up with systems of power that are not coterminous with sovereign states. Drawing on Gramsci's conceptualization of hegemony, Cox suggested that these systems of power could be meaningfully distinguished depending upon the relative balance of coercive and consensual forms of power. The rethinking of world politics produced by Cox and other neo-Gramscian scholars has provided a critical alternative to conventional understandings which take sovereign states – understood as territorially based wielders of coercive power – to be axiomatic.

The state and the interstate system

More orthodox Marxian scholars of world politics have in recent years made important contributions to understanding the historical production of the state and interstate system as modern social forms historically bound up (if not genetically twinned) with capitalism. In his incisive critique of orthodox realist International Relations (IR) theory, Rosenberg (1994) argues that 'geopolitical systems' are not independent of, and cannot be understood in abstraction from, the social organization of material life and its processes of reproduction. Rosenberg challenges realism's reification of the state as a transhistorical essence, and its typical reduction of political agency to state policy. Abstracting the modern state from those social relations in which it is embedded, such that the state may be determining without itself being determined, realism understands the politics of economic relations in terms of the instrumental machinations of states extracting resources for deployment in international geopolitical competition. This reveals a crucial theoretical weakness at the heart of orthodox IR theory, its blindness to the political relations intrinsic to the capitalist world economy that are not reducible to the interests or actions of sovereign states. Following the logic of historical materialist critique, Rosenberg (1994: 14) situates the sovereign state and its geopolitics – as well as the seemingly separate sphere of the capitalist economy – in the historically specific social relations of capitalist modernity:

The separation of the political and the economic indicates precisely the central institutional linkage between the capitalist economy and the nation-state: that is, the legal

structure of property rights which removes market relationships from directly political control or contestation and allows the flow of investment capital across national
boundaries.

It is through these latter processes of transnational economic activity that the privatized
powers of capital have been projected on an increasingly global scale.

While acknowledging Rosenberg's insight that capitalist geopolitics are qualitatively
different from absolutist or feudal geopolitics, Lacher (2002) offers a powerful theoretical and historical argument against the thesis that the modern state – and, by extension,
the system of states – had its genesis in the very historical processes which gave rise to
capitalism. He argues instead that the emergence of a system of states – a process driven
by the historically distinct politico–economic imperatives of absolutist rule – preceded the
emergence of capitalist production relations and cannot adequately be understood as their
product. On this view, the modern state emerged from irreducibly geopolitical processes
rooted in the precapitalist milieu of absolutist states. Subsequently, with the emergence
of capitalist agriculture and primitive accumulation in Britain, the pressures of interstate
political competition contributed to the articulation of this geopolitical state system with
capitalism, integrating and transforming both and generating thereby the primary structural
forms of modern social life. Following the emergence of capitalist production relations
in England, the dynamics of absolutist geopolitics were transformed by the competitive
dynamics characteristic of capitalism, and the system of territorial states was internalized within, and became integral to, a distinctly capitalist system of social relations. In
this historical system, political authority was organized through territorially defined states
even as economic transactions – and capitalist competition – overflowed state boundaries.
Geopolitical competition among states thus became bound up with transnational processes
of competitive capitalist production.

Imperialism: Then and now

Among the most familiar and long-standing contributions of Marxist theory to the understanding of world politics are its theorizations of imperialism, initially developed in
the early twentieth century. By the dawn of the twenty-first century, the concept of
imperialism appeared to have lost much of its currency, displaced by a focus upon the
less directly coercive mechanisms of capitalist globalization. Recent episodes of military
adventurism by major capitalist powers, however, serve as a reminder that this branch
of Marxian theory, even if no longer novel, remains significant for contemporary world
politics (Halliday 2002).

Since capitalism entails a structural separation between the economic and the political
aspects of social life (the de-politicization and privatization of the economy which makes
possible capitalist property and wage labor), the state in a capitalist context is generally
dependent upon the economic activities of capitalists in order to generate resources which
it can tax and to create enough economic growth and prosperity within its territory to
minimally legitimate the government and the social order as a whole. The state has,
therefore, a compelling interest in the overall success of accumulation by capitalists whose
operations are based within its territory. But since capitalist economic activity routinely
overflows those boundaries, and encounters in the world market capitalist competitors based
in other states which may well be geopolitical rivals of the home state, the imperatives
of capitalist and geopolitical competition may converge to generate imperialism – the

deployment of military power in the service of capital accumulation. This has entailed forcibly integrating new areas into the world market, destroying noncapitalist ways of life and commodifying social relations to create an exploitable proletarianized labor force, or enforcing the dominance of private property and capitalist access to important resources.

Capitalist imperialism, as distinct from precapitalist tribute-extracting or commerce-controlling empires, involves the use of coercive power in order to create and maintain conditions necessary for capitalist production, exchange, and investment – in short, for capital accumulation – to occur on a transnational scale (Wood 2003). This is not to say that all modern instances of imperialism have had a purely capitalist character. As a consequence of the globally uneven development of capitalist social relations we may identify historically hybrid instances such as the British Raj with its militarily enforced mercantilism and tributary taxation, or King Leopold's Belgian Congo, where partial commodification was attended by outright extortion and the massive and ruthless exercise of coercive force to compel hyper-exploited labor. Viewed from a world historical perspective, however, the spatial expansion of capitalist social relations and processes has prepared the way for the recession of explicitly political coercive force into the background of global capitalism, never entirely absent but not as a rule directly present or transparent.

Globalization

When conditions of transnational accumulation have been more or less secured, capitalism can function without regular recourse to directly coercive exploitation: rather than the sharp point of a bayonet, it relies on what Marx called 'the dull compulsion of the economic', the relentless pressure in a commodified society to earn enough to secure the material necessities of life. Robinson (2004) argues forcefully that by the late twentieth century, much of the globe had been successfully integrated into the capitalist world market, such that the commodification of labor and of the conditions of material life was very nearly complete. On this view, globalization represents an 'epochal shift' in which the displacement of precapitalist relations is completed and capitalist commodification is universalized, national circuits of accumulation are subsumed within global circuits (through the globalization of commercial, productive, and financial capital), a transnational capitalist class emerges, and the nation-state is tendentially transformed, superceded by and incorporated within a multilayered 'transnational state' as the political aspect of capitalist social organization. Patterns of nation-state-based political accommodation between capitalist and popular classes (such as the Fordist accommodation), and the constraints on accumulation that these have represented, have been increasingly vitiated by the transnational reorganization of capitalist power, displaced by the hegemonic project of the neoliberal Washington Consensus.

Despite the perhaps overly confident tone of his extrapolations regarding the emergence of a qualitatively new transnational capitalism and transnational state, Robinson explicitly acknowledges the continuing presence and significance of nationally based phenomena, and ongoing contradictions between national and globalizing aspects of capitalism. Increasingly global, capitalism is nonetheless a deeply contradictory system and faces recurrent accumulation crises and political tensions among fractions of the global capitalist bloc as well as between that bloc and the great bulk of the world's people who are politically and economically marginalized by this system of power.

Wood (2003), another important contemporary Marxist theorist, is resistant to Robinson's strong 'transnational state' thesis, and suggests that under capitalist conditions market-mediated economic relations readily outdistance the social organization of political rule, so that globalizing capitalism is increasingly reliant on nation-states for the political mediation of unevenly developed and variously regulated local spaces. On this view, contemporary capitalism is likely to generate an intensification of the contradiction between economic expansionism and the territorially defined forms of political authority upon which capitalism depends for social stability and political reproduction. Wood sees the US quest for unquestioned military supremacy as a response to this contradiction, an attempt to exert control over the system of states in order to maintain conditions of profitability for US-based firms operating in a world economy.

Empire: Marxism for the twenty-first century?

Hardt and Negri's *Empire* (2000) has been celebrated as a brave theorization of new social horizons, a visionary statement of the revolutionary politics of a postmodern global era. An international literary sensation, *Empire* is undeniably a monumental work; but despite its philosophical density it suffers from a profound political hollowness.

Hardt and Negri contend that social life is undergoing a passage of world historical significance: the transition from territorial systems of rule characteristic of modernity and imperialism to the qualitatively distinct postmodern form of Empire, entailing the decentering and deterritorialization of rule *via* the globalization of capitalism and the emergence of pervasive, information-saturated networks of social production, governance, and control. Hardt and Negri infer from the alleged presence of a new global Empire the necessary preexistence of a globally productive and rebellious form of human subjectivity – the multitude. And if *Empire* necessarily presupposes the multitude – imbued not only with socially productive powers but also with a primordial will to resist the containment of those powers – can revolutionary global emancipation be far off?

Empire is animated by the activist commitments characteristic of the autonomist strain of Marxian thinking, insisting that after all and before anything else, our world, social life itself, is a product of human social subjectivity, of associated human producers 'autonomous from the dictates of both the labour movement and capital' (Wright 2002: 3). In Tormey's (2004: 116) admirably clear summary, autonomism emphasizes

> the 'open' nature of historical process and thus the importance of political struggle over economic forces... [t]he significance of such a move theoretically is that it leads to an 'open' account of how resistance to capitalism arises, and thus to a less doctrinaire account of who as well as what can be considered 'progressive' from the point of view of developing anti-capitalist resistance... [a]utonomists argue that it is the concentration of political and economic power that has to be combated, whether this power be in the hands of the capitalist class or 'representatives' of the working class itself such as trade union leaderships or communist party bosses.

Thus they celebrate the capacity of ordinary people for self-organization and anticapitalist struggle in a variety of contexts, and the historical significance of such resistances in driving the development of social institutions. For Hardt and Negri this historical subjectivity takes the form of a pluralized, postmodern, globalized proletariat – the multitude: 'The subjectivity of class struggle', they assert, 'transforms imperialism into Empire' (Hardt and Negri 2000: 235). Emphasizing the historical priority of the multitude's socially productive powers, and hence its transformative potential, Hardt and Negri argue that the multitude 'is the real productive force of our social world, whereas Empire is a mere apparatus of capture that lives only off the vitality of the multitude' (Hardt and Negri 2000: 62). This implies that the multitude, as producers of the postmodern world of Empire, is capable of transforming global Empire into global liberation.

Despite *Empire's* apparent commitment to an insurgent global politics, the presumed globality of the multitude – the producers and gravediggers of Empire – has the effect of flattening politics to correspond with Hardt and Negri's smoothed imagination of Empire. Insofar as it represents 'a superficial world' of diffuse and omnipresent power, they suggest, 'the construction of Empire, and the globalization of economic and cultural relationships, means that the virtual centre of Empire can be attacked from any point' (Hardt and Negri 2000: 58, 59). In the postmodern world of Empire, politics is always already global. In effect, then, the politics of concretely situated social agents becomes redundant insofar as it is subsumed within the multitude's already global struggle against an already constituted global enemy. For Hardt and Negri, the omnipresence of power and resistance implies the possibility of globally transformative politics. But it seems to me that this formulation presumes what must be explained: it supposes the preexistence of a rebellious global subjectivity on the cusp of self-emancipation, and in so doing it begs the question of politics. Having imagined globalization as seamless and omnipresent Empire, they look for sources of political hope and claim to find it in a curiously transhistorical and effectively asocial abstraction – the impulse to resist.

> One element we can put our finger on at the most basic and elemental level is the *will to be against*. In general, the will to be against does not seem to require much explanation. Disobedience to authority is one of the most natural and healthy acts. To us it seems completely obvious that those who are exploited will resist and – given the necessary conditions – rebel.
>
> (Hardt and Negri 2000: 210)

But can resistance and rebellion be abstracted in this way from historical grounding in the complexity of concrete social relations, specific articulations of economic and political, pubic and private, global and local, colonizer and colonized? For (self-)transformative politics is not just a function of resisting oppression as such, but of concrete processes of building solidarities on the basis of overlapping (if not congruent) oppressions, and the construction of these solidarities requires the negotiation of difference and in particular the ways in which people are differentially situated on multiple axes of social power and privilege. From the perspective of a potentially (self-)transformative politics, it matters a very great deal how these potentially rebellious communities are socially situated within particular contexts, how they understand themselves, their oppressions, and their resistances, and how they negotiate with others in order to begin to envision and move toward common horizons of action, creating what Gramsci referred to as an historical bloc, a collective agency capable of enacting a transformative political project. In other words, if politics is a process of collective self-production by concretely situated social agents, then their presumed will to resist or rebel cannot substitute for the complexities of politics concretely enacted and understood. If progressive forces are unable creatively to confront the political problems of transnational solidarity, the abstract possibility of global transformative politics will be moot. For the purposes of such an emancipatory political project – entailing the problematic self-construction of a global social subject (potentially unified but hardly uniform) – I find a neo-Gramscian approach more challenging and much more promising than the postmodern global nostrums of Hardt and Negri.

Conclusion

Although not without its tensions and limitations, Marxian theory provides critical leverage for understanding the structures and dynamics of capitalism, its integral if complex relationship to the modern form of state, the class-based powers it enables and the resistances these entail; and Gramsci's rich legacy suggests a conceptual vocabulary for a transformative politics in which a variety of anticapitalist movements might coalesce in order to produce any number of future possible worlds whose very possibility is occluded by capitalism. In the present context of globalizing capitalism and neoimperialism, such resistance has taken the form of a transnational confluence of movements for global justice and peace. It not only contains elements that are explicitly based on class, but also encompasses a rich variety of social forces opposed to the depredations of globalizing neoliberal capitalism and the US power that enforces it. Insofar as the multifarious movements for global justice and peace inhabit common ground, it is a world where massively unequal wealth and divergent life chances are underpinned by historical concentrations of both economic and military power; an implicitly undemocratic world that, while historically real, is neither natural nor necessary. In their diverse but convergent challenges to this concentrated power these social forces embody a rejection of capitalism's abstract individuals in favor of more relational and process-oriented visions of social reality, and an affirmation of the historical situatedness of political knowledge and practice. To the extent that they are forging a transnational culture of solidarity across meaningful social differences, and together effect resistance to the power relations which variously and commonly oppress them, they may represent the germ of a transformative political process which need not be contained by capitalism's reified separations of economics/politics, state/society, and domestic/international.

Further reading

Hardt, M. and Negri, A. (2000) *Empire*, Cambridge, MA: Harvard University Press.
Kolakowski, L. (2005) *Main Currents of Marxism*, New York: Norton.
Wood, E. (2003) *Empire of Capital*, London: Verso.

5   Critical theory

Andrew Linklater

Introduction

The ceremony that opened the *Institute of Social Research* in Frankfurt, Germany, on 22 June 1924 marked the official beginning of Frankfurt School critical theory (although it should be understood that the term 'critical theory' now refers to a very broad worldview in the study of International Relations (IR)). The principal members of the School have included the founders of the Institute – Max Horkheimer (1895–1973) and Theodor Adorno (1903–1969) – Herbert Marcuse (1898–1979), the major 'New Left' theorist of the 1960s; Jurgen Habermas (b. 1929), the foremost critical theorist of recent times; and Axel Honneth (b. 1949). Their writings have developed an approach to society that is faithful to the spirit but not to the letter of Marxism. Marx and Engels used the 'paradigm of production' to analyze particular social systems and to comprehend human history. This paradigm maintained that the forces of production (technology) and the relations of production (class relations) provide the key to understanding political systems and historical change. In particular, class conflict was thought to have been the greatest influence on how societies have developed.

Marx and Engels argued that the struggle between the bourgeoisie (the class that owns the means of production) and the proletariat (the class that has to sell its labor-power in order to survive) is the central dynamic of capitalist societies. They believed that class conflict would destroy capitalism and lead to a socialist system in which the forces of production would be used to benefit the whole of society rather than to maximize profit for the bourgeoisie. They also had a vision of global political progress in which the whole of humanity would come to be freely associated in a socialist world order. Crucially, Marx and Engels thought the purpose of social inquiry was to promote the emancipation of the exploited proletariat and other oppressed groups. This commitment to emancipatory social science is also defended by the Frankfurt School. Its members have sought to preserve this conception of social inquiry while breaking with the fatal limitations of the paradigm of production. It was plain to Horkheimer and Adorno in the 1930s that the stress on the centrality of production and class conflict could not explain violent nationalism in the Fascist societies, the rise of totalitarian states and the outbreak of total war. Their writings displayed increasing pessimism about the prospects for emancipation. To them, the promise of emancipation that had united the members of the Enlightenment (such as Kant) with their successors (such as Marx and Engels) seemed impossible to realize in the modern era in which society is increasingly dominated by pressures to administer the social world more efficiently and more economically.

Later members of the Frankfurt School sought to recover the emancipatory project without relapsing into classical Marxism and without ignoring the dangerous side of modernity. Marcuse (1964) analyzed how capitalism created 'one dimensional man' caught up in the satisfaction of manufactured material needs, but he believed that the student movement of the 1960s and struggles for national liberation and socialism in the Third World represented major political efforts to create the free society. Habermas has focused on how efforts to administer capitalist societies have resulted in the 'colonization of the life world' – that is, in the encroachment of administrative rationality on everyday life – but he sees in social movements that promote human security, equality for women and environmental degradation the promise of a new kind of society, which replaces the quest to control nature and administer society with the effort to expand human freedom.

Habermas regards the European Union as an important new experiment in developing 'postnational communities' that are linked by shared commitments to world citizenship and cosmopolitan law. These are political communities in which the state is no longer primarily linked with a dominant nationality or dedicated to promoting selfish interests. States in the European region are not alone in coming under pressure to create political arrangements that respect the multicultural nature of modern societies. The greater mobility of peoples in recent decades has encouraged this 'postnational' development, as have globalization and the growing realization that democracy may have to be established on a world scale if it is to survive. Cosmopolitan democracy must link peoples and cultures that do not have a common language, common symbols or the shared history that have underpinned nation-states for the past two centuries.

The influence of Kant's ideal of perpetual peace and Marx's internationalism is evident in Habermas's vision of postnational communities – and indeed Habermas has been more concerned than earlier members of the Frankfurt School with commenting on international affairs. Marx largely neglected this dimension of human affairs. Engels recognized the importance of war and military strategy without wrestling with the problems they raised for the paradigm of production. Horkheimer and Adorno were well aware that nationalism, totalitarianism and war had shattered the vision of a socialist utopia, but they did not theorize these phenomena. Habermas has not set out to develop a critical theory of world politics but his many interviews and journalistic essays have addressed global issues such as the 1991 Gulf War, NATO's intervention over Kosovo in 1999 and the recent war in Iraq. His main theoretical ambition has been to furnish the critical project with ethical foundations and with universal moral commitments that were either absent from earlier Frankfurt School inquiry or inadequately theorized by leading proponents. By developing critical theory in this way, Habermas (1990) turns to Kant's ethical doctrine that he reworks in the 'discourse theory of morality' (see Traditional and critical social theory). This is a controversial standpoint, and Habermas's critics have argued that the search for ethical universals contains the danger of privileging one cultural standpoint or imposing ethnocentric values on presumed inferiors. The question of ethical universalism has been the central controversy surrounding Frankfurt School critical theory, and the importance of this controversy for the study of IR is immense. It is necessary to analyze Horkheimer's distinction between 'traditional' and 'critical' theory before considering these issues in more detail.

Traditional and critical social theory

Horkheimer set out the aims of the Institute of Social Research in a famous essay entitled 'Traditional and Critical Theory', which was first published in 1937. In that paper, he defended critical theory from the rising tide of positivism (traditional theory). In broad terms, positivism is an approach to society that aims to emulate the natural sciences by using scientific methods and quantitative means to uncover social laws and to predict human behavior. The status of positivism remains controversial in the philosophy of social science. Horkheimer's main objection was that positivism produces knowledge that makes the more efficient administration of society possible. With the results of social scientific inquiry at their disposal, those that administer the social world can have greater confidence in their ability to steer society. This may seem a curious objection given that nineteenth-century positivists such as the French sociologist Auguste Comte believed that the application of science to the study of society could improve human circumstances. An unprecedented ability to predict how human actions would affect society, and a unique capacity to control unanticipated consequences, would make it possible to realize the Enlightenment ambition of increasing human freedom. Horkheimer's belief, however, was that positivism cannot keep faith with Enlightenment ideals.

The main problem, as he saw it, was that positivists believed that objective knowledge of society was possible while visions of moral preferences were subjective and arbitrary. Positivism could explain the most rational means of achieving chosen ends, but it denied that human beings could have objective knowledge about what they should do. Max Weber made this point in *Science as a Vocation* (1919) when quoting Tolstoy's observation that science cannot tell us what we should do and how we should live. Horkheimer drew the conclusion that positivism left human beings at the mercy of those with the power to use knowledge to administer social relations and to maximize economy and efficiency. It offered no challenge to what Weber called the 'iron cage' in which the inhabitants of modern society seemed destined to be trapped because of the dominance of administrative rationality (whether their society was capitalist or socialist was immaterial in his view). Indeed, it left human beings in the grip of a form of rationality ('instrumental reason') that represented the greatest threat to the project of emancipation. In *Dialectic of Enlightenment* (1947), Horkheimer and Adorno argued that the triumph of instrumental reason was the main achievement of the Enlightenment, but greater success in mastering the physical world had the effect of extending the political control of society and diminishing human freedom. The tragic consequence of the development of the unrivaled technological mastery of nature (which Marx had regarded as the key to freedom from exploitative labor) was that individuals had become subjects of increasingly bureaucratized and disciplined forms of life.

The Frankfurt School has long been associated with envisaging future social conditions in keeping with the view that the Enlightenment ideal of universal emancipation should drive political inquiry. As Bottomore (1984: 49) has argued, its members have hoped to recover 'subjectivity against the idea of an objective, law-governed process of history'. But Horkheimer and Adorno came to believe that the Enlightenment project was lost in the 1930s, not least because of the demise of the revolutionary proletariat, which Marx and Engels had proclaimed to be the historical subject that would realize universal human emancipation. As noted earlier, the main legacy of the Enlightenment for Horkheimer and Adorno was the emergence of the 'totally administered society' because of the triumph of instrumental reason. Adorno believed all that remained was a 'negative dialectics' in which the theorist could highlight the inadequacy of social arrangements (e.g., by showing how art could expose the absurdity of the world of instrumental reason and represent human suffering) while at the same time conceding that there was no evidence that the Marxian vision of the good society would ever be realized.

The importance of Marx's thought for the Frankfurt School cannot be overestimated although its actual relationship with Marxism has been marked by great ambivalence. One of the Frankfurt School's central complaints about Marxism in the twentieth century, and specifically about Soviet Marxism, was that it had been transformed into a positivist social science. It was thought that the antecedents of that positivism could be found in Marx's discussion of how the iron laws of capitalist development would lead to political crisis and engender the transition to socialism. It is true that Soviet Marxism became crudely positivist in its approach to the transition from capitalism to socialism. Horkheimer's claim that positivism left human beings at the mercy of those that wield political power seemed to be confirmed by the Soviet Union where the idea that the revolutionary elite could use the most advanced technology to promote freedom resulted in totalitarian domination. For later theorists such as Habermas, the question was how to preserve the emancipatory ideals of critical theory from the challenges of positivism and the curse of Soviet Marxism.

How then do critical theorists defend themselves from the positivist criticism that it is impossible to have knowledge of the ends and ideals that human beings should promote? How do they ground moral claims about freedom, and how do they ensure that political efforts to promote human freedom do not degenerate into cruelty and domination? How should the commitment to human freedom inform social and political inquiry, and what can it contribute to understanding IR? Habermas is the main critical theorist to deal with these questions. Although he has not analyzed contemporary theories of IR, and barely refers to the relevant literature, his writings have influenced efforts to apply critical theory to world politics. To understand his approach it is useful to describe Marx's position on how to criticize actual social and political arrangements, and how to envisage realisable alternatives. Then it is important to discuss how Habermas has tried to overcome not only the limitations of Marx's approach but also Horkheimer and Adorno's renowned pessimism about the irreversible dominance of instrumental rationality.

Marx was mainly concerned with the critique of ideology (*ideologiekritique*), an approach that is evident in his analysis of capitalist ideology, according to which private property, the division of labor and the free market were natural phenomena rather than socially constructed and changeable features of human life. Crucially, for Marx, capitalist society used the idea of the freedom and equality of all of its members to justify social practices. In so doing, it provided the victims of capitalism with the language with which to criticize capitalist exploitation and with which to imagine a world in which human beings could enjoy the freedom and equality which capitalism, according to bourgeois theorists, already realized. For Marx, a central task of critical theory was to criticize ideology; it was to show how the terms in which societies legitimated their arrangements clashed profoundly with existing social and political conditions; it was to analyze the particular revolutionary social forces which emerged from the tension between ideology and practice; and it was to both comprehend and support their efforts to create a society in which the principles of freedom and equality would no longer be contradicted by capitalist forms of exploitation and domination.

The critique of ideology is linked with 'immanent critique' – the notion that it is necessary to judge societies with the same terms they use to describe and legitimize themselves. The main alternative to his position is to criticize society by appealing to moral standards that are thought to be inherent in human nature or human reason. Marx and Engels rejected the belief, which is defended by Kant for example, that reason can uncover immutable and universal ethical standards for the purpose of criticizing and condemning actual social arrangements. Their preferred approach, which was developed by the first generation of the Frankfurt School, aimed to subvert society from within by showing that the moral principles of freedom and equality which were said to govern all capitalist social relations actually worked to promote sectional interests – those of the bourgeoisie which exploited subordinate classes in the labor process. One can see in this approach how the critical standpoint that was defended by the Frankfurt School differs from traditional theory or positivism. Critical theory focuses on political struggles that reveal in broad outline how an alternative society is already immanent within the current social order (already present in its 'womb', to use one of Marx's recurrent metaphors), whereas positivism aims to explain social laws or recurrent processes and, on this basis, to predict future behavior. For the Frankfurt School, the decision to concentrate on the repetitive features of social life – on law-like regularities – can have the dangerous effect of perpetuating unjustifiable constraints on human beings and of reinforcing existing inequalities. Traditional theory is inadequate then because it lacks the emancipatory intent and interest in immanent possibilities, which define the critical-theoretical standpoint.

The critical approach outlined above does not explain why it is right to judge society by the ideals it uses to legitimize its arrangements and to map future developments. Why should these ethical ideals be privileged? There is an implicit assumption in the Frankfurt School that freedom and equality are the highest moral ends, but they are not valued everywhere and they are understood in rather different ways in those parts of the world where they enjoy most support. Habermas's reworking of critical social theory endeavors to overcome this lacuna in Frankfurt School thinking.

To understand Habermas's position it is necessary to analyze one of the main themes in his reconstruction of historical materialism, namely that Marx and classical Marxism were correct to highlight the importance of class and production in human history, but wrong to regard the labor process as the key to social and political organization and mistaken in depicting class struggle as the driving force behind significant social change. The parallel error was to assume that the conquest of nature held the key to human emancipation (specifically, by abolishing material scarcity). The rise of totalitarianism in the interwar years revealed major errors in their thinking. For Habermas, classical Marxism elevated the importance of labor only to downgrade the significance of interaction – the sphere in which human beings negotiate principles of coexistence within actual societies. His view is that the reproduction of society depends as much on the level of success that actors have in reaching some agreement about the principles of social interaction as on their collective achievement in shaping the natural world in accordance with their basic material needs. The reconstruction of historical materialism to produce a fully comprehensive study of society and history must therefore focus on both processes and the interplay between them: on how societies use technological resources to satisfy fundamental needs and on how they employ language to reach some understanding about the principles that bind their members together in particular ways of life. To put this differently, the classical Marxist commitment to the 'paradigm of production' must be complemented by the 'paradigm of communication' that recognizes the importance of language or 'communicative action' for preserving actual social relations and for imagining improved social arrangements.

The irreducibility of communication to labor is central to Habermas's attempt to recover critical theory from Horkheimer and Adorno's pessimism – not only because communication plays a central role in the preservation and development of forms of life, but because human beings can be said to learn in this domain just as they can be said to learn more about the natural world and about how it can be exploited for human purposes. Marx and Engels believed that learning in the technological sphere explains the mystery of human development; Habermas suggests that learning in the communicative domain is the real key to how human societies can realize the immanent possibility of higher levels of freedom.

In a striking formulation, Habermas argued that the first use of language or the first 'speech act' already promised the unification of the human race. What he meant by this idea was that participants in communicative interaction are committed to the same four presuppositions: that what is said is intelligible; that it is true; that it is said sincerely; and that speakers are entitled to advance their claims and have a right to communicate. Of course, actors do not always behave in this way. But those who use language for the purposes of deception can only hope to succeed because others are committed to these four basic principles (and believe that the liar has a similar commitment to them). Moreover, it is apparent that most societies in human history have not supported the principle that every member has an equal right to speak and an equal right to be heard. Special rights to communicate are thought to reside in male elders or in spiritual leaders with esoteric knowledge in many social systems. The commitment to open, public dialogue that recognizes each person's formal right to express views is the exception, not the rule, in human history. But according to Habermas, the possibility of societies which organize themselves around these convictions – and the possibility of a 'universal communication community' in which all persons have equal rights of representation – was present in the first use of language between human beings. This, he claims, is where one finds the moral standards for judging existing conditions and for envisaging social and political relations that liberate human beings from unnecessary structural constraints. The immanent possibility of advanced forms of society is found then in the properties of communication which are not specific to any particular time and place but which are genuinely universal. This belief that certain moral principles have this universal or transcendental quality marks Habermas out as a Kantian.

Habermas has used the terms 'ideal speech' or 'undistorted communication' to describe the possibilities for radical, deliberative democracy which are immanent in everyday speech. It is crucial to stress that Habermas is not a dreamy utopian who believes that any society will ever succeed in eliminating relations of power and domination so that all policies and decisions can be determined by ideal speech. The more modest point is that the notion of ideal speech (in which all human beings possess an equal right to express their views about matters that affect them, in which all have equal possibilities of success and where decisions will be made on the basis of the 'unforced force of the better argument') provides a way of highlighting major deficiencies in social life and of encouraging public debate about how such defects can be removed. The conviction that underlies the approach to society and politics is that human beings can learn how to replace relations of domination and coercion with relations of dialogue and consent. Contrary to the more reductionist forms of Marxism, they do not learn simply in the realms of labor. Human beings do not only learn how to be more successful in exploiting the physical environment. In the sphere of interaction they also learn how to develop more sophisticated ways of assessing the legitimacy of institutions, policies and decisions and of weighing up competing arguments about how separate societies, and indeed the whole species, should organize their affairs in future. Habermas calls this 'moral-practical learning' as opposed to 'technical-instrumental learning' that occurs in the relationship between society and nature. The former involves an appreciation of how ideal speech should be conducted and also the rather different phenomenon of breaking down 'scope restrictions' that have barred some human beings from participation in dialogue (and which at their worst even deny that some persons belong to humanity). The ways in which societies have excluded persons from the moral community, and the ways in which some have come to include the previously excluded within their ethical world, can also be regarded as key elements of moral-practical learning (Linklater 1998).

Modernity, for Habermas, has made progress in advancing the ethical claim that the legitimacy of social arrangements depends on how far they are answerable to everyone who is affected by them. Important as it is to promote democratic accountability between the members of the same political community, answerability cannot be confined to those who are already citizens of a specific nation-state. Since people everywhere are affected by decisions concerning the global environment or the world economic system that are made in distant places, the relevant moral constituency must include the whole human race. On these grounds Habermas has added his voice to the recent defence of cosmopolitan democracy (Habermas 1997).

It is important to note that Habermas builds on Kant's moral philosophy to create new ethical foundations for critical social theory and to promote the development of more adequate normative codes. He breaks with Kant's belief that each moral agent must reflect separately on whether preferred principles of action can apply to all human beings in similar circumstances. Decisions about such matters can only be taken in forms of open dialogue in which moral agents search for the best possible argument using public reason. Despite this break with Kant's univocal perspective, Habermas shares his belief that the proper task of moral philosophy is to search for universal principles – principles that hold for all persons and which are capable of moving the human race closer to perpetual peace. This controversial line of argument preserves the method of immanent critique because, as noted earlier, Habermas invokes moral principles which are said to be latent within structures of communication which exist in all human societies. They are not the unique possession of modern liberal democracies although these social systems may have done more than most to place commitments to dialogue at the center of political life. Their universality holds out the promise of a global political system in which all persons and collectivities face each other as equals in forms of open dialogue in which no one knows 'who will learn from whom' in advance.

To develop this last point, it is useful to stress that the globalization of economic and social life has transformed the status of the cosmopolitan principle that every human being has an equal right to be heard in communication communities which make decisions that affect them. Given the dominance of the state and the prevalence of national loyalties, this was once regarded as a utopian ideal. Globalization turns the institutionalization of the ideal of a universal communication community into a practical necessity. The need for progress on this front has become especially urgent because radically different moral perspectives and cultural orientations come into daily contact, underlining the need for mutual comprehension in the context of growing hostility to all attempts to impose one set of values on other cultures. Disputes between radically divergent groups cannot be resolved by appealing to the self-evident superiority of any one way of life. In this context, it is futile to appeal to some notion of the good life or good society or to hope that the fundamentally different can agree on a shared vision of how all persons should live. The emphasis needs to be placed instead on procedures for resolving disputes or for reaching a compromise on which the supporters of discrepant conceptions of the good can agree. Given their common commitments as language users, Habermas argues, the radically different can agree on basic procedures that uphold the right to communicate contrasting positions and create the possibility of reconciling competing claims (or reaching a compromise which seems fair to different parties). Whether radically different groups can agree on the procedures of the discourse theory of morality – a theory that is concerned with how moral agents should communicate their claims and not with advocating any particular standpoint which all can agree – is keenly debated however.

Critics have argued that the Habermasian account of discourse has a liberal bias which favors moral agents who think that the highest forms of morality search for universal principles which treat all human beings as equals – a standpoint that is clearly not universally shared (Linklater 2005; Shapcott 2001). Supporters of the discourse approach argue that it is not limited in this way (Linklater 2005; Lynch 2000). These debates are far from over. They have profound implications for Habermas's claim that the commitment to 'undistorted communication' is not limited to existing liberals or to potential converts to liberalism but can apply across all worldviews. Globalization, he argues, presses the advocates of all standpoints to confront the partiality of their views and to take a multiperspectival stance that is open to diverse standpoints. In his defense of dialogic cosmopolitanism, Habermas seeks to recover the belief in the possibility of human progress from the pessimism of earlier years while recognizing that some groups (specifically fundamentalist religious movements) respond to the challenge of globalization by asserting exclusionary and totalizing worldviews (Borradori 2004).

Critical international theory

Critical theory has been a central element in the challenge to the neorealist claim that anarchy forces all states to behave in much the same way, so perpetuating a world in which distrust, competition, and conflict dominate. Echoes of Horkheimer's distinction between traditional and critical theory are evident in the critique of neorealism. Neorealism has been associated with the positivist interest in understanding law-like regularities and with predicting behavior. This is a legitimate interpretation since Waltz (1979) was emphatic that the purpose of a theory of international politics is to understand patterns of behavior that have survived for millennia and which will endure for as long as the world is divided into independent political communities. In his criticism of neorealism, Ashley (1982) argued that the approach is predicated on a 'technical interest' in controlling the social world as far as possible. What is sacrificed is the commitment to the 'emancipatory interest' in removing political constraints which appear immutable but which can be worn down through the exercise of human agency. This stress on the human interests that shape approaches to understanding the social world has the purpose of showing that explanations of the social world are not objective but are anchored in sectional political interests and aspirations. Habermas made this claim in his account of 'knowledge-constitutive interests', which Ashley was the first to apply to IR.

Cox (1981, 1983) applied the critical method to the study of IR in his celebrated discussion of the difference between 'problem solving' and 'critical' theory. The principal influences on Cox are the twentieth-century Italian Marxist Antonio Gramsci, and the eighteenth-century Italian philosopher of history Giambattista Vico. There are parallels, however, between Horkheimer's distinction between traditional and critical theory and Cox's identification of two main approaches to IR. Cox argued that problem-solving approaches take the world for granted and ask how it can be made to function as smoothly as possible. This method informs neorealism, which maintains that international anarchy is unalterable and which asks how order can be maintained in the face of geopolitical competition and rivalry. For neorealists, order ultimately depends on a balance of power that imposes external constraints on state interests.

By contrast, critical theory asks how current global arrangements came into being and whether they are changing, not least because of political contestation and struggle. The approach aims to identify what Cox calls 'counter-hegemonic movements' that challenge dominant structures and principles, and strive to realize alternative ways of organizing world politics. The most promising political actors for Cox when he developed this analysis in the early 1980s were states (especially in the Third World) and social movements that challenged the global capitalist economy along with forms of labor exploitation and social inequality that are intrinsic to it. In common with the long tradition of critical theorizing, Cox has been concerned with the alternative principles of world political organization that are already immanent within existing structures and carried forward by counter-hegemonic forces. The emphasis, it should be noted, is not on the political actors which have the greatest impact on the world as it currently is (these are the great powers, as Waltz has argued) but on political movements which are in the vanguard of efforts to imagine and create global structures which address the plight of the most vulnerable members of humanity.

Cox's critical approach shifts attention from the anarchic political system, which is Waltz's main object of analysis, to the organization of the world political economy and to forms of dominance and hegemony within it. Whereas Waltz argues that political actors have no choice but to resign to the constraints inherent in international anarchy, Cox argues that many political actors are already involved in collective efforts to change the principles of world political organization. In Marx's language, the latter are actively involved in trying to make more of their history under conditions of their choosing. This led Cox (and Ashley in his early writings) to advance a central claim which has its origins in Marx's thought – that theories of the social world can have the ideological effect of aiding the perpetuation of arrangements that benefit some members of humanity while disadvantaging others. Cox argues that neorealism has the pernicious consequence of inviting human beings to resign to an allegedly immutable condition of international anarchy. This criticism is reminiscent of Marx's argument that bourgeois political economists assisted the maintenance of material inequalities by characterizing private property, the division of labor and market competition as natural and unalterable phenomena. As noted earlier, the point is that theories of the social world are not neutral accounts of an external reality. In Cox's much-quoted phrase, theories are 'always for someone and for some purpose' (Cox 1981: 128) and invariably work for some interests and against others. A central task of critical theory then is to uncover the political implications of claims to analyze the world in the spirit of neutrality. It is to show that theories of the social world do not stand outside the sphere of politics but have profound consequences for the distribution of power, material resources and significant opportunities in domestic and global society.

Cox sets out a broadly materialist interpretation of the nature of world politics, but he does not support a return to a reductionist form of 'the paradigm of production'. Although his starting point is labor and production, he does not regard these phenomena as more influential than state power or the structure of world order in shaping society and politics. Each level (production, the state and world order) influences the others, and shapes the environment in which the struggle between hegemonic and counter-hegemonic movements is conducted. Although Cox seems to privilege labor over interaction – in Habermas's use of these terms – his later writings have turned to the role that different civilizational perspectives play in world affairs (Cox 1996, 2003). Other approaches to the critical theory of IR have attached more significance to the sphere of interaction and, specifically, to the idea of dialogue as featured in Habermas's writings.

An alternative, but complementary, approach to Cox's perspective starts with the Habermasian notion of learning in the moral and cultural sphere. The emphasis shifts to the evolution of more cosmopolitan tests of the legitimacy of political institutions, policies and decisions. To return to an earlier point, the argument is that all human beings have a right to be represented in dialogue whenever decisions affect them. The accent here is on 'the triple transformation of political community' at the national and global levels so that communities are not only more cosmopolitan for the reasons just mentioned, but also sensitive to cultural and other differences, and strongly committed to the reduction of material inequalities. New forms of political community are needed in the 'postWestphalian era' to ensure that vulnerable persons and groups everywhere have a greater opportunity to influence decisions which harm their vital interests (Linklater 1998). There are important parallels here with 'critical security studies' which replace problem-solving approaches to national security with an emancipatory orientation to 'human security' (Booth 1991, 2005; Wyn Jones 1999, 2001).

Critics of the Habermasian approach doubt that this cosmopolitan commitment can avoid erecting new forms of domination and power. Postmodern or poststructuralist approaches, and feminist critiques of the discourse theory of morality, have claimed that the project of including all human beings in the 'universal communication community' may lead to different forms of social exclusion – for example, to the banishment of those who do not subscribe to what they regard as Habermas's essentially Western liberal belief that decisions should be reached through processes of dialogue in which the interests of all persons receive equal consideration and where no persuasion is ruled out in advance as transparently illegitimate. The critics agree with the idea that political life should be determined by dialogue, but they are not convinced by Habermas's version of unconstrained communication or 'non-repressive deliberation'. Some of the most important debates between Habermas and his critics are concerned with whether there are firm foundations for ethics, and also with the extent to which all forms of knowledge – including knowledge geared toward human emancipation – may accomplish anymore than the reconstitution of hierarchies of power (Devetak 2005). Despite these differences with critical theory, feminist and poststructuralist approaches to IR are no less opposed to neorealism. They are also broadly committed to showing how claims about the immutable nature of international politics can help to reproduce forms of competition and conflict and to explaining how these claims obscure the prospects for political efforts to remove unnecessary social constraints and end needless suffering.

Suffering and solidarity

Members of the Frankfurt School have argued that the desire 'to lend a voice to suffering' and to 'abolish existing misery' should stand at the center of political analysis (Horkheimer 1993: 32). The stress on needless suffering, which had been pivotal to Marx's writings, raises important possibilities for the critical theory of world politics, specifically by foregrounding undeniable realities of human vulnerability or 'injurability'. In the critique of Hegelian idealism, Marx emphasized that human beings are *embodied selves* with physical needs that link them to the wider natural world. Recent sociological thinking has sought to recover physical embodiment for social inquiry, highlighting the susceptibility of persons to physical pain and suffering, and contending that these inescapable features of social existence can provide a solid foundation for the idea of universal human rights (Turner 1996).

These themes have not received the attention they deserve in past discussions of critical theory and world politics.

The rediscovery of the body highlights a fundamental feature of human existence, namely the widespread desire to avoid pain, anguish and misery, which often gives dialogue its content in politics within and between separate political communities. Habermas (1998: 25) has observed that discourse ethics reflects the struggle for 'recognition' that results from the suffering that is caused by 'concrete cases of denigration and disrespect'. In this formulation, the idea of the 'injurable animal' refers not only to a capacity to feel pain (which human beings share with other sentient creatures) but also to species-specific susceptibilities to humiliation and degradation. Honneth (1995) has made these considerations central to his project of recovering the Hegelian idea of the 'struggle for recognition' for the contemporary critical theory of society. Social and political struggles, he argues, are fuelled by the 'moral injury' which results from 'the withdrawal or refusal of recognition'. Actions that cause physical pain or injury, or aim to humiliate or exclude persons from the entitlement to social resources, are a recurrent cause of the 'moral injury' that inspires resistance (Hacke 2005).

A robust defense of an ethic of vulnerability that unites 'materialism and morality' can be found in Horkheimer's essays. Horkheimer argued for grounding human solidarity on a shared experience of suffering (see Bronner 1994: 332–35 on the importance of such themes for the Frankfurt School more generally). The recognition that human beings are 'finite beings whose community consists of fear of death and suffering' and 'of the struggle to improve and lengthen the life of all' was the only basis, he argued, for 'correct solidarity' (Horkheimer, quoted in Stirk 1992: 178). Injurability was more than the possible basis for 'the solidarity of those who are suffering . . . the community of men lost in the universe' (Horkheimer 1974: 75). It could underpin 'solidarity with life in general' and the sympathy for all sentient creatures (Horkheimer 1993: 36). The idea of sentience serves to check the anthropocentrism of much moral and political theory. Similar themes pervade Adorno's claim that the Holocaust required a return to an ethic that begins with the inescapable fact of the 'injurable animal'. The purpose of a 'new categorical imperative', he argued, was to ensure that Auschwitz could not happen again. A foundational claim was advanced for an ethic centered on injurability, one that is encapsulated in the thesis that although human beings 'may not know' what the 'absolute good' is, they can still agree on what counts as 'inhuman' behavior and on what constitutes the 'bad life' (Adorno 2000: 167ff). Whether Adorno overwrote the argument is an interesting issue, but he raised important questions about human frailty and vulnerability that are central in the writings of many contemporary moral and political philosophers. These include Barry (1995: 87–8), who maintains that rules of justice prohibiting injury can 'be easily agreed upon' by persons who have different conceptions of the good life; Butler (2003), who emphasizes human vulnerability in her critique of the treatment of the detainees in Guantanamo Bay; and O'Neill (2000), who adapts Kantian ethics in the light of the precariousness of human existence. It is important to note that several world religions have regarded the capacity for suffering, and the potential for sympathy with the distressed, as the most natural point of solidarity between strangers (Bowker 1975). Secular standpoints have echoed this belief stating that the best prospects for human solidarity may lie in shared susceptibilities to physical pain and mental anguish rather than in conceptions of a allegedly universal good life, which often do more to divide than to unify human beings.

We have seen that Habermas maintains that discourse ethics resonates with struggles for 'recognition' that seek to break the shackles of 'denigration and disrespect' – and we have noted his claim that the first 'speech act' already contained the promise of the eventual unity of humankind. It is necessary to ask whether the same might be said about the first protests against bodily injury, social exclusion and humiliation. After all, most human beings can understand the desire to avoid unnecessary suffering. How far persons sympathize with the suffering of others is a different matter. Actors may have religious grounds for thinking that other persons deserve to suffer for their sins, because they are a threat to the former's survival or because their recklessness absolves all others of any responsibility to help them. That said, in general, human beings do not have to have been socialized into the same way of life in order to empathize and sympathize with others, faint though these emotions may be in comparison with regard for those that belong to the same family or community. The individual experience of pain and suffering – or the ability to imagine such misery – creates the possibility of the sympathetic dispositions that make some form of global solidarity possible. That commonality – rather than the resemblances between language users – has every claim to be regarded as containing the *immanent possibility* of the unity of humankind.

The main forms of exclusion in world history (national, racial, gender, etc.) have blocked the development of this universal potentiality, most obviously by denying 'the other' access to the relevant communication community – the association of persons who are entitled to protest against hurt. Widening participation in communication communities is essential so that human beings can protest against the imposition of ethnocentric notions of significant suffering and harm (Shapcott 2001). Dialogue is the key to designing a universal moral language which expresses the common ground between societies and which also ensures that global political arrangements recognize the existence of diverse cultural conceptions of human suffering (McCarthy 1993: 144–9).

Conclusion

How the global awareness of common vulnerabilities has emerged from the shadows of pernicious systems of exclusion is an intriguing sociological question, one that invites some final comments about Habermas's project of reconstructing historical materialism. Habermas (1979) stressed the priority of analyzing the evolution of cosmopolitan moral orientations in the development of society. These are orientations that believe in universal moral principles which can command the consent of persons everywhere. On this argument, the move beyond Marxist sociology points toward an analysis of domestic and international political arrangements that investigates the extent to which the support for cosmopolitan ethical ideals broke through pernicious distinctions between those who did and did not count morally. This is not an area that Habermas has developed, and analyzing these dimensions of human history remains a key part of the unfinished business of the Frankfurt School. The potential for developing solidarity with other members of the human race has existed in all societies. How far such attitudes to suffering have shaped contemporary IR and how far they distinguish the modern states system from earlier systems are intriguing questions for a sociological approach which is influenced by the Frankfurt School's defense of universal solidarity (Linklater 2004). Investigating this area is a core element in understanding how the human race may yet come to organize its affairs so that all persons and communities are released from those constraints which are not absolutely necessary for the reproduction of society, but which are grounded instead in gross asymmetries of power, in the dominion of sectional interests, in disrespect for other persons or groups and in the forms of fear, distrust and insecurity which are associated with intractable conflicts. The purpose of this critical sociology is to understand how human beings can learn to live together without such afflictions.

Further reading

Habermas, J. (1990) *Moral Consciousness and Communicative Action*, Cambridge: Polity.
Linklater, A. (1998) *The Transformation of Political Community*, Columbia, SC: University of South Carolina Press.
Wyn Jones, R. (ed.) (2001) *Critical Theory and World Politics*, Boulder, CO: Lynne Rienner.

6 Constructivism

Andrew Bradley Phillips

Introduction

International Relations (IR) is a discipline of the twentieth century. Forged in an era that saw the advent of the total state and total war, and reaching maturity in an environment marked by systemic ideological conflict and the pervasive threat of nuclear Armageddon, the discipline's historic mission has been to divine insights that might facilitate the realization of a modicum of order in an obstinately anarchic world. The durability of anarchy, the state's retention of a monopoly of legitimate violence, and the perennial possibility of Great Power war are foundational assumptions of the discipline. Already subject to intense scrutiny following the Cold War's peaceful conclusion, these assumptions have been further called into question in the post-9/11 era. The advent of unipolarity has spawned numerous interpretations emphasizing the quasi-imperial position now occupied by the American colossus in world affairs, a position that arguably confounds the dichotomy between the domestic and the international that has historically been constitutive of IR as a distinctive field of inquiry (Cox 2003; Katzenstein 2005; Mann 2003). In addition, while the threat of Great Power war appears to be in abeyance, the international community now confronts in transnational *jihadist* terrorism a threat that differs fundamentally from the powerful revisionist states that threatened international peace and security in the twentieth century (Fishel 2002; Mendelsohn 2005). Finally, the traditionally state-centric focus of IR has been problematized by both globalization as well as the increasing prevalence of state failure across large swathes of the developing world (Fukuyama 2004; Rotberg 2002).

It is in this more fluid global context that constructivism has matured as a distinctive approach to the study of global politics. Constructivists are defined by their emphasis on the socially constructed character of actors' interests and identities, and by their concomitant faith in the susceptibility to change of even the most seemingly immutable practices and institutions in world politics. In this chapter, I argue that precisely because of these commitments, constructivists are well placed to enhance our understanding of fundamental normative and institutional transformations that are currently reshaping the world polity. The widespread failure of the IR community to anticipate either the fall of the Berlin wall or the collapse of the Twin Towers (the two iconic bookend events demarcating the immediate post-Cold War era) reflects the need to readjust the discipline's orienting assumptions in ways that can accommodate the more complicated and less state-centric environment in which global politics is now played out. Fortunately, such a readjustment need not come at the expense of theoretical diversity. Constructivists' analytical emphasis on the determining influence of nonmaterial factors in world politics and their sensitivity to possibilities of transformative international change have the potential to enrich the work of researchers writing from a range of divergent theoretical perspectives. Moreover, given the diverse character of constructivists' normative commitments and their prescriptive claims about world politics, I will also argue that constructivism is unlikely to emerge as a coherent and commensurable competitor to the established grand traditions of IR theorizing (realism, liberal internationalism, and to a lesser extent Marxism and critical theory). Finally, notwithstanding the historic centrality of paradigmatic debate as a means of catalyzing intellectual advances within the discipline, I will suggest that the rationalist–constructivist divide (Ruggie 1998) has outlived its heuristic usefulness as the field's orienting polarity. The partial transcendence of this polarity through the growing popularity of analytical eclecticism should ideally encourage acknowledgment of the far more stimulating normative disagreements dividing constructivists from realists, liberals, and others, for such an acknowledgment is essential if IR is to reengage with the prescriptive as well as the explanatory tasks that initially formed its twin *raisons d'etre*.

The following discussion proceeds in five parts. I first review constructivism's origins in the 'third debate' between rationalists and critical theorists that dominated the field in the 1980s, before identifying the common ontological, epistemological, and methodological assumptions that have historically differentiated constructivists from their rationalist counterparts. Second, I examine the argument for permanent estrangement between constructivism and rationalism as it has been articulated from both sides of the rationalist–constructivist divide. Third, I consider arguments for a possible convergence between rationalist and constructivist approaches to the study of IR. Fourth, having reviewed both sides of the debate, I then advance an alternative view, suggesting that debates between 'fence builders' and 'bridge builders' are fundamentally miscast to the extent that they remain preoccupied by differences in analytical approach to the exclusion of the more fundamental normative differences that separate the various strands of IR theory from one another. Far from being mourned, these fundamental disagreements should be celebrated inasmuch as their recognition enables IR theorists to more vigorously engage with the ethical as well as the explanatory challenges that are raised by the contemporary transformative processes now reshaping the state system. Finally, I argue that while the discipline has been enriched by the turn toward analytical eclecticism inspired by constructivism's emergence, constructivism's full promise will only be truly realized once the tasks of critique as well as explanation are comprehensively reintegrated into the mainstream of IR theory.

In the beginning – the 'great divide'

Constructivism's origins are traceable to the 'third debate' between rationalists and critical theorists that dominated the discipline in the 1980s. Critical theorists attacked what they perceived to be the inherently conservative stance assumed by mainstream IR scholarship in its engagement with world affairs (Ashley 1984; Cox 1981). These authors dismissed as analytically naïve and politically irresponsible the view that IR scholars should devote themselves to providing 'policy relevant' insights about the world 'as it really is'. To the extent that scholarship naturalized and thereby fortified existing power structures, taking concepts such as the sovereign state and the condition of anarchy to be objective and immutable features of global politics, it was to be opposed as an expression of existing relations of domination (Ashley 1988). In contrast, critical theorists proposed that the real task of IR scholars should be to critique existing power structures, opening up the possibility of imagining more emancipatory alternatives (Cox 1981).

That this meta-theoretical critique was initially received so coolly by mainstream IR scholars is unsurprising, given that the critique coincided with the ascendancy of neorealism and neoliberal institutionalism, variants of realism and liberalism that owed their conceptions of human agency less to the canonical works of their respective traditions than to theories of human behavior borrowed from microeconomics. The commitments to parsimonious explanations, systems-level theorizing, and anthropomorphic conceptions of the state as a rational egoist that distinguished the 'neo' ascendancy corresponded closely with critical theorists' caricatures of positivist social science. While rationalists insisted that critical theorists demonstrate the practical relevance of their claims by applying their insights to the empirical study of problems of immediate concern to social scientists, critical theorists conversely protested that the ontological, epistemological, methodological, and normative assumptions of mainstream and critical approaches were so divergent as to preclude a fruitful synthesis of perspectives (Price and Reus-Smit 1998).

Fortunately, the Cold War's abrupt and peaceful termination exposed weaknesses on both sides of an emerging critical-rationalist divide, ensuring that this condition of mutual estrangement was destabilized before it could ossify. On the one hand, the rationalists' failure to anticipate or account for the Cold War's peaceful end seemingly confirmed critical theorists' claims that rationalists were incapable of adequately imagining or explaining large-scale changes within international politics (Price and Reus-Smit 1998). Conversely, that rationalists had been so obviously wrong-footed by history also suggested that critical theorists had overstated the significance of IR scholarship in naturalizing and sustaining global structures of domination (Price and Reus-Smit 1998). The Cold War's end thus served as an intellectual circuit breaker, exposing the limitations of existing approaches and providing an opening for the development of a more diverse range of explanations for contemporary international phenomena.

Constructivism thus emerged in the more fluid disciplinary context of the immediate post-Cold War period. Nonetheless, insofar as constructivism shares similar concerns to those expressed by critical theorists, a recapitulation of these differences is necessary before the debate on bridge-building across the rationalist–constructivist divide may be evaluated.

Ontologically, constructivists and rationalists differ on three points. First, constructivists are philosophical idealists rather than materialists. They argue that material structures acquire social significance only *via* the intersubjectively shared meaning structures through which they are mediated (Finnemore and Sikkink 2001). Constructivists do not deny the phenomenal reality of material processes such as nuclear proliferation, but they suggest that one can only understand actors' behavioural responses to said phenomena by reference to the shared meaning structures through which these processes are perceived and understood. Whether nuclear proliferation will be perceived as threatening international stability, enhancing it, or even exercising a neutral effect will depend on actors' interests and identities, which are socially constructed rather than being logically inferable from one's structural position within the international system.

Second, constructivists posit a mutually constitutive relationship between agents and structures (Hopf 1998: particularly pp. 172–3). Drawing from the insights of sociology, constructivists argue that the question of 'who am I?' is both logically and ontologically prior to the question of 'what do I want?' and that agents' identities are in turn governed by the normative and ideological structures that they inhabit (Hopf 1998: 175). These structures themselves are not ontological primitives, but are rather sustained patterns of social practice that are produced and reproduced through the actions of these agents. The international system is therefore seen by constructivists as being a constitutive rather than merely a strategic domain (Reus-Smit 1996: 209–30). States' conceptions of who they are and what interests they possess as a corollary of these identities derive from intersubjectively shared meaning structures rather than forming prior to social interaction (Reus-Smit 1996). This position contrasts with rationalists' belief that agents are analytically separable from the environments they inhabit, and that the study of international politics consists of the study of agents' instrumental pursuit of presocial interests that remain constant over the course of social interaction.

Finally, rationalists and constructivists diverge in their conceptions of the dominant logics governing agents' actions. Behavior through constructivist eyes is seen as essentially norm-driven, with states seeking to ensure a correspondence between their own conduct and internalized prescriptions for legitimate behavior that states have derived from their identities (Finnemore 1996; March and Olsen 1998). Far from being of purely ornamental value, norms exercise a profound influence on state behavior both by helping to constitute states' identities and interests in the first instance, and by conditioning and constraining the strategies and actions undertaken by states in the furtherance of these interests. This position contrasts with rationalists' belief that agents' behavior is governed not by a logic of appropriateness but merely by a logic of consequences. States through this optic are conceived as rational egoists pursuing interests formed exogenously to social interaction in a rationally instrumental manner, with cooperation or conflict being determined not by the presence or absence of norms but rather by a combination of resource constraints (owing to states' finite capabilities) and the congruity, or lack thereof, that states perceive between their own interests and those of other states (Baldwin 1993).

Ontological disagreements between rationalists and constructivists are mirrored in epistemological and methodological differences. Most constructivists endorse a postpositivistic approach to the social sciences, arguing that the socially constructed character of agents' interests and identities and the attendant diversity of possible meaning structures through which these interests and identities might be constituted preclude the possibility of developing all but the most elementary transhistorically or transculturally valid claims about international politics (Finnemore and Sikkink 2001: 394). This contrasts with rationalists' conviction that there exists sufficient commonality in state behaviors across different cultural and historical contexts as to warrant the development of law-like generalizations about international politics, and their concomitant belief in the possibility of developing robust predictive claims about global politics on the basis of these generalizations. From the mid-1990s onward, many constructivists have moderated their hostility toward positivism by pursuing contingent rather than universal generalizations about international phenomena in the course of their empirical research. Nevertheless, aversions to both prediction and the development of nomothetic covering laws about global politics remain distinctive features of constructivist scholarship.

Methodologically, rationalists' commitment to a positivistic epistemology has manifested itself in recourse to quantitative methods such as statistical regression analysis and game theory, in addition to more traditional methods such as the use of analytic narratives. Conversely, in light of their emphasis on the centrality of shared structures of meaning in constituting agents' identities, interests, and actions, constructivists draw from a highly eclectic range of methodologies – including discourse analysis, comparative historical case studies, ethnographic research, and qualitative and quantitative content analysis – in order to excavate these meaning structures and thus better enable them to apprehend the underlying power dynamics of the international system.

Condemned to division?

In light of the differences outlined above, the scope for potential dialogue across this latest disciplinary 'great divide' would seem limited. Indeed, even as constructivism has matured as a distinctive approach to the study of global politics, many of the disagreements that defined the 'Third Debate' between rationalists and constructivists have been revisited in the claims of scholars from both sides arguing for the inevitable and perpetual irreconcilability of the two approaches.

Turning first to constructivists, the divide between modern and postmodern constructivists needs to be recognized, particularly with regard to their disagreements regarding the compatibility of the tasks of explanation and critique. For postmodern constructivists, the task of critiquing structures of power, hierarchy, and domination, as they inhere both within global structures (e.g. the sovereign state system, the global capitalist economy) and within the discipline of IR itself, remains primary (Hopf 1998: 183). Postmodern constructivists are deeply concerned with the presumed nexus between power and knowledge, and are principally committed to excavating the sociolinguistic practices through which particular 'truth regimes' in international politics are constructed and alternative discourses rendered unimaginable (Price and Reus-Smit 1998: 262). This overriding emphasis on critique contrasts starkly with modern constructivists' attempts from the early 1990s to provide competing (and occasionally even complementary) solutions to empirical puzzles in IR that have long preoccupied rationalist scholars. In engaging with rationalists, modern constructivists have frequently pursued the development of contingent rather than all-embracing generalizations, and have employed a more eclectic range of methods than the sociolinguistic approaches favored by postmodern constructivists (Finnemore and Sikkink 2001: 394). Unsurprisingly, these developments have not been welcomed by postmodern constructivists, who maintain that a fundamental incompatibility exists between the task of critiquing power and the attempt to intellectually engage with rationalists, whose very commitment to positivism and the search for objective truths is seen to implicate them in the reproduction of global structures of power, hierarchy, and domination (for examples of postmodern constructivist scholarship, see Bartelson 1995 and Campbell 1998).

From the other side of the epistemological divide, rationalist purists have also emphasized the supposed incompatibility of explanation and critique, and have further sought to downplay the scope for productive dialogue (much less synthesis) between rationalist and constructivist approaches to IR. Initially, rationalist purists marshaled a range of criticisms, from constructivism's perceived utopianism through to its allegedly inadequate treatment of agency and operationalization of ideational variables, to discredit claims that constructivism could serve as a commensurable complement or competitor to established theories. Increasingly, however, as constructivism has adapted in response to these criticisms, some rationalists have reverted to a hegemonic assimilationist position, whereby rationalists are encouraged in their explanations to draw on an *ad hoc* basis upon stereotypically 'constructivist' ideational factors to account for residual variance in outcomes after the causal influence of rationalist variables has been exhausted (Desch 1998).

In form if not in spirit, the hegemonic assimilationist position bears some resemblance to the calls by epistemological centrists for convergence and greater analytical eclecticism. This fallback position has emerged only in light of constructivism's resilience in the face of earlier attempts to downplay its explanatory potential. The attempt, particularly favored by realists, to associate constructivism with the utopian idealism of the interwar period enjoyed some early credence given the disproportionate emphasis on the genesis and evolution of 'good' norms (e.g. human rights norms, the antiapartheid norm) that initially character-ized the constructivist research agenda (on the critique of constructivists as utopians, see Mearsheimer 1994/1995). However, as constructivists have turned their attention to topics such as the militarization of gender roles in armed conflicts (Enloe 1998), the production of cultures of insecurity (Weldes 1999), and the resort of states to pathological practices of population management including ethnic cleansing and genocide (Rae 2002), the intel-lectual plausibility of this criticism has declined and its primarily polemical character has become more apparent. Constructivists' growing willingness to explore the dynamics of 'bad' as well as 'good' norms, of pathological as well as progressive social identities, puts paid to the suggestion that an analytical focus on the socially constructed (and thus potentially changeable) character of agents' interests and identities need necessarily be antithetical to a comprehension of the often-grim realities of IR.

Similarly, criticisms of constructivism's alleged neglect of agency have also become less persuasive as constructivism has matured. In emphasizing the link between an existing norm or identity and a state's subsequent actions, the work of early constructivists was subjected to the criticism that it failed to seriously engage with questions of intentionality and active decision-making on the part of social agents (Hopf 1998: 198). Critics further pointed to the multiplicity of norms and identities to which agents are routinely subject, and the attendant dilemmas that are raised when actors are forced to reconcile the incompatible logics of appropriateness that might be mandated by these disparate norms and identities (Kowert and Legro 1996: 451–97; see especially pp. 486–8). In such instances, agents would appear to be compelled to make conscious and calculated decisions about the most appropriate course of action, suggesting a degree of self-consciousness and selectivity in norm compliance that was not always adequately accommodated within constructivist accounts.

Admittedly, early empirical applications of constructivism drew disproportionately from sociological institutionalists' insights about the determining power of norms in guiding actors' behavior, thus lending a surface plausibility to the above criticisms. Neverthe-less, as constructivists have integrated questions of agency more systematically into their explanatory frameworks, the persuasiveness of this criticism has progressively declined. With regard to the genesis of normative structures, constructivists have investigated the crucial role played by actors such as epistemic communities and Transnational Advocacy Networks in generating and diffusing international norms (Keck and Sikkink 1998). From the late 1990s, constructivists have also attempted to more explicitly elaborate the micro-foundations underpinning broader processes of norm genesis, diffusion, and transformation. Increasing attention has been paid to identifying the respective roles played by communic-ative action (argument, deliberation, and persuasion) and various social influence mechan-isms (e.g. backslapping and shaming) in securing actor compliance with norms (Johnston 2001). The variability of actor compliance with norms has also been acknowledged, with scholars increasingly seeking to trace out the different sources of norms at an organiza-tional, unit, and systemic level in order to better establish which norms matter and when in accounting for states' actions (Legro 1997).

Criticisms relating to constructivists' alleged imprecision in operationalizing ideational phenomena have also become more muted with time. The very multiplicity of diverse norms and identities in social life prompted early critics to observe that it was possible for constructivists to provide *post hoc* explanations for virtually any outcome by reference to a corresponding norm or identity, thereby threatening to render constructivist arguments nonfalsifiable (Kowert and Legro 1996: 486). Rationalists further pointed to the difficulties associated with quantifying ideational variables, arguing that these difficulties seriously complicate efforts to measure the relative importance of ideational variables *vis-à-vis* other factors in influencing agents' conceptions of interest and the attendant strategies and actions undertaken in pursuit of these interests (Desch 1998: 160–1).

In response to both these criticisms and the post-Cold War resurgence of ethnonationalist violence and religious fundamentalism, which captured the attention of rationalists as well as constructivists, scholars working on both sides of the analytical divide have sought to render intangible concepts such as social identity more amenable to empirical analysis. Scholars have employed a range of methods to capture the precise pathways of influence through which different ideas, norms, and identities condition actors' conceptions of self and interest, their decision-making procedures and causal beliefs, and their resulting strategies and actions.

Admittedly, constructivism's maturation as an explanatory approach has been poorly received by those who believe that such developments detract from its true tasks of under-standing, interpreting, and critiquing structures of power and domination in global politics. The hegemonic assimilationist position – whereby norms, values, ideas, and culture may be invoked to mop up residual variance only once rationalist explanations have been compre-hensively exhausted – also remains well represented, particularly within the North American academy. Nevertheless, owing in part to constructivism's increasing sophistication and in part to a growing interest in the role played by identity, norms, and culture in international politics (an interest that has only intensified following 9/11), the debate on construct-ivism's place within the discipline is increasingly being dominated by 'bridge-builders' emphasizing the possibilities of complementarity or convergence between rationalist and constructivist approaches.

Bridging the great divide

From the mid-1990s, a growing number of scholars occupying the epistemological center have argued in favor of constructivism's complementarity with existing rationalist approaches to global politics (Kahler 1998; Katzenstein and Sil 2004: 1–33). Scholars arguing the case for complementarity have contrasted constructivists' focus on processes of identity and interest formation with rationalists' focus on the dynamics of strategic action and have suggested the possibility that these different emphases might be productively combined. Specifically, a model of 'stage complementarity' has been proposed, whereby constructivists focus on the genesis of identities and interests, while rationalists explicate the strategies and actions adopted by agents in accordance with these identities and interests (Jepperson *et al.* 1996: 33–75).

Unsurprisingly, given the ontological disagreements dividing rationalists from construct-ivists, proposals for stage complementarity have not escaped criticism. Detractors have noted that stage complementarity assumes the existence of universally valid conceptions of instrumental rationality, overlooking the possibility that strategic and instrumental ration-ality may share with identities and interests the quality of being saturated by culturally and historically specific values and meanings (Reus-Smit 1999: 159–62). Proposals for stage complementarity would also seem to be predicated on the possibility of analytically isolating processes of interest and identity formation from processes of strategic interaction, presumably through recourse to some form of temporal-sequential bracketing. However, this analytical move jars with constructivists' ontological claims that identity and interest formation occur endogenously to strategic interaction. Disagreements over the extent to which norms, values, and ideas permeate logics of strategic interaction, together with disagreements over the extent to which identity and interest formation might be analytically bracketed from processes of strategic interaction, are reflective of deeper differences between rationalists and constructivists that are not easily susceptible to reconciliation within the one explanatory framework.

It is important to note, however, that these difficulties are not necessarily insurmountable. For example, in some instances, it may be possible to distinguish periods in which identities and interests are in an extreme state of flux from those in which identities and the interests that they prescribe are relatively stable. Ultimately, the question of whether or not identities and interests are ever sufficiently stable as to make strategic interactions between players amenable to rationalist analysis should be settled empirically on a case-by-case basis rather than being automatically prejudged on the basis of scholars' ontological leanings.

While some have sought to cultivate a complementary working relationship between rationalists and constructivists, others have welcomed in constructivism's emergence the apparent rise of a commensurable competitor with mainstream rationalist IR theories. Debates within the discipline on topics such as the end of the Cold War (Brooks and Wohlforth 2000; Evangelista 1999) and NATO's post-Cold War expansion (Kydd 2001; Williams and Neumann 2000) have been enriched by the emergence of competing rationalist and constructivist explanations. This discussion has been facilitated in part by rationalists' increasing willingness to countenance the possibility of ideas playing a role as *intervening* variables in their causal explanations, coupled with recognition of the fact that constructivists do not oppose interests to identities but rather see one as being constitutive of the other (on the constitutive relationship between norms and interests, see Finnemore 1996: 27). This recognition has in turn opened up the possibility of productively juxtaposing constructivist and rationalist 'interest-based' explanations, a possibility that has been further strengthened by constructivists' increasing willingness to present causal as well as constitutive explanations for empirical puzzles in global politics.

Notwithstanding the potential commensurability of rival rationalist and constructivist explanations with respect to specific research questions, two factors militate against constructivism's emergence as a commensurable peer competitor with established grand traditions. First, unlike other established theoretical traditions within the discipline, constructivism is not anchored within a distinctive political philosophy; consequently, the normative commitments that give realism, liberalism, or even Marxism the degree of internal coherence necessary for them to serve as distinctive rival approaches to the study of IR are absent from constructivism. This point is persuasively made by Barkin (2003), who combines constructivists' analytical focus on ideational influences in global politics with realists' moral skepticism and concern for unequal power dynamics. Second, while constructivists have increasingly sought to mount causal as well as constitutive explanations for phenomena in world politics (much to the chagrin of epistemological absolutists in both the rationalist and the constructivist camps), constructivism is nevertheless distinguishable from rationalist IR scholarship in its preparedness to explore 'how possible' as well as 'why' questions. Attempts to shoehorn constructivism into the category of commensurable competitor to existing approaches thus need to be qualified by the recognition that one of constructivism's most valuable contributions to the discipline has been its willingness to ask hard questions about the very processes through which entities such as the state are constituted and how constitutive norms such as sovereignty become established and evolve over time. To the extent that these types of questions are engaged in only marginally if at all by rationalist IR scholars, attempts to construe constructivism as a commensurable competitor to established traditions understate constructivism's distinct contribution in destabilizing dominant practices and institutions in global politics that are taken for granted by the rationalist mainstream.

The final argument in favor of 'bridge-building' across the rationalist–constructivist divide points to the increasing blurring of this division manifest in the growing popularity of analytically eclectic explanations for phenomena in global politics (on the case for analytical eclecticism as an approach to the study of global politics, see Katzenstein and Okawara 2001/02; Katzenstein and Sil 2004). This trend has occurred within a post-Cold War disciplinary context characterized by the decline of neorealist and neoliberal institutionalist hegemony in the field, and the concomitant emergence of variants of realism and liberalism that are arguably more sensitive to both the possibilities of large-scale change in global politics and also the significance of nonmaterial factors as determinants of social phenomena. In the instance of realism, Nina Tannenwald has cogently observed that realists have long relied on concepts such as 'socialization' and 'perceptions' to do the heavy lifting in their explanations, concepts that would appear to be particularly amenable to analysis along constructivist lines (Tannenwald 2005: 23–4). With the emergence of neoclassical realism, which emphasizes the role played by domestic state institutions, ideologies, and shared elite-level threat perceptions in explaining international behaviors that deviate from neorealist expectations (e.g. predatory expansion, under-balancing against imminent threats), one can see more overt evidence of realists' recourse to factors that were formerly the preserve of constructivists in developing their arguments (for examples of neoclassical realist scholarship, see Schweller 2004; Snyder 1991; Zakaria 1998). Similarly, in the case of liberalism, research on the democratic peace has increasingly emphasized the role played by mutual identification between democracies and the externalization of domestic norms of nonviolent conflict resolution in accounting for the absence of wars between democratic states (Huth and Allee 2002; Russett and O'Neal 2001). In both of these instances, constructivists' focus on the role played by ideational factors in accounting for behavioral regularities in world politics has been assumed (albeit partially and with serious qualifications) by realists and liberals, further strengthening the claims of those arguing for the increasing permeability of the rationalist–constructivist divide in the empirical research of IR scholars.

The increasing willingness of realists and liberals to incorporate nonmaterial determinants of social action into their analyses is particularly significant. It suggests a genuine blurring of the rationalist–constructivist cleavage that has defined the discipline in the post-Cold War era. Nevertheless, irrespective of their increasing analytical sensitivity to nonmaterial determinants of social action, realists and liberals will continue to remain distinct both from each other and from constructivists to the extent that their analyses remain grounded in distinctive normative claims about the essence of global politics (e.g. as in the realists' struggle for power and survival between states or as in the liberals' struggle by self-interested actors to realize common interests in the absence of central authority). Ultimately, debates on constructivism's place in the discipline that emphasize themes of complementarity, commensurable competition, or even convergence remain problematic to the extent that they obscure the essential normative differences that separate distinguish realists, liberals, and constructivists from one another. An unfortunate consequence of the 'bridge-building' discourse is that even in those cases where it has self-consciously sought to transcend the rationalist–constructivist polarity, it has paradoxically implicitly reaffirmed its centrality as the discipline's defining fault-line. In so doing, it has directed our attention toward the differences in analytical approach dividing theorists from one another, overlooking the irreducibly incompatible normative claims and discordant political anthropologies that inform different theoretical perspectives. Rather than perpetuating this lacuna, I will now argue that it is imperative that these irreducible incompatibilities be acknowledged and their implications explored if the discipline is to fulfill the prescriptive as well as the explanatory roles that initially formed its twin *raisons d'etre*.

A bridge too far

From its inception, IR has contained a normative as well as an explanatory agenda, seeking to prescribe as well as to describe – it has focused, to paraphrase E.H. Carr, not only on what is but also on what ought to be (Carr 1946: 5). Already, it is apparent that constructivism's emergence has advanced the explanatory component of this agenda by both spurring the rationalist mainstream to become more sensitive to the possibility of large-scale change in global politics and also by forcing them to pay greater attention to nonmaterial factors that are incapable of unproblematic incorporation within an unmodified rationalist and materialist framework. By contrast, however, the scope for advancing the discipline's normative agenda will remain stymied while the rationalist–constructivist divide remains the discipline's primary fault-line. For ultimately this division funnels discussion on possibilities for productive exchange between theoretical approaches toward meditations on the extent to which rationalist–constructivist disagreements over ontology, epistemology, and methodology might or might not be capable of being set aside to enable an incremental, puzzle-driven convergence based on the existence of shared research interests. In so doing, it occludes the fact that constructivists are fated to remain distinct from liberals and realists on account of the different political anthropologies from which their explanatory frameworks derive, as well as the differing prescriptive claims that these divergent conceptions of human nature entail. Given the dramatic institutional and normative changes that are currently reshaping the international system, a reengagement with both the normative as well as the explanatory goals of the discipline is crucial. However, such a reengagement can only occur once the irreducible *differences* and *incompatibilities* as well as the similarities and complementarities between the different theoretical traditions are acknowledged.

Considerable and potentially insurmountable differences exist between constructivists, realists, and liberals, pertaining to their underlying assumptions regarding the nature of human agency, the purposes of collective association, and the essence of the political as a distinct field of human endeavor. Unfortunately, the 1980s 'Third Debate' and its contemporary echoes have obscured these essential differences. Realism and liberalism have historically been differentiated by their subscription to radically divergent conceptions of the state of nature and of the range of behaviors that are to be expected of social agents in the absence of a central authority. Whereas realism draws its insights from a Hobbesian conception of the state of nature and is imbued with a pessimism regarding the prospects for human progress that has its foundations in theology as much as in the social sciences, liberals subscribe to a Lockean conception of the state of nature and are conversely informed by an optimism about humanity's capacity to effect transformative social change that is anchored firmly within the tradition of the Enlightenment (on realism's distinct intellectual genealogy, see Louriaux 1992 and also Vincent 1981 and Williams 1996). That these two approaches could plausibly be yoked under the common banner of rationalism is explicable only through reference to the fleeting convergence of traditions that accompanied the 'neo' ascendancy of the 1980s (Ruggie 1998: 4–11). The convergence in analytical approach (commitments to systems-level theorizing, parsimonious explanations, and conceptions of states as rational egoists) that marked the 'neo' ascendancy substantially narrowed differences between the two traditions, but only temporarily. Whereas both neorealists and neoliberal institutionalists sought to account for patterns of continuity in the context of the 1980s (the stability of bipolarity and the stability of international economic regimes, respectively, in the wake of declining American hegemony), realists and liberals now seek to account for processes of change (e.g. the rise of predatory revisionist states, the global spread of democracy) that resonate strongly with the very different conceptions of human nature and understandings about the potential for human progress that underpin realism and liberalism as broader theories of politics.

Unlike realism and liberalism, and in keeping with its rejection of essentialist claims about human nature, constructivism is not explicitly anchored within a broader philosophical tradition, its origins in critical international theory notwithstanding. Consequently, constructivism lacks the internal coherence necessary for it to be situated as a commensurable paradigmatic alternative to realism, liberalism, or Marxism (Finnemore and Sikkink 2001: 393). Nevertheless, a consideration of individual strands of constructivism reveals assumptions about the character of human agency and possibilities for progressive social change that contrasts strongly with those informing realism and liberalism. In their emphasis on the capacity for social agents' interests and identities to be transformed by the force of logical argument, Habermasian constructivists imbue communicative action with a significance that is absent from both realism and liberalism; this in turn leads them to infer far greater possibilities for expanding the moral boundaries of political community than may be discerned in either realism or all but the most radical streams of liberalism. This emphasis on the transformative potential of communicative action differs again from the pessimism of postmodern assessments of agents' capacity to permanently transcend relations of power and domination that flows from this.

The foregoing observations are far from novel, but a renewed recognition of these differences between and within different theoretical traditions is crucial if the discipline is to escape the confines of an increasingly sterile debate over the scope for productive dialogue between constructivism and rationalism as analytical approaches to the study of global politics. Realism, liberalism, and the various strands of constructivism are each predicated on divergent conceptions of human agency, the underlying purposes and character of collective associations, and the essence of the political as a distinctive field of endeavor. Given their deep foundations in substantive political philosophies, I would further argue that realism and liberalism are far from incapable of engaging in critique as well as explanation (although this may be true of neorealism and neoliberal institutionalism). However, a renewed engagement by realists, liberals, constructivists, and others with the tasks of prescription and critique *in addition* to explanation is possible only once the divergent philosophical claims animating these different approaches are acknowledged.

Global transformations, IR, and normative political theory

I have argued above that a reintegration of the explanatory and normative objectives of IR theory is possible. I have also suggested that a transcendence of the rationalist–constructivist polarity, and a concomitant appreciation of the diversity of normative positions that characterize diverse strands of constructivism, realism, and liberalism, makes this reintegration possible. I will now conclude by arguing the case for the necessity of this reintegration, owing to the operation of three global macro-processes that undermine the discipline's analytic assumptions about the nature of the international system, and thus necessitate a reappraisal of the associated normative assumptions currently informing the explanatory agendas of different IR theories.

The IR theorists have conventionally understood the modern state system as being predicated on a distinction between domestic hierarchy, deriving from the state's monopolization of the legitimate use of force, and international anarchy, reflecting the absence of a global Leviathan and the concomitant decentralization of war-making capabilities between multiple sovereign states. The post-Cold War advent of unipolarity and the widespread prevalence of state collapse in many postcolonial societies together challenge this understanding of global politics. In its unchallengeable military superiority, its willingness to use force unilaterally to advance its interests, and its aggressive export of its preferred regime type via a 'forward strategy of freedom', the United States presently occupies a role in global politics that is without a modern historical parallel, that of the revisionist hegemon. This revisionism, implicit in the United States' involvement in humanitarian interventions and in its democracy promotion initiatives in the 1990s, has become explicit following 9/11 and the link drawn by the Bush administration between tyrannical, weak, and failing states in the Greater Middle East and the contemporary wave of transnational Islamist terrorism.

The concentration of conventional war-fighting capabilities in the hands of a revisionist hegemon, the weakening of the state's coercive monopoly in many postcolonial societies, and the diffusion of destructive capabilities to transnational nonstate networks such as *al Qaeda* substantially undermine the Weberian assumptions of statehood that have traditionally informed IR theories. Conventional assumptions about the state are being further unsettled by the continuing diffusion and consolidation of norms that increasingly circumscribe states' internal exercise of their sovereign prerogatives. The accelerated diffusion of democracy as the internationally recognized standard of legitimate statehood (120 of the world's 192 countries encompassing nearly two thirds of the world's population are now electoral democracies), the increasing acknowledgment of a 'responsibility to protect' circumscribing states' domestic use of force, and the United States' growing assertiveness in insisting upon states' active cooperation in suppressing terrorism and WMD (weapons of mass destruction) proliferation (Feinstein and Slaughter 2004) all reflect the increasingly conditional character of sovereignty in the modern state system. While international enforcement of democratic and humanitarian norms in particular remains selective and inconsistent, the post-Cold War era has nevertheless witnessed a progressive shift away from the negative sovereignty regime and blanket rhetorical acceptance of nonintervention as the meta-norm governing interstate relations that prevailed during the Cold War.

Finally, in the face of globalization, the link between collective identities and territoriality has become increasingly attenuated, or at the very least rearticulated through a global frame. Transnational terror networks like *al Qaeda* and *Jemaah Islamiyah* purport to act in the interests not of a specific territorially bounded nation, but rather in the name of an imagined global *ummah* encompassing all of the world's Muslims in justifying their attacks against the United States and its allies (on this point, see Mendelsohn 2005: 60). Conversely, Western states' increasing recourse to forcible humanitarian intervention depends on popular subscription to the notion that the thin moral obligations one owes to an imagined universal humanity are occasionally sufficient to warrant costly military action in support of these duties. Finally, even in the case of ostensibly localized ethnonationalist conflicts (e.g. the war between the PKK and the Turkish government, Sri Lanka's war against the Tamil Tigers), nonstate protagonists now exploit the long-distance nationalism of globally dispersed diaspora networks to source the funding, the *materiel*, and even the personnel needed to prosecute prolonged struggles against state authorities (Adamson 2005; Gunaratna 2003: 197–223).

Transformations in patterns of organized violence, the consolidation of democratic and humanitarian norms at the expense of unconditional state sovereignty, and the increasingly contingent relationship between territoriality and collective identity – these processes together confound the discipline's foundational assumptions about the nation-state as the primary locus of coercive power and popular loyalty within the international system, as well as threatening to destabilize the distinction between domestic hierarchy and international anarchy that has traditionally been constitutive of the discipline. As such, these processes impinge directly upon questions of core concern to realists, liberals, and constructivists alike.

For realists, the progressive erosion of the state's coercive monopoly from above and below surely cuts against the analytical state-centrism of realism. In addition, however, this process also impinges upon realists' ethical assumptions in favor of the state as the 'hard shell' providing the citizen's ultimate guarantee against the twin threats of foreign conquest and civil disorder. The prerogative that realists grant to rulers to sacrifice other moral values to the overriding imperative of national security presupposes a degree of domestic control over organized violence that is increasingly being eroded through the activities of Private Military Companies, transnational criminal and terrorist networks, and globally connected domestic rebel movements. Conversely, the normative preference for anarchy over global hierarchy that already informs neorealism may if anything be being further reinforced by the destabilizing consequences flowing from post-Cold War rise of an informal American imperium and the Bush administration's aggressive attempts to transform domestic authority structures of other states along democratic lines.

For liberals as well, the processes sketched above carry significant analytical and normative implications in their train. The global diffusion and consolidation of democratic and humanitarian norms is a cause for celebration for liberals. Nevertheless, given these norms' status as constitutive standards of legitimate political authority and their profoundly transformative effects on institutionalized domestic authority structures, liberals could profit from constructivists' analyses of the social processes through which such constitutive norms emerge and become diffused throughout international systems. At a normative level, the creeping demise of a negative sovereignty regime and the growth of strong states' intervention into the domestic affairs of weak states – processes that have accompanied the diffusion of humanitarian and democratic norms and have partially depended on them for legitimation – sit uneasily with the liberal commitment to national self-determination. Given liberals' historic dependence on functioning states as the natural guarantors of human liberty, the phenomenon of state failure also unsettles liberals' prescriptions for the ordering of world politics. Markets, democracy, and international institutions, emphasized by liberals either individually or in combination as palliatives for the perils of anarchy, are each predicated on the prior existence of functioning states, thus the growing prevalence of state failure impinges directly on the prescriptive as well as the descriptive and explanatory claims of the liberal tradition (Fukuyama 2004).

Finally, for constructivists, the very fluidity of the international system at present raises considerable analytical and normative challenges. Norms that have historically been central to the operation of the state system such as sovereignty and nonintervention are currently in the process of revision or rearticulation, while globalization is increasingly attenuating or reframing the relationship between territoriality and collective identity. While constructivists are well positioned to observe and analyze such changes, both the speed of these transformations and the simultaneous operation of multiple and often-conflicting norms and identities upon social agents significantly complicate attempts to explain agents' behavior in world politics at present. The extent to which constructivists' normative agendas are being advanced by contemporary developments is also open to interpretation. While globalization might potentially expand the scope for exchange and dialogue between social actors, thus serving Habermasian constructivists' goals of promoting radical deliberative democracy, these prospects are significantly circumscribed by the current domination of the world polity by a revisionist hegemon led by an administration whose activism is unlikely to be tempered by the force of the better argument.

Conclusion

The foregoing comments are not intended to suggest that contemporary IR theories are incapable of productively engaging with changes in global politics. On the contrary, I suggest that the emergence of constructivism and the parallel decline of the 'neo' hegemonies within realism and liberalism have spawned exactly the level of theoretical diversity that will be needed to effectively make sense of world politics in the twenty-first century. The constructivist emphasis on the centrality of nonmaterial factors as determinants of phenomena in global politics can and should serve the agendas of realists and liberals, just as it has informed the works of feminists, critical theorists, Gramscian Marxists, and others writing from outside the theoretical mainstream. For realists, the crucial question of the durability of American hegemony can only be addressed by considering whether other states will balance against or bandwagon with the United States; this question in turn can only engaged by considering the systemic and unit-level determinants of state identity that inform leaders' threat perceptions and thus condition their decisions to balance or bandwagon. Similarly, constructivist insights regarding the origins and diffusion of norms are of obvious relevance to liberals interested in accounting for the rapidity with which democracy has established itself as the world's most common regime type over the last three decades. Finally, given constructivists' frequent tendency to fall back by default on the state-centric assumptions of IR theory, continuing processes of globalization and state failure are likely to necessitate further constructivist engagement with both the works of historical sociologists and also theories of state formation informed by a variety of theoretical standpoints, including those that bear certain family resemblances with realism and liberalism.

The dramatic changes currently convulsing the international system also pose serious challenges to the normative commitments of IR theorists, challenges that will hopefully engender a reengagement between IR and normative political theory. In concentrating on the ontological, epistemological, and methodological disagreements between constructivists and their critics, commentators have generally overlooked the far more interesting normative disagreements that separate constructivists from realists and liberals and that also internally divide these schools of thought. To the extent that a growing analytical eclecticism undermines the rationalist–constructivist divide as the discipline's orienting polarity, it is possible that the incessant debate on possibilities for bridge-building and theoretical synthesis will be partially displaced by a more vigorous dialogue on the different moral visions informing the explanatory claims of the different theoretical traditions. The weakening of the Weberian template of organized violence from above and below, the diffusion of democratic and humanitarian norms at the partial expense of norms of unconditional sovereignty and nonintervention, the increasingly tenuous relationship between territoriality and collective identity – each of these changes has a fundamental bearing on the ethical as much as the explanatory dimensions of the discipline's agenda, and both sides of this program must be satisfactorily engaged if IR is to effectively capture the full complexity of global politics in the twenty-first century. Only once constructivism's emergence has reignited a sustained focus on the ethical questions that were initially a core part of the discipline's *raison d'etre* will its promise be realised.

Further reading

Finnemore, M. (1996) *National Interests in International Society*, Ithaca, NY: Cornell University Press.

Weldes, J. (1999) *Cultures of Insecurity*, Minneapolis, MN: University of Minnesota Press.

Wendt, A. (1999) *Social Theory of International Politics*, Cambridge: Cambridge University Press.

7 The English School

Alex J. Bellamy

Introduction

There are three main ways to assess the English School's contribution to International Relations (IR) theory. The first is to follow Barry Buzan in arguing that the English School is an 'underexploited resource' and that 'the time is ripe to develop and apply its historicist, and methodologically pluralist approach' to the subject (Buzan 2001: 472). Buzan argues that the English School has become recognized as a distinctive worldview that has much to offer the discipline. At the other end of the spectrum, some writers call for the School's closure. The 'English School' label was first written down by Roy Jones in 1981 in an article calling for the School's closure (Jones 1981). More recently, Hall (2001) went one step further and argued that the School no longer existed because it had been distorted by contemporary proponents such as Dunne (1998) and Wheeler (1992). According to Hall, Dunne and Wheeler's commitment to solidarism and constructivism eschew some of the English School's foundational ideas such as the centrality of states, importance of power politics and a deep skepticism about the possibility of different political communities reaching agreement on substantive political matters. A third perspective, somewhere between these two poles, has arisen as a result of the increased dialogue between English School ideas and other worldviews – most notably realism and constructivism. Both realists and constructivists alike have called for the further development of English School thinking to give it a more 'refined' theory capable of identifying the motors for change and lines of causation in world politics (Copeland 2003; Finnemore 2001).

The purpose of this chapter is to evaluate these positions by investigating the English School's contribution to IR theory in the twenty-first century. A frequent source of confusion about the School stems from the idea that there is a single common view within it. By contrast, as this chapter will demonstrate, there is not one but many theories and accounts of IR embedded within the School, which is united by 'family resemblances' (Dunne 1998). Thus, as Suganami (2005: 29) argues, the English School is best understood as 'a historically constituted and evolving cluster of scholars with a number of plausible and interrelated stories to tell'. This chapter substantiates this claim by focusing on core contemporary debates within the English School. It does so in four parts. The first briefly considers the School's evolution and relationship with constructivism. The second and third focus on the School's defining ideas of three traditions of international thought and three pillars of world politics respectively. The final part evaluates a central question about contemporary international society (is it under threat from US hegemony?) in order to illuminate how English School theorizing can help make sense of IR today and the potential for conversations with other disciplines and approaches.

Evolution, contribution and link to constructivism

The purpose of this section is to briefly describe the evolution of English School thinking in recent years and its relationship with constructivism. One of the most significant developments in the recent history of IR theory has been the elevation of the English School from the margins to the center. Originally pioneered by the British Committee in the 1960s and 1970s and developed by writers based largely at Oxford and the London School of Economics, by the end of the 1980s the English School had been effectively consigned to the history books of IR theory. For many, the School's professed methodological pluralism made many of its key writers difficult to discern from realists (Fierke 2002: 133; Molloy 2003), and its commitment to interpretivism (Bull 1966a) meant that it could not rival the causal, ostensibly scientific, theories put forward by neorealism and neoliberalism.

In short, when Roy Jones called for the 'closure' of the School in 1981 there was little dissent. Indeed, there was no reply at all until 1988, when Grader (1988) insisted that the School could not be closed because it did not exist – a claim rapidly and convincingly disputed by Wilson (1989). The School's key thinkers of that period – Hedley Bull, Martin Wight, Adam Watson and R.J. Vincent (amongst others) – were more concerned with unraveling contemporary political puzzles than explicitly identifying themselves within schools of thought. Bull spent the early 1980s grappling with questions of order and justice and the 'revolt against the West' (Bull 1984a,b); Wight identified three traditions in international theory (1991); Watson's work tended to focus on the historical evolution of the international system (1992) – a marginal issue until very recently – and the conduct of international diplomacy (1984), whilst R.J. Vincent moved from detailed analyses of the principle of nonintervention (1974) to a landmark study of justice and human rights in international society (1986). The important point to make here is that during this period none of the central writers made the defense of their collective worldview a central component of their research, though Bull and Vincent did in passing identify themselves as part of a common tradition of inquiry – labeled the 'British School' by Bull (Dunne 1998: 7; Vincent 1983).

The reemergence of the English School after the end of the Cold War changed all this significantly. Since 1981, when Jones' article was published, there has been an exponential growth in the number of people who either identify themselves within the School's tradition of inquiry or are engaged in dialogue with it. Today, the number of scholars who fall into one of these categories can be counted in the 'hundreds' (Buzan and Little 2001: 944), whereas in earlier years only a handful of scholars identified themselves as part of a loose-fitting common worldview. Over the past two decades the School's intellectual content has been elaborated on and more carefully demarcated from other approaches.

This process of self-identification was pioneered by Tim Dunne's important study on the British Committee. Here, Dunne (1998: 5–11) identified three 'preliminary articles' of the English School which should be understood, he argued, as 'family resemblances'. First is a self-identification with a particular tradition of inquiry. Although the key early thinkers such as Bull, Wight and Vincent did not expend much energy justifying their common ideas (with the possible exception of Bull 1966a), since the 1990s writers have increasingly identified themselves in relation to a common tradition usually by referring to and utilizing the concept of international society. Second is the adoption of an interpretive approach to the study of IR. Scholars within or related to this common tradition are deeply skeptical about 'scientism' in IR. Instead, they prefer to use a variety of methods drawn from historical, legal and diplomatic studies. This has left the tradition exposed to the criticisms of some constructivists and realists who insist that the English School needs to develop 'better' (more scientific) theories. However, the English School can make a strong case for rejecting scientism, and Little (2003) has convincingly argued that its broad historical canvas makes scientism and the quest for causal variables less useful. Third, international theory is understood as normative theory. English School writers recognize that ethical inquiry lies at the heart of international theory. From Carr onward, writers associated with this tradition of inquiry have acknowledged that the proper study of IR not only involves questioning 'what is' but also 'what ought to be' (Reus-Smit 2001b). By identifying the common features of the English School tradition, Dunne made an important contribution to the development of a self-conscious school of thought, able and willing to defend its key claims and characteristics.

In short, since the end of the Cold War, the English School has developed from a loose collection of a handful of scholars, who pursued similar interests and shared a common mode of thought, into a significant, self-identifying intellectual movement. In so doing, however, the overlap between the English School and the most popular 'new' IR theories – collectively labeled 'constructivism' – has become more apparent (Reus-Smit 2005: 81–96). Indeed, the reemergence of the English School and its incorporation into IR debates outside the United Kingdom and Australasia is largely due to its relationship with constructivism. It is important to recognize at the outset, however, that not all constructivists and English School theorists accept these common interests or origins. Emmanuel Adler, for instance, argues that the English School approach 'had little to do with the construction of social facts by socially constructed knowledge and language' (2005), a view disputed by Buzan (2005b: 189), who claims that 'the very act of taking society as one's object of study requires a form of constructivist understanding'. Reus-Smit (2002) argues that both sides of the English School/constructivism debate tend to inaccurately caricature the other.

Despite these disputes, and although constructivism is a broad church, constructivists share three common concerns (Reus-Smit 2001c: 216) that also resonate with English School theorists. First, they argue that normative and ideational structures are just as important as material structures, an idea that relates closely to the English School's ideas of international theory as normative theory and the importance of interpretivism. The second common concern is that ideational structures shape the identities and therefore interests of actors in world politics. The third common view is that the relationship between agents and structures is mutually constitutive. It follows from the previous two observations that meaning is socially constructed (thus granting agency to actors) and that identities, interests and behavior are conditioned by ideational structures. Constructivism attempts to find a synthesis between approaches that focus on the actions of actors and the way that they create political institutions and ideologies and structural approaches, including neorealism and Marxism, which hold that political action is shaped by socioeconomic and historical structures (Cerny 2000; Dessler 1989; Wendt 1987). The idea of mutual constitution holds that although actors are constituted and constrained by ideational and material structures, 'those structures would not exist were it not for the knowledgeable practices of those actors' (Reus-Smit 2001c: 218). The social structures that constitute and constrain states in international society are themselves constructed and maintained by social interaction between states, a point commonly accepted by English School theorists. It is important, however, to recognize that the English School and constructivism are not synonymous. In particular, the School is committed to methodological pluralism and a tripartite conception of world politics.

Three traditions

English School approaches to world politics insist that there are three images or traditions of world politics, labeled 'realism, rationalism and revolutionism' by Wight (1991) and 'Hobbesian, Grotian, and Kantian' ideas by Bull (1977). Although Wight came to identify most closely with the 'rationalist' tradition, he insisted that all three (realist, rationalist and revolutionist) were necessary components of the proper study of world politics. As Wight (1991: 260) himself put it,

> The three traditions are not like three railroad tracks running parallel into infinity. They are not philosophically constant and pure like three stately, tranquil and independent streams ... [t]hey are streams, with eddies and cross-currents, sometimes interlacing and never for long confined to their own river bed ... They both influence and cross-fertilize one another, and they change without, I think, losing their inner identity.

The 'three traditions' idea was Wight's response to his own observation that there was no discrete body of international theory separable from legal, historical and philosophical forms of knowledge (Wight 1966). We therefore have broad *traditions* of thought rather than formal theory. The traditions prompt us 'to notice illogicalities and discontinuities because exigencies of political life often override logic' (Wight 1987: 226). Before proceeding to look at the traditions themselves, it might be useful to reflect on the nature of intellectual traditions themselves.

There are two ways to understand the meaning of tradition. The first is to see a tradition as a form of intellectual inheritance. A tradition is a mode of thought handed down through generations. Participants in a tradition believe that what they are doing and how they are thinking can be traced to past generations. From this perspective, a tradition's authority is derived from its past so that, as MacIntyre (1990: 116) put it, the 'superiority of the formulations of [each epoch's] predecessor, and that predecessor in turn is justified by a further reference backwards'. This type of thinking is evident throughout IR theory. The problem is that it can read the present into the past, looking for signs from history to confirm modern predilections. As Bleiker (2005: 184) has commented, 'an outsider examining the English School is struck by its strict and consistent citational rules, by who needs to be quoted for the scholarly work to count as a contribution to English School inquiry'. This comment suggests an alternative, more pragmatic way of understanding traditions, as 'unintentionally invented' (Jeffrey 2005: 69). Drawing on Oakeshott, Jeffrey (2005: 72) insists that

> all tradition is invented in the sense that it is a function of present thinking ... there is no sense in which traditions of thought can be said to really exist in the past ... [some] traditions are not invented in an explicit and self-conscious manner but rather evolve somewhat organically.

In my view, the three traditions are therefore best understood as externally imposed analytical categories that enable the identification and study of the key dilemmas of world politics. There are two main points here. First, traditions are externally constructed and imposed – they are not descriptions of the way things really are but categories to enable our understanding. Second, they are sets of ideas or modes of thinking, not really existing objects. The importance of these two points for clearing up the confusion about the relationship between the English School's 'three traditions' and 'three pillars' will become clearer below.

For Wight, 'realist' worldviews and practices are based on 'power politics' (Wight 1979: 23–30, 1991: 15–24). They emphasize the inherent conflict between states, the anarchical condition of world politics and the role of war as the ultimate arbiter. 'Rationalism' sits somewhere between realism and revolutionism though there is considerable debate over which pole it is closest to (Dunne 1998: 58–9). Rationalism is based on the notion that the world's diverse communities and cultures are housed in states that together form an international society. Rationalists insist that states can agree to construct and follow rules that facilitate their mutual existence and prosperity (Wight 1991). One of the most influential advocates of rationalism was Hedley Bull. He argued that states were necessary to fulfill the basic human goals of security and welfare (Bull 1977). Without states, the human condition would indeed resemble the Hobbesian state of nature. States, he argued, inhabited an *anarchical society*. Because international society is anarchic, states developed rules and norms that allowed them to cohabit and achieve their fundamental goal: provision of security for their citizens. The most fundamental rule is that of nonintervention enshrined in Article 2(4) of the UN Charter. Without the nonintervention rule there would be nothing to stop states constantly intervening in each other's affairs. States would quite literally go to war because there would be nothing to stop them (Waltz 1954). Therefore, states abide by the rules because they have a shared interest in maintaining international order.

Whilst rationalism is often dubbed the 'Grotian conception' of international society (Bull 1966b: 51–73), it is important to recognize that there are at least two rationalist 'strands' within the English School. Both accept the idea that states form an international society, but they disagree about what type of society it is. Those that accept a Vattelian or pluralist view of international society argue that states are only bound by whatever rules they consent to (Ralph 2006). Others hold a Grotian or solidarist view. The Grotian view differs from the Vattelian in at least two ways. First, Grotius argued that international law comprised elements of natural law, sometimes referred to as 'common morality' (Nardin 2005: 247–64) or an 'overlapping [moral] consensus' (Rawls 1993). He argued that states had an inherent right to defend themselves and to punish those who commit basic wrongs. Thus, Grotius argued that intervening on behalf of an oppressed people might be justified (Bull 1984a: 2–3). Second, the Grotian perspective holds that states are bound to obey international law irrespective of whether they consent to be so bound.

The third tradition is revolutionism, which can be either benign (Bull's 'Kantian' perspective) or malevolent (e.g. Marxist or Islamic fundamentalist). Revolutionists share a belief in moral universalism (Wight 1991: 8). Whereas rationalists insist that moral values derive from the society and state in which they exist, revolutionists argue that certain moral principles are universal. As Bull put it, the universal imperative has been 'fed by a striving to transcend the states system so as to escape the conflict and disorder that have accompanied it' (1977: 38). Wight and Bull were both skeptical about revolutionism. Wight associated it with fascist and communist movements that wanted to replace international society violently with a global government in its own image. Bull was concerned that revolutionism or the quest for global distributive justice would ultimately destroy global order and replace it with unmitigated anarchy (Bull 1984b; Wheeler 1992). More recently, however, revolutionism has become associated with a Kantian conception of world politics based on the idea that there is a world society of individuals that comes prior to the society of states. From this perspective, sovereignty and other international rules should be understood as instrumental values because they derive from states' responsibility to protect the welfare of their citizens, and when states fail in this duty, they lose their sovereign rights (Tesón 2003: 93). There are a variety of ways of arriving at this conclusion. Some draw on Kant's concept of the rational individual to insist that all individuals have certain prepolitical rights (Caney 1997: 34). Others argue that today's globalized world is so integrated that moral obligations cross boundaries along with interactions.

The three traditions are therefore three broad ways of thinking about how world politics is and how it ought to be. As Jackson (1995: 110–28) pointed out, each tradition could be thought of as a layer of responsibility confronting political leaders which taken together point to the important normative and pragmatic dilemmas that shape world politics. Realism refers to a leader's primary responsibility for the welfare of citizens. In contractarian terms, a state can be understood as having a contract to secure its own citizens. Rationalism refers to a state's responsibility to abide by international law, and its constitutive rules in particular. If we take seriously the claim that modern states and contemporary international society are mutually constituted then there is a very strong imperative for states to abide by the core principles of law. We should not underestimate the importance of Bull's insight that states have a vested interest in the maintenance of international society and hence in the preservation of its constitutive rules. Finally, Jackson takes revolutionism in its benign form to refer to the idea that states, particularly liberal states, feel a sense of moral responsibility for the welfare of individuals across borders. From this perspective, then, world politics is a site of perpetual contestation between three levels of responsibility.

Three pillars

Whilst realism, rationalism and revolutionism are sets of *ideas* about the way the world is and how best to shape it, 'international system', 'international society' and 'world society' are analytical devices to help us understand the global polity at any particular historical juncture. I label this triad the three *pillars* of English School theorizing. According to Bull, an international system is formed whenever states are in regular contact with one another and where 'there is interaction between them, sufficient to make the behaviour of each a necessary element in the calculation of the other' (Bull 1977: 10). By contrast,

> a *society of states* (or international society) exists when a group of states, conscious of certain common interests and common values, form a society in the sense that they conceive themselves to be bound by a common set of rules in their relations with one another, and share in the working of common institutions.
>
> (Bull 1977: 13)

Beyond the simple assertion that states comprise an international society, there are important differences about the type of international society we live in today and the type we *ought* to live in. As Buzan (2004: 61) argues, it is a debate about both the 'degree and institutionalization of shared interests and values' and about the 'collective enforcement of rules'. Both pluralist (Vattelian) and solidarist (Grotian) conceptions contain descriptive as well as prescriptive components. To date, both of these approaches have tended to assume that international society is a society of states and to focus on the types of diplomatic and legal intercourse and historical analyses that informed early English School approaches. The dialogue between pluralism and solidarism helps to highlight the important tension between conceptions of order and justice in IR. However, this debate needs to become broader (recognizing that international society deals with a wider number of questions than has hitherto been acknowledged) and deeper (recognizing that international society, even narrowly conceived, is no longer solely a society of states – and probably never was). Moreover, taking a lead from Buzan (2004), we need to recognize that the two sides are not mutually exclusive. That is, at any given moment contemporary international society is neither pluralist *nor* solidarist but is more or less one or the other (conceived as points on an axis rather than 'black boxes') in different *sectors* (i.e. economic, environmental, military) and different *regions*.

By contrast, 'world society' is much less well defined. Manning (1962: 177) describes it as the society of 'all mankind' which exists 'within, beneath, alongside, behind and transcending' the society of states. Martin Wight, too, has a vague concept of a world society united by a thin common culture. For Wight, all international societies are subsystems of this wider world society (1991: 49, 137). Bull himself identified world society as 'a degree of interaction linking all parts of the human community to one another' and insisted that it was held together by 'a sense of *common interest and common values*' (1977: 279). Later, Bull even went as far as identifying 'human rights' as the basic value that bound world society together (1984a: 13).

As I conceive them, the three traditions are modes of thought carried by diplomats, politicians, intellectuals and other individuals in the three pillars that comprise global politics (international system, international society and world society). Thinking of international system, international society and world society in this way raises important questions about the relationship between the three pillars.

International system/international society

Bull's definition of international systems and international societies permits considerable overlap between these pillars, and his argument is somewhat contradictory in places. Occasionally, Bull argues that international systems precede societies but elsewhere he suggests that international systems and societies 'necessarily coexist' (Little 2005: 48). According to Jackson, the distinction between the two is flawed because if states establish the diplomatic relations necessary to constitute a system, it must follow that they have also established a society because diplomacy is only possible if common rules and languages have been established. As Jackson puts it, '[a]ll relations between human beings – including people who speak and act in the name of states – necessarily rest on mutual intelligibility and communication' (Jackson 1990: 112). Moreover, Alan James has criticized the argument that the distinguishing feature of international systems and societies is the presence of common values in the latter. By contrast, he claims that all international societies comprise units that hold different values, with the system itself being held together by rules regulating their coexistence (James 1993).

If one of the key characteristics of international society is a shared identity among states based on their mutual recognition of the principle of sovereign equality (Buzan 1993; Reus-Smit 1999: 6), there are at least two problems with this view. First, states have never recognized sovereign equality, either formally or customarily. Since the origins of European international society, members of international societies have recognized hierarchies of power and authority, almost always granting special rights and responsibilities to great powers (Simpson 2004). Second, insisting on a shared set of principles as a precondition for international society is problematic. Ostensibly 'shared' values may in actuality be imposed on the weak by the powerful. In such circumstances, if they are able to maintain a degree of independence, units may be able to participate in the common diplomatic culture without establishing common values beyond a shared interest in preserving the society and agreement about rules of coexistence. Moreover, this approach rules out the possibility of radical difference within an international society. In practice, however, many different types of unit have inhabited the same society (empires, states, city-states, 'private' states, etc.) as have many different types of state (capitalist, communist, Islamic, etc.). For these reasons, I share James' skepticism about the differentiation between an international system and society which, we will see later, has important ramifications for the way we understand what Dunne (2003) fears is an assault on international society by US hegemony.

International society/world society

It is perhaps the relationship between international society and world society that presents the most pressing contemporary problems for English School theorists. Many of the School's critics (Paterson 2005: 163–78; True 2005) complain that international society, conceived as a society of states, is too narrow to accommodate the needs of human emancipation, the fact of gendered identity or the governance of the global environment. There can be no doubt that today there is little utility in thinking about world politics in terms of a society of states alone. This raises the important question of whether the English School is attempting to construct a grand theory of everything in world politics or whether it is merely trying to explain one aspect of it (state-to-state relations). In many ways, as I noted earlier, the English School's founding fathers avoided this problem by insisting that international society was only one of three elements that comprised world politics, with the revolutionist or Kantian strand incorporating civil societies and nonstate actors.

There remain, however, three important problems with this perspective. First, the majority of nonstate actors in world politics are neither revolutionists nor Kantians. Many of them are transnational business organizations that support and strengthen the underlying economic structures of international order. Second, contemporary 'international' and 'world' societies are not easily separable domains. Are global environmental or trade summits that comprise state and nonstate agencies features of the 'international' or the 'world society'? Third, maintaining the division means that international society will continue to be seen as constituted on one plane, that of state-to-state relations. In its place, we need a multilayered account of international society to make sense of contemporary world politics.

Whilst it certainly seems appropriate to conceptualize international society and world society as different realms when we are studying earlier periods, and world society remains a useful vehicle for interrogating the global and transnational processes that create change in world politics, the distinction is becoming less useful today. When thinking about contemporary international society, it is perhaps better to follow Buzan (2004) in asking whether it is necessary and justified to exclude particular actors from our worldview. It seems to me that there is no reason why regional organizations, business groups, nonstate organizations, civil society movements, human rights activists and others could not (and should not) be incorporated *within* our conception of international society rather than as an adjunct. Or, alternatively, why our understanding of state-to-state relations embedded with the idea of international society could not be incorporated within a new concept of world society. This would mean conceiving international society as constituted on vertical as well as horizontal planes and as a much more complex collection of actors, institutions and rules than we have hitherto acknowledged. Such a move would mark a significant step away from Bull's conception of international society or theories of world society, but just as his theory was a product of his time so must ours be. It may be appropriate, therefore, to eschew the international society – world society divide in favor of a conception of either international society or world society that incorporates different types of actors operating at different levels. At very least, there is a need for a careful and expansive articulation of the relationship between the two domains.

The central danger with such an approach is that by broadening the scope of study, the concepts would lose their analytical utility. As Dunne (2005a: 71) argues, the problem with what he calls the 'hedgehog' account is that international society becomes 'an undifferentiated category' as 'too much is folded into this account'. However, the concept of international society that we use today does not, by itself, provide a useful vehicle for exploring state-to-state relations in most policy domains. Political argument and change often involves coalitions of actors from both domains acting within a common setting (Dunne 2005b: 166). The key point is that, in practice, retaining two distinct domains may obscure more than it illuminates.

In this section, I have made two key claims about the three traditions and three pillars that form the basis of English School theorizing. First, the three traditions reflect three distinctive ways of thinking about how world politics is and how it ought to be. My second argument is that international system, international society and world society are best understood as overlapping analytical constructs. Because it is difficult to have a system without social relations, there is a good case for eroding the distinction between international system and international society. It is also important to recognize that in today's globalized era international society is itself embedded in a broader world society. Finally, world society should be understood as encompassing much of the nongovernmental sector and transnational interactions across state borders. World society is itself codependent on international society because cross-border interactions are regulated by states, and individuals are always under the legal jurisdiction of states wherever they are on the world's surface.

International society and the lone superpower

Is international society is under threat from forces emanating from the other two pillars of world politics? There are many potential sources of threat to international society, including globalization and Islamic recidivism, but for reasons of space I will focus on the claim that US hegemony poses a distinct threat to international society. Dunne (2005a: 75; 2003) argues that the concentration of power in the hands of a single actor threatens international society because the founding justification of international society was antihegemonic; that is, 'international society exists to protect diverse political communities from being overrun by more powerful neighbours' (Dunne 2005a: 75). In the absence of a world government, Dunne argues (as Bull did) that it is the responsibility of great powers to maintain international society's constitutive rules, especially the principles of sovereign equality and nonintervention. Dunne acknowledges the point I made earlier, that hierarchies have always existed, but argues – on essentially Vattelian lines – that there are at least three grounds for thinking that the threat this poses to international society is more prescient today than in earlier times. First, the practice of 'legalized hierarchies' – to use Simpson's (2004) term – was traditionally reciprocal. That is, such structures were constructed with the consent of the weaker parties (Dunne 2005a: 76). By contrast, the US has not sought consent for its post-9/11 reordering of international hierarchy. Second, whilst anarchical societies require a degree of inequality, that should not extend to one state being able to lay the law down to the others (Dunne 2003; Hurrell 2002). Bull argued that international law depended on reciprocity: states recognize the rights of others because others recognize their rights (Bull 1977: 108). A hegemonic state, by contrast, can override others' rights without fearing for its own rights. If it does so, it removes the basic reciprocity essential for the functioning of international law. Third, traditionally international society has comprised more than one great power, meaning that it comprises actors and institutions willing and able to challenge hegemonic power. Dunne argues that there are now no bodies to counter US hegemony. This does not mean that the US will simply disregard international rules and institutions but that 'it will retain an option to disregard the rights of other members' (Dunne 2005a: 76). This does not necessarily mean the end of international society, Dunne argues, but it does suggest a reordering wherein international society becomes secondary to forces traditionally associated with the international system.

To what extent is US hegemony a challenge to international society? I suggest that contemporary US foreign policy constitutes less of a challenge than Dunne suggests primarily because the Bush administration's articulation of a new world order where sovereign rights are conditional on three measures of responsible sovereignty (WMD proliferation, support for terrorism and pattern of domestic human rights abuse) is much less radical than Dunne and others suppose. I will address each of Dunne's three points in turn.

First, the idea that international society's rules are predicated on consent is, by and large, a legal fiction. At question are two points – the origin of international society's foundational rules and their global dissemination. Their origin was distinctly European. As Bull observed, 'international legal rules ... were not only made by European and Western powers, they were also in substantial measure, made *for* them' (Bull 1984b: 217). Their dissemination, during the period of decolonization, was both consensual and coercive. Colonized political communities were granted freedom and recognition only if they adopted a particular mode of governance and 'consented' to international society's basic rules. This process left little space for the legitimization of alternative forms of community or the renegotiation of the constitutive rules (Seth 2000: 221–5). If consensus is understood in a Habermasian sense as a general agreement freely arrived at, the idea of a consensus on international society's constitutive rules at the point of decolonization is a fiction. In international society, consensus has always been mediated by power. Decolonizing states did not subscribe to international legal rules because they necessarily agreed with them or shared the values that they underpinned, but because subscription to those rules was the precondition for decolonization. This does not invalidate those rules but it does cast doubt on the claim that the contemporary era is a uniquely dangerous one for international society because states are not being asked to consent to rules changes.

Dunne's second argument is that the US is 'laying down the law' in international society. To support this case, he points to the 2003 war in Iraq as evidence of the US being 'willing and capable of laying down the law to those it sees as rogue states, even when it has conspicuously failed to persuade the majority of Security Council representatives' (Dunne 2005a: 76). In this argument, Dunne elides two separate claims: that the US has set itself up as a lawmaker and that the US has claimed for itself a right to interpret and enforce the law. I will deal with each in turn. The Iraq case does not substantiate the first claim, principally because the formal legal justification for war was based on existing Security Council resolutions. In other words, the US did not make a novel legal argument or advocate changing the rules. Instead, it justified its case by reference to the commonly accepted legal rules governing *jus ad bellum*. The Bush administration's attempt to articulate a new interpretation of the right of preemption might be a clearer case of unilateral rule-making, but this too is hotly contested with others disputing the novelty of American arguments or arguing that the US is claiming *exceptions* for itself rather than indulging in lawmaking (Bellamy 2006; Wheeler 2003).

The second element of the claim is also problematic. The idea that the US did not have the authority to use force to enforce its interpretation of the law because it failed to persuade significant others of its case assumes an answer to the question of where authority lies, and overlooks the fact that the US did persuade a significant number of states (approximately 42) of its legal case, and endured economic and political costs when actors in both international and world society deemed US actions to be illegitimate.

According to Higgins, international law can be understood either as a set of rules or as a process. The 'law as rules' or positivist approach holds that legal judgments involve simply finding the appropriate rule and applying it. This formulation assumes that there is a 'correct legal view' that can be discerned in an objective fashion by applying the rules (Higgins 1994: 3–4). This view, Higgins argues, is untenable because it overlooks the element of choice. That is, legal judgments involve choices about the meaning and purpose of rules, the 'facts' of the case, which rules apply, which rules and facts are most important and past decisions. In contrast, the law-as-process approach suggests that legal discourse provides a common language for debate, but that political and social factors play a significant role in shaping decisions (Higgins 1994: 5). Because international law is decentralized, states are free to interpret the law however they see fit but are obliged to justify their actions to their peers by reference to the law. Their peers (other states) will judge for themselves whether they accept those arguments and will choose to act accordingly. Dunne's argument is that the US chose to override the 'correct legal view' which was that a further UN Security Council resolution was necessary to authorize the use of force (Bellamy 2003). This view is problematic because it relies on an untenable account of international law.

The intersubjective version of the argument is much more persuasive but begs the question of why this poses a particular challenge to international society. This perspective assumes that there is consensus about the source of authoritative pronouncements about international law, which is commonly held to be the Security Council, and that ostensibly illegitimate acts undermine the social rules. However, the Council's exclusive authority to determine the legality of force has often been challenged: during the Cold War, both the Organization of American States and the Warsaw Pact argued that they took precedence over the Security Council within their spheres of influence (Bellamy and Williams 2005), and more recently, during the debate about whether or not to intervene in Kosovo in 1999, Slovenia argued that the Council had 'primary' but not 'exclusive' responsibility for the maintenance of international peace and security (Wheeler 2000: 279). Indeed, the Council has sometimes itself tacitly deferred decisions about the use of force by implicitly authorizing force and issuing intentionally ambiguous resolutions (Byers 2004). According to Byers, such resolutions, including Resolution 1199 on Kosovo (1998) and 1441 on Iraq (2003), take the debate outside the realm of law and international society's constitutive rules and place them within the realm of politics. Referring to Resolution 1441, Byers argued that 'the Security Council succeeded in effectively de-legalizing the situation, and thus protecting the international legal system from the damage that would otherwise have resulted when politics prevailed' (Byers 2005: 45). The preservation of international society only requires that states justify their actions by reference to the common rules or that *utter disregard* for the foundational rules incurs some kind of costs. Although many states rejected the American argument and acted accordingly, many other states – not all of them obviously coerced – accepted the argument. In other words, international society and world society themselves are the arbiter. When states proffer justifications for their actions, other actors serve as 'judges and juries' weighing the balance of the different claims (Franck 2002: 185). 'Judges' are those entities capable of backing up their judgments with serious material rewards or punishments; in particular, the world's most powerful states. 'Juries' comprise the rest of world opinion. Jurors debate and form their own opinions, can impose some relatively minor penalties and rewards, and can attempt to influence judges' decisions. The point here is that even powerful actors will incur political and economic costs for perceived rule-breaking (Reus-Smit 2004). Of course, powerful actors are able to bear more costs than weaker actors, but even the world's lone superpower cannot bear costs indefinitely. The war in Iraq, for instance, has had significant negative effects on the US economy, US attempts to forge consensus on issues such as terrorism and humanitarian intervention, and domestic support for the Bush administration – demonstrating once again the interconnectedness of the interstate and nonstate domains. To summarize, the US did not take on the role of lawmaker in the Iraq case, and its case for being a law enforcer was based on a plausible if not wholly convincing legal argument that enabled international society and world society to judge the invasion on its political and moral merits and act accordingly, leaving international society's constitutive rules intact.

The third component of the argument that international society is threatened by US hegemony is the suggestion that there are no countervailing forces and that maintaining this imbalance has become a pivotal feature of US grand strategy (Dunne 2005a: 76). This argument implicitly draws on Bull's claim that 'a balance of power is an essential condition of the operation of law' (Bull 1977: 108), and is closely connected to the idea that law requires the threat of punishment to be effective. There are a number of difficulties here. On the one hand, I am not wholly convinced that the absence of countervailing forces is a particular novelty in world politics. During the nineteenth century, Britain publicly espoused the balance-of-power doctrine whilst maintaining its clear supremacy at sea. During the Cold War, although there were *global* countervailing forces, there were very few – if any – countervailing forces *within* the superpowers' spheres of influence. In Latin America and the Soviet Union's 'near abroad', the superpowers were free to act with impunity – much more so than the US does today – and yet there was little suggestion that this constituted a challenge to international society itself. Indeed, Bull acknowledged that spheres of influence, especially where the great power has an acknowledged right to assert its special interests and responsibilities, made a contribution to international order (1977: 219–25). On the other hand, the argument that international law requires a balance of power is also problematic and sits uncomfortably with the idea that a defining feature of solidarism is the level of law enforcement. Commitment to a balance of power does not equate to a commitment to law enforcement unless violations of the law threaten the balance itself. Indeed, with its tendency toward 'spheres of influence', balances of power might mitigate against global law enforcement, as they did during the Cold War. Moreover, as solidarism itself suggests, law enforcement requires common values, identities and interests. Finally, I would suggest that the chorus of opposition to the Iraq war in both international and world society suggest that there are indeed countervailing forces to US hegemony.

Conclusion

The principal purpose of this chapter has been to evaluate the English School's contribution to IR theory by charting its main ideas and debates, articulating a way of understanding the three traditions, the three pillars and the relationship between them, and asking a big and important question about contemporary international society: is it under threat from US hegemony? I have argued that the English School shares a close affinity with constructivism although there are important differences between them. Its main ideas focus on the three traditions (realism, rationalism and revolutionism), which are ways of thinking about the way the world is and how it ought to be, and the three pillars (international system, international society and world society), which are analytical constructs. Recent English School debates have focused on the meaning of the traditions as well as the pillars, and whether they should be revised. I have argued that there is a good case for eroding the system/society distinction and thinking about international society and world society as codependent.

In future, the School needs to move beyond the introspection that has characterized much of its scholarship in the past decade. On the one hand, its writers need to embrace pluralism more fully in their methodologies and to engage in dialogue with the other major traditions of thought within IR theory. On the other hand, however, the approach needs to yield more in the way of empirical analysis of contemporary international society. In that sense, it is important to either think more carefully about the relationship between international society and world society, or to erase the distinction and replace it with a wider and deeper concept of either international society or world society that is able to accommodate the wider range of actors and issues that inform contemporary world politics. After all, the crucial test in the IR marketplace of ideas is not so much the theoretical sophistication of a particular perspective but its ability to shed light on our current predicament.

Further reading

Bellamy, A. (ed.) (2005) *International Society and its Critics*, Oxford: Oxford University Press.

Dunne, T. (1998) *Inventing International Society*, London: Palgrave.

Linklater, A. and Suganami, H. (eds) (2006) *The English School of International Relations: A Contemporary Reassessment*, Cambridge: Cambridge University Press.

8 Poststructuralism

Jenny Edkins

Introduction

Poststructuralism now comprises a substantial body of work within International Relations (IR) that has developed rapidly over the past three decades. There are disputes and disagreements between poststructuralists, of course, but in recent years the emphasis has moved away from a critique of the mainstream of IR theory toward a more direct and practical engagement with a wide range of specific questions and issues. There are many scholars in IR using approaches that might be described as 'poststructuralist', even though some of them might prefer not to be subsumed under this label. Their work examines the full diversity of topics that come under the rubric of IR; for example, security (Dillon 1996; Stern 2005), war and militarization (Dalby 1990; Shapiro 1997; Zehfuss 2002), political economy (De Goede 2005), international ethics (Campbell and Shapiro 1999), diplomacy (Der Derian 1992), international institutions (Debrix 1999), popular dissent (Bleiker 2000), humanitarian intervention (Orford 2003), development (Escobar 1995, Ferguson 1994), postcolonial politics (Doty 1996), famine (Edkins 2000), environmental politics (Dalby 2002; Kuehls 1996; Bennett and Chaloupka 1993), foreign policy (Campbell 1992), conflict resolution (Bleiker 2005), borders (Shapiro and Alker 1996), refugees (Soguk 1999), nationalism (Campbell 1998; Shapiro 2004), identity (Connolly 1991) and citizenship (Cruikshank 1999). Poststructuralism is probably best described as a worldview (or even an antiworldview). Scholars working within this worldview are skeptical of the possibility of overarching theoretical explanations for things that happen in the world. They prefer not to look for grand theories but rather to examine in detail how the world comes to be seen and thought of in particular ways at specific historical junctures and to study how particular social practices – things people do – work in terms of the relations of power and the ways of thinking that such practices produce or support. Formulating grand theory is seen as a social practice among other social practices: theories of how the world works are regarded as part of the world, not detached from it, and are studied by poststructuralists alongside other practices. A starting assumption of poststructuralist thought is that there is no point outside the world from which the world can be observed: all observations and all theoretical systems, in physical theory or natural science as well as social theory, are part of the world they seek to describe or account for, and have an effect in that world. For example, theories are not and cannot be politically neutral, but rather inevitably have a social and political impact. In this picture of the world, then, the theorist of IR is not a detached observer of world politics but inevitably a participant in it.

As well as being skeptical of theoretical explanation, poststructuralist thinkers tend to be unconvinced by a number of other assumptions that were taken for granted in most social and political theory up until the first part of the twentieth century – as well as in the natural sciences up to the end of the Newtonian era – and that are still unquestioned in much thinking in IR theory today. The assumptions that poststructuralist thinkers are doubtful of remain part of everyday common sense, and because poststructuralism challenges these assumptions, it can be difficult to grasp. Understanding poststructuralist ways of analyzing global politics requires the reader new to this way of thinking to be willing, if only temporarily, to relax deeply held convictions about the nature of the world and of politics. It asks those interested in understanding what poststructuralism is trying to say to think about what it would mean to begin from new and rather uncomfortable or counterintuitive assumptions about 'life, the universe and everything'. Of course, there are many people unfamiliar with poststructuralist thought who have already in their own thinking found much of what is often assumed to be obviously commonsense disturbing and unconvincing: to them the encounter with poststructuralist writing often brings relief and a feeling of finally having found an approach that they can work with. For those who are content with their current assumptions, understanding poststructuralism calls for a willingness to be adventurous and to imagine, just for a while, what it might be like to think in a completely different way.

What are these assumptions that poststructuralist scholars are unconvinced by? One of them has already been discussed: the assumption that it is possible to step outside the world and observe it or, to express the same thing differently, that the scholar can adopt a God-like detachment or otherworldliness. If there is no possibility of observing from outside, then the goals of academic inquiry have to be seen very differently. The other assumptions are all linked with each other: traditional, modernist approaches assume a world that comprises distinct entities (such as individuals, material objects, processes, events and structures) that can be said to possess some form of essence or nature and that exist unproblematically in time. The job of political and social theory then becomes to describe and account for the relations and interactions that take place between objects and/or structures, and the job of normative theory to consider how we might decide what form those relations and interactions should take. Poststructuralist ways of thinking, in contrast, do not start from this point. Rather, they are interested in the processes and practices that produce entities as distinct in the first place. For example, rather than starting from the individual human being and asking how these individuals come together to form social groups, they ask how it is that we come to think in terms of people as separate and distinct individuals in the first place. The idea of the individual can be shown to be geographically and historically located. 'The individual' has not existed in all places and in all periods. The question 'what is a human?' or 'what is an individual?' is not one that makes sense outside specific historically and geographically situated ways of thinking. And thinking in terms of already distinct individuals as a starting point limits the questions that can be asked about social and political life, and the answers that will make sense. Poststructuralist thinkers want to ask why we think in terms of entities or beings that are distinct one from another – why we see the world as made up of such entities existing against the background of a neutral flow of time – but they also want to dislodge this view, and suggest the possibility of thinking differently. The latter is a more radical move, one that requires a taking apart of commonsense notions of time and existence and replacing them with new ways of thinking.

This is all rather abstract. To give some sense of how it translates into poststructuralist writings in IR, this chapter begins by tracing a series of themes that run through poststructuralist work. The themes that are chosen here, all of them closely interrelated, are subjectivity, language and discourse, power relations and biopolitics and the notion of excess or lack. The discussion of themes is then followed by a review of two of the research 'methods' or tools that are used in poststructuralist analysis: genealogy and deconstruction. This is not so much a 'how to' section as an outline of these two approaches in very general terms, with examples. Finally, the chapter concludes with an overview of work in IR that has used poststructuralist approaches, and a discussion of the relation of this work to other traditions in the study of IR.

Subjectivity

Poststructuralist notions of the subject or 'personhood' represent a series of moves away from the 'modern' subject: the fully self-present, though self-doubting, Cartesian subject, the subject who could say with certainty 'I think therefore I am'. The first move away from the Cartesian subject took place under the influence of sociology (Hall 1992). The sociological 'self' is shaped significantly by the social and economic environment. In other words, the subject does not arrive in the world fully formed. Rather, the subject is developed by upbringing and socialization. It is in this context that the nature–nurture debate arises. How much of the self is a product of social upbringing and how much is due to its inherent (genetic or spiritual) nature? The poststructural 'move' is far more radical, abandoning any residual notion of preexisting subjectivity. According to this way of thinking, the 'subject' and the 'world' are not distinct. Instead, they are produced, as 'world' and as 'subject', through social, cultural and particularly political practices. This is often expressed by saying that subject and social order are 'mutually constituted' or 'co-constituted'. The important thing is that neither subject nor environment is ontologically privileged. The subject is not born into a world. The subject produces the world of which it is a part at the same time as it is itself produced. As Jacques Derrida puts it, there is nothing outside the text (Derrida 1976: 158–9).

It is important to note the difference between concepts of the subject that retain a core of essential subject-hood and those that do not. After all, seeing the subject as fragmented or as the potential holder of a diversity of identities or possible subject-positions, which is often how poststructuralist thinking is characterized, retains the concept of an essential subject. How else could there be fragmentation? What is there that could 'possess' a range of identities? Once the notion of an essential core is abandoned, however, identity can no longer be 'possessed' nor subjectivity 'fragmented'. Several strands of thinking contributed to the move from a Cartesian subject through a sociological subject to a postmodern or poststructural subject, as Hall (1992) notes. Sigmund Freud's work proposed that people were not in control of their thoughts in quite the way that Descartes assumed (Freud 1991). To account for certain symptoms that he observed in his patients and for common phenomena such as dreams, slips of the tongue and jokes, it was helpful to propose that a large part of thinking takes place in a separate realm, which Freud called 'the unconscious'. In this realm, to which there is no conscious access, thinking processes are structured very differently. Moreover, Freud argued, conscious thought is to be regarded as in many ways the lesser in importance: it is only the tip of the iceberg.

In a second strand of thinking, De Saussure (1966) demonstrated that language was not a simple case of nomenclature or transparent communication of preexisting ideas. The naming of objects in the world is arbitrary, and, moreover, the process of naming produces the object named as something that is separate from the continuum of things in the world. Objects, in other words, are not presented as distinct, ready for naming. This can be seen by the way in which each language not only names objects differently, but has a distinct set of objects that it enables its speakers to 'see'. This means that people do not speak language. Rather, language 'speaks' people. What is said or thought depends on what the specific language, and its way of seeing the world, makes it possible to say or think. This means that thinking, which for Descartes was intimately related to his individual existence – it was the one thing he could be sure of – is an inherently social activity that relies on language.

Language and discourse

An acknowledgment of the significance of language, discourse and interpretation is the second feature that approaches labeled as 'poststructuralist' share. As well as pointing out the importance of language in constituting the world, De Saussure (1966) noted that meaning in language depends not on positive value but on differences. Words mean what they do not because of any link in sound with the object they represent but because of the difference between one word and the next. What is said is meaningful because of the associations with what is not said. This notion is taken further in the study of discourse that takes place in Michel Foucault's work. Whereas De Saussure was interested in what *could* be said in any particular language, Foucault was interested in what *is* said in any specific epoch. He explored the connection between the various things that were said, and the other social practices in which these 'things said' were embedded in any particular era or episteme (Foucault 1970). He argued that different epistemes could be characterized by different ways of looking at the world, and in particular by distinct ideas of what might constitute an ordering principle, or a way of making sense of the world. Whereas 'a history of ideas' traces the gradual evolution of a particular concept over time, Foucault's archaeology of knowledge, which he also designated a history of the present, aimed to demonstrate the discontinuity between different ways of ordering the world in different epochs.

A Foucauldian approach is also concerned to demonstrate the continuity between discursive practices and other social practices. Discourse is not confined to written forms or to language in the narrow sense, but extends to all symbolic systems and to any form of social practice that by definition involves such systems. One of Foucault's key contributions to contemporary thought and political analysis is his demonstration of the way in which knowledge is tied up with the forms of subjectivity or subject-hood to which it gives rise. He showed this in the case of the penal or prison system (Foucault 1991). He examined the way in which the prison as a form of punishment displaced earlier forms that had involved public executions and the demonstration of the sovereign's power over the subject's body by practices such as hanging, drawing and quartering. The penal system in contrast involved a form of punishment that entailed disciplinary practices: confinement to an institution, continuous surveillance, the collection and storage of information about prisoners, their involvement in compulsory work programs and so forth.

The image of the panopticon is exemplary of this disciplinary practice: prisoners were held in cells structured in such a way that each prisoner could be seen by the prison guards at any time, but no prisoner could see another prisoner or the source of surveillance. As a result, prisoners behaved as if they were continuously observed: they disciplined themselves. Foucault also crucially observed that although prisons always failed in their declared aim of rehabilitation – levels of reoffending by released prisoners were always high – they nevertheless continued as institutions. For Foucault, the crucial question was not 'Why did they fail?' but 'What was their function?' His response was that prisons delineate a class of person – the delinquent – as a distinct group that has no political voice.

Analogous forms of argument and analysis have since been applied to institutions of IR. It has been proposed, for example, by Escobar (1995) that Third World development is a process that fails to produce its stated result (the economic development of 'underdeveloped' areas of the globe), but that continues nevertheless because it serves to delineate certain countries as in need of development and thus intervention. Aid practices in complex emergencies have been analyzed in the same way.

Power relations and biopolitics

Michel Foucault's work has also been of significance in relation to the third strand that is shared by the so-called 'poststructuralist approaches' to IR: a different view of power (Foucault 2000). Traditionally power has tended to be thought of as something that can be possessed: states or individuals *have* power, and some have more than others. It therefore makes sense to talk of a balance of power and to discuss different forms of power (political, military, economic or cultural). Foucault suggests a new way of thinking of power. He argues that power should be seen not as something that preexisting entities possess but as something produced in relationships. Thus Foucault does not speak of 'power' but of 'power relations'. Power is not held centrally but produced in a dispersed way, through a series of power relations that take place on a micro-level during social interactions. To understand how power works – fundamental of course to understanding global politics – it is necessary to examine the microphysics of power relations. This enables scholars to understand how relations of domination, when power is sedimented over long periods, arise, and how they might be challenged. It also makes it possible to analyze resistance. In the Foucauldian view, power is not separate from resistance but rather implies it: were there no resistance, there would be nothing that could properly be called 'a power relation'.

Foucauldian thinking insists on a close relation between power and knowledge or, more accurately, on the inseparability of what he calls 'power/knowledge'. He talks in terms of 'regimes of truth', systems of power relations that determine what mechanisms are used in any particular era to determine what counts as true. Each society has its own way of authorizing 'truth'. Intellectuals are closely implicated in these regimes. And each system of power relations produces particular subjects and at the same time generates knowledges about those subjects. For example, in the criminal justice system, records are kept of offenders. The sum of these records produces the delinquent as subject, as described above.

The detailed analysis of power relations leads to the identification of a series of different practices of power. Foucault argues that sovereign power, which he regards as entailing the power over death – the sovereign can put to death those it chooses – has more recently been supplemented by biopower, the power over life or, more specifically, the power over populations. Biopower is expressed in disciplinary practices, such as are found in the prison, the barracks, the school or the hospital, and in forms of governmentality. The state increasingly operates through these practices, which are addressed to entire populations, rather than through the direct expression of sovereign power in relation to the individual subject.

Excess or lack

In addition to the shared interest in subjectivity, linguistic or discursive practices and power relations, scholars working within the poststructuralist tradition share a fourth concern, one that is perhaps more difficult to specify. This is an interest in what has been called variously 'the excess' (or lack), 'the real' or the 'mystical'. What is alluded to here is an interest in that which falls out of language and discourse, that which has to be excluded in order for what we call 'social reality' to constitute itself or that which occurs at the moment of the founding of the state but is then forgotten (Lacan 1980; Zizek 1991, 1992).

The lack or the excess can be explained by noting that once something has been named, that something both *never lives up to* the name it is given and *is always more than* the name can encompass. For example, if people are described as 'political activists', what does that mean? One might say, well, if they are activists, why do they not stand in elections, or go on demonstrations: surely writing letters to one's representative or delivering election manifestos is not sufficient? Alternatively, the term does not exhaust that which it names. The people concerned are not just activists. Consider all the other things they do, being fathers and mothers and employees, for example. More broadly, in poststructuralist thought, attention is drawn to the 'mystical foundation of authority', the way in which the 'origin' of a state or a system of laws is a 'non-founded founding moment' that has nothing to rely on to justify or legitimate itself because it is the very point at which the source of law or legitimation will have been established (Derrida 1992).

One of the features of poststructuralist thinking is the way it questions conceptions of politics and the political. In much of this work there is an attempt to distinguish *politics* (something that takes place in elections, political parties and government institutions, and forms part of the realm distinguished from the economic or the social) from *the political*. The latter is more concerned with specifying what counts as 'politics' and establishing the institutional setting through which it can take place. Whereas politics operates within a settled agenda or framework that is taken for granted, the political takes place when that agenda itself is called into question; the political also refers to the processes that take place every day in order to reproduce that order, once established. The political moment is unsettled and unsettling, the moment of excess or of trauma (Edkins 2003). There have been a number of attempts within poststructuralism to rethink 'the political'. There are also scholars who draw our attention to processes of repoliticization and depoliticization. Ferguson (1994), for example, looks at the way in which development practices in Lesthoto function to depoliticize a series of social practices and thus place them beyond political challenge. The political moment is sometimes likened to the moment of decision (Derrida 1992). This is the moment of ethico-political responsibility. It is the point at which it is necessary to take an action that is not guaranteed, or indeed cannot be guaranteed, by rule or by law. Only such actions can be said to be responsible, not actions that follow rules, whether contained in legal or moral codes. The latter are not ethico-political acts but rule-following technologies.

Research methods

What is called 'poststructuralism' does not translate neatly into research methods, although it does give rise to certain ways of working and specific approaches. Despite the mythology surrounding these approaches, they are often highly practical, and most poststructuralists are engaged in detailed empirical analyzes involving, for example, meticulous readings of texts, in-depth participant observation, elite interviews, oral history, archive research and so on. Methods such as deconstruction, interpretative analysis, discourse analysis and genealogy are used to analyze the data that is gathered through empirical work. Often the focus of study will be the practices of other academics, as well as those of policy makers and workers in government or nongovernmental organizations.

It is important to note that poststructuralism is not just a method of textual analysis in the narrow sense of the study of written or spoken texts or discourses. It is an approach that treats social practices, objects and institutions as 'texts' in the broadest sense, in that they are capable of being interpreted in terms of their production of meaning, their discursive function and the power relations and structures they produce and in which they are embedded. James Ferguson's work on development in Lesotho is again an excellent example here. He examines the way in which the development discourse produces a particular picture of Lesotho, and how interventions organized on this basis strengthen and expand bureaucratic state power while at the same time presenting a depoliticized view of the processes involved (Ferguson 1994).

These types of analysis can also lead to policy engagement, but they do not lead to policy advice of the form 'if such and such a situation is found, do this'. Rather, they caution us to be suspicious of this kind of policy advice, which can often be harmful and counterproductive. In other words, poststructuralists eschew prescriptive generalizations and encourage a focus on the specifics of particular situations. In ethical terms they advocate a focus on the singularity of the practice, the singularity of the situation in which policy decisions have to be made. In this way what is argued is not very different from the way in which many, perhaps most, people act in practice, but what is explicitly refused is the idea that there is a possibility of 'expert', objective, nonpolitical knowledge that can provide impartial and universally applicable guidance for action. All knowledge is seen as situated in terms of power relations as well as in terms of the social and cultural background against which it is produced. Two modes of analysis that are often associated with poststructuralist work are genealogy and deconstruction.

Genealogy

When approaches to IR labeled 'poststructuralist' or critical mention 'genealogy', they are generally referring to the work of Michel Foucault, who himself borrowed the notion from Friedrich Nietzsche (Foucault 1998). Unfortunately the term 'genealogy' is often used broadly and inaccurately to refer to any history of a concept or a social practice. Foucault's notion of genealogy is quite specific. He draws our attention to the problematic nature of any attempted history of ideas. For him history is always 'a history of the present'. It is inevitably composed from the perspective of the time in which it is written, and it views the past from the worldview of the present. What is more, the purpose for which it is compiled is located in the present. Foucault opposes any attempt to search for origins, or to trace the 'history' of an idea or concept through the ages, as if that concept somehow retains an identity through several periods, each with distinct ways of thinking. His work demonstrates that outlooks in different epochs – or *epistemes*, as he calls them – are radically incompatible with each other. It is not just that distinct concepts are recognized in each historical period but that what counts as rational thought, or as a suitable topic of study, changes. Ways of thinking, explaining and understanding change, as do ways of ordering. For example, although at present the human being – 'man' – is considered an appropriate subject of study, this was not always the case, and, according to Foucault, will not always be so. Hence his famous remark that man may well 'be erased, like a face drawn in sand at the edge of the sea' (Foucault 1970: 387). A genealogy attempts to trace these differences and discontinuities.

What is accepted as rationality and what is necessary for something to be considered 'true' is dependent on the prevailing *regime of truth*. This term emphasizes the way in which the mechanisms and conventions for validating knowledge are tied up with systems of power. For Foucault, power and knowledge are so closely related that he speaks of *power/knowledge*. He argues that there is no way in which 'truth' can be seen as separate from power; on the contrary, systems of power are needed to produce truth, and, in turn, truth induces effects of power (Foucault 2000: 132). What counts as 'true' in any particular historical period depends on the social structures and mechanisms that are in place to validate particular methods or certain people or institutions as capable of producing 'truth'. In the contemporary world, it is 'science' as a practice and a method that is credited with the ability to produce 'truth' (Foucault 2000: 131).

A distinction is sometimes made by commentators on Foucault between his *archaeology* – for example, his work on the human sciences in *The Order of Things* (1970) – and his *genealogy*, including his later work such as *Discipline and Punish* (1991b). The later work is said to introduce the question of power relations into the study of discursive practices. There may or may not be this contrast between the early and the later Foucault, but certainly genealogy as Foucault practices it is closely concerned with power relations. It analyzes not only how discourse works at a particular time, but how discourse produces relations of power. For example, in *Discipline and Punish*, Foucault not only points to the way in which incarceration delineated 'the delinquent' as a distinct and criminal group, but also indicates the political consequences of this delineation, which facilitated the extension of surveillance, control and the depoliticization of an entire group. Because of the way in which genealogy attempts to uncover ways of thinking entirely distinct from each other and unfamiliar to current thought, it requires extensive and detailed historical research: 'Genealogy is gray, meticulous, and patiently documentary' (Foucault 1998: 369). Often, it means examining thinkers, writings and practices not generally considered important from the perspective of the present day. It also includes the uncovering of ways of thinking that, while taking place in the present, do not accord with generally accepted positions. In addition, and most importantly, it entails establishing the functionality of social practices in terms of power relations and the production of subjectivities.

This type of work brings to light the possibility of intervening in regimes of truth. Exacting, meticulous historical scholarship leads to the rediscovery of the history of struggle and conflict. It also involves the resurrection of local, marginal knowledges, which Foucault calls 'subjugated knowledges', disqualified or regarded as insignificant by the current regime of truth, repressed memories of struggles and so on. As Foucault puts it, 'the coupling together of scholarly erudition and local memories … allows us to constitute a historical knowledge of struggles and to make use of that knowledge in contemporary tactics' (Foucault 2003: 8). This is what he calls 'genealogy'. And this is what he claims can be effective in fighting 'the power-effects characteristic of any discourse that is regarded as scientific' (Foucault 2003: 9). Genealogies are antisciences.

Of course, genealogy is not an unproblematic enterprise, since it is a struggle against forms of power that are associated with certain forms of (scientific) knowledge. Often, as soon as genealogical fragments are excavated, they will be recolonized by the unitary, scientific discourses that previously rejected them. They then become part of the power/knowledge effects of the dominant discourse into which they are incorporated.

A related danger is the risk of building the fragments of subjugated knowledges themselves into an alternative unitary system, which would then exhibit all the problems of the 'sciences' that genealogy was attempting to fight.

Deconstruction

'Deconstruction' is a specific, technical term elaborated in the work of Jacques Derrida and is much in evidence in poststructural approaches to IR. It is occasionally used very loosely to mean the opposite of 'construction'; in other words, to mean 'taking apart', but this is not what it means in the work of Derrida. Another confusion is that it equates 'deconstruction' with 'destruction', which again is very misleading. Indeed, it is ironic to attempt to define 'deconstruction' and specify what it might consist of as a 'method'. Derrida's work, and his discussion of deconstruction in particular, is a critique of the very possibility of definition and an analysis of the outcomes of attempts to delineate concepts and specify methods and programs. He claims that such attempts to produce certainty are totalizing moves that endeavor to close off the possibility of the ethico–political. To understand what this means it is necessary to examine the basics of Derrida's critique of Western metaphysics, or 'logocentrism'.

Logocentrism, a way of reasoning that is fundamental to contemporary thought, specifically that derived from the European world, operates through the production of dichotomies such as inside/outside, man/woman, memory/forgetting and presence/absence. Every dichotomy of this sort is more than just an opposition between two terms. Each sets up a hierarchy in which the first term of the pair is seen as primary and is valued more highly than the second. However, as Derrida points out, the prioritized term cannot operate without its shadow. It only has meaning in relation to the 'spectral' second term, which is sometimes called 'the constitutive outside'. In other words, the second term has to be excluded to bring the first term into being. For example, 'memory' only has meaning if we also have in mind the concept 'forgetting'. In a sense 'memory' is *haunted* by 'forgetting'. Derrida's work suggests that rather than thinking of *ontology*, or what exists, we should be looking at *hauntology* (Derrida 1994: 10).

Most importantly, Derrida uses this analysis to critique the centrality of the notion of presence in Western thinking. He suggests that 'presence' is something that is brought into being by a particular way of thinking, and that the drive for presence has certain political implications. Through endless debates and discussions of what *exists* or how things should be *defined* (questions like 'What *is* the state?' or 'What *is* terrorism?') structures of authority are put in place. These structures of authority have no foundation other than the violence of the hierarchies or the dichotomies and exclusions on which they are based. In the end, though, since dichotomies and the structures they authorize are unfounded and reliant on concepts that cannot by definition be pure but rather are always haunted by their opposites, they have an in-built tendency to collapse or, to use the terminology, to *deconstruct*. In other words, *deconstruction happens*. Deconstruction takes place of its own accord, as the structures set up by logocentric thinking falter and collapse.

A deconstructive approach can examine what is set to one side in a piece of writing in order for the analysis to continue. What has to be excluded is instructive, and bringing this 'back in' can reveal the contingent nature of the analytical frame that has been set up. It demonstrates how the argument relies on the very thing that it excludes. As noted above, deconstruction is not an option or a choice: it is inevitable. Importantly, this means that those adopting this 'approach' to analysis are not destroying something. Deconstruction is not destruction. Deconstruction as a method involves no more than gently nudging or helping along a process *that is inevitable at some point*. Deconstruction involves drawing the attention of logocentric thinking to the way in which its foundations are unstable or indeed untenable, and demanding instead a properly political approach. Logocentric thinking proceeds on the assumption that knowledge and 'truth' are attainable, and can be arrived at through various forms of logic, reason and analysis. A deconstructive approach points out that this way of thinking can be problematic and calls instead for a recognition of the need for ethico–political decisions and an acknowledgment of the impossibility of full knowledge or ontological presence (Campbell 1994). A philosophical or metaphysical analysis based on abstractions or general rules gives an illusion of certainty and closure that can be politically dangerous. Derrida calls for an acceptance of openness, and a recognition of the importance of the ethico–political process of making decisions. Specific decisions must be taken in a particular case, even though 'knowledge' will not be sufficient to guarantee them. Derrida is emphatically not calling for indecisiveness or relativism, but demanding the recognition of the impossibility of specifying in the abstract what action should be taken.

Conclusion

The way of studying IR that has been called 'poststructuralist' can be loosely characterized by a shared view on a series of themes. These include subjectivity, language, new ways of analyzing power relations and politics, and a sensitivity to the importance of what cannot be spoken: the excess or the lack. Scholars working in this way use a variety of methods to analyze empirical information. Two of the most distinctive methods include genealogy and deconstruction. Poststructuralist thinking in the study of IR is closely related to other strands of work. Many writers within the feminist worldview count poststructuralist thinkers among those in their toolbox. Of course there are a number of different aspects of feminist and gender thinking in political theory and IR. Some feminists hold a more or less essentialist view of 'woman', though in most cases this is quite likely to be a strategic essentialism that can sit happily alongside poststructuralism. Other writers in the feminist tradition are critical of the way in which much poststructuralist thinking can appear to be gender blind. There are similar issues concerning the relation of the poststructuralist tradition in general to questions of race and ethnocentrism. There is a rich literature in postcolonial studies that takes poststructuralism very much to heart and uses it to analyze colonial and postcolonial practices (Doty 1996). It is invaluable in drawing attention to areas of the world that have been largely ignored by IR scholars in the past, and practices of imperialism and colonialism whose analysis has been neglected despite their intimate relation to contemporary practices of intervention and globalization. Much poststructuralist work draws strongly on certain elements of Marxism. In particular, poststructuralist critiques of ideology are closely linked to Gramscian notions of hegemony (Gramsci 1971), although poststructuralism refuses to make an abstract distinction between the material and the ideational (Deleuze and Guattari 1983).

Many of the writers in IR that draw on the assumptions that have been described in this chapter as 'poststructural' remain uncomfortable with the label. The label draws a series of disparate thinkers under one banner. To call them all 'poststructural' conceals important differences between them. Significantly, the process of labeling is not just homogenizing and totalizing; it can be a means of disciplining and control. Poststructuralism is rarely seen by its practitioners as one of a series of contending approaches to the theorization of IR. On the contrary, it is opposed to such a project. It goes about its work differently, intervening in specific locations and in particular debates. Many 'poststructuralists' seek ways of acting outside academia or outside standard academic forms of writing; others engage in critique within and with the discipline. Much poststructuralist work is interdisciplinary, and draws on work from sociology, geography, anthropology, literary studies, film and fine art. But many poststructuralists are concerned to engage with similar questions that draw other scholars to the field of IR. Including poststructuralism in a text like the present one, which presents an account of different IR worldviews and theories, can have the effect of domesticating it and glossing over the radical nature of its critique. We should remind ourselves that poststructuralism is not so much a 'theory' of IR amongst others, but an approach that presents a critique of the viability, value and ethico–political implications of theorizing IR in the first place. Rather than being one among a series of contending worldviews in IR, poststructuralist thought is best seen as offering a critique and an analysis of the project of 'viewing the world' itself.

Further reading

Campbell, D. (1998) *National Deconstruction: Violence, Identity and Justice in Bosnia*, Minneapolis, MN: University of Minnesota Press.

Edkins, J. (1999) *Poststructuralism and International Relations*, Boulder, CO: Lynne Rienner.

Hindess, B. (1996) *Discourses of Power: From Hobbes to Foucault*, Oxford: Blackwell.

9 Feminism

Cynthia Enloe

Introduction

Feminism is a multidimensional yet coherent worldview. It is an approach to investigating the world. It also generates prescriptions derived from those findings. Feminism is an achieved mosaic of understandings, yet it is still unfolding. Feminism puts women – their experiences, their ideas, their actions, thoughts about them, efforts to convince and manipulate them – on center stage, while feminism also makes 'men-as-men' visible and masculinity problematic. Feminism takes 'women-as-women' seriously, yet it acknowledges and explicitly explores women's own myriad, often unequal, locations. In short, feminism is a complex set of understandings about how power operates, how power is legitimized and how power is perpetuated. Feminists investigate forms of power that are constructed and wielded in what are conventionally imagined as 'private' spaces (inside homes, within families, among friends), as well as forms of power wielded in what are presumed to be 'public' spaces (elections, courts, schools, television companies, banks, garment factories and military bases). What distinguishes a feminist curiosity is its concern with the causal links *between* power in private spaces and power in public spaces.

The idea that public and private spaces' power dynamics can causally influence each other is one of the reasons that feminist studies are interdisciplinary. Feminism employs research skills drawn, yet recrafted, from political science, history, sociology, philosophy, anthropology, biology, film and literary criticism, geography, economics and psychology to create a genuinely feminist investigation of, say, nuclear weapons policy making or global trade bargaining. This realization that feminist investigations call for multiple skills has nurtured the interdisciplinary character of many feminist International Relations (IR) scholarly projects: organizing conferences, designing research, publishing journals, developing curriculum, advising graduate students and drafting academic job descriptions. These are the activities that launch and sustain any academic research and teaching field. Feminist scholars have not found narrower disciplinary 'gatekeeping' in any of these activities to be fruitful.

Feminism, gender and power

It is because feminism explores power in all its forms that feminist explorations and understandings are not just about gender, even though gender is one of the crucial building blocks of feminist analysis. Gender refers to socially constructed (not biologically produced), disparate and historically contested meanings that both women and men assign to masculinity and to femininity. For instance, what does it mean to be 'manly' in an early-twenty-first-century Chinese automobile factory? Using a gender approach to understand the rise of the auto industry in China today would include asking this important question, and then asking how this particular meaning of masculinity has gained such widespread acceptance and how this idea of manliness might be influencing the interactions between junior men and senior men in the factory and in the international corporate joint venture as a whole. One might push further, not just sustaining a focus on the factory floor and the corporate headquarters. With a gender approach to the Chinese political economy of an emerging auto industry, one would look carefully into the relations between those male employees and the women in their lives, not only as coworkers (even highly masculinized automobile factories employ women) but also as those male employees' and executives' wives, mothers, girlfriends or labor union allies.

In doing this gender analysis, one would ask several hard questions. What is the dominant idea about being manly doing to all of these relationships inside and around the auto company? How do those results help shape the power dynamics of Chinese industrial policy? Welded into every car – not only in China, but in Canada, the United States, Germany, Korea and Japan – are distinctive gendered relations, usually unequal, between women and men, derived from contested ideas over what it means to measure up to notions of masculinity. Now add some curiosity about power in general. Turn this gender analysis into a feminist investigation. What are the power relationships between men and women flowing from these complex relationships between masculinities and femininities in the growing Chinese automobile industry? That is doing feminist IR.

Here is another example. Using a gender analysis, an investigator of nationalism would find the following question analytically fruitful. Why did some early-twentieth-century Egyptian women who became nationalist feminists continue to wear their veils even when they confronted the British-controlled armed police during their public rallies on the streets of Cairo in 1919, while other Egyptian activist women decided to shed this symbol of feminine respectability? A gender analysis would enable one to better understand how contested standards for feminine respectability shaped both the mobilization of a major male-led nationalist movement against British colonial rule and the efforts by a masculinized colonial state to maintain its imperial control (Badran 1996). Gender, therefore, is never just about women and never just about contested meanings attached to femininity. Gender is always about both masculinities and femininities, and the relationship between them. Thus in contemporary IR, referring to 'gender and the small arms trade' should never prompt questions only about where women and notions of femininity belong in this complex political economy of rifles, handguns, grenade launchers and land mines. 'Gender and the small arms trade' *should* provoke those questions, but it should also raise questions about how notions of masculinity sustain those profitable international weapons sales (Buchanan 2005).

Still, 'feminist analysis' and 'gender analysis' are not synonymous. They are complementary – each enhances the other – but they are not synonymous. A *gender analysis* explores meanings attached to femininity and masculinity and about how those contested meanings shape relations between women and men, men and various institutions, and women and various institutions. By contrast, *feminist analysis* digs into all of those questions, plus how they shape the distribution of and uses of *power*. There is nothing inherent in gender analysis that prevents any of its users from being curious about power, but it is a feminist analysis that explicitly puts power at the center of analysis.

Over their last two centuries of observing and theorizing, feminists have discovered how and when ideas about femininity and masculinity have not just been held; they have been wielded by particular people to create and sustain male privilege and the marginalization of most women. Those findings – by women reformers, philosophers, activists, investigators – have brought feminists to the conclusion that a perpetual interest in the uses and consequences of power must be integral to any exploration of the workings of gender. A gender analysis, therefore, that omits a feminist analysis is inadequate. An analysis of politics inside or between countries that ignores both gender analysis and feminist analysis is even more inadequate. It is politically naïve. Today, a university course or a special journal issue titled 'Gender and IR' is presumed to include, even be chiefly informed by, a self-conscious feminist approach to IR. However, despite this widely held assumption, it is useful to untangle gender analysis and feminism in order to be clear about how 'Gender and IR', if it is understood too narrowly, will be inadequate. Its inadequacy lies in its insufficiently explicit commitment to investigating power – what forms power takes, how exactly it is wielded in any given setting, who wields power, who gains from it and who is silenced by it, or excluded, marginalized or oppressed by it, and who is able to contest and resist those uses of power, and how. Thus gender analysis is crucial to feminist inquiry and explanation, but gender analysis alone is not sufficient. To make full and adequate sense of any aspect of IR, feminist analysis requires an explicit investigation into the public and private gendered workings of power.

When is a revolution not so revolutionary?

In her sensational late-eighteenth-century publication *A Vindication of the Rights of Woman* (1792), Mary Wollstonecraft launched a scathing critique of the hidden patriarchal presumptions within French male revolutionaries' seemingly radical thinking. She spelled out – and chastised both British and French middle-class and aristocratic women for accepting – how allegedly revolutionary ideas about 'rational man' and 'the rights of man' meant just that the male of the species were, allegedly, the sole possessors of the capacity to think and act rationally. This patriarchal revolutionary logic suggested that only men could be trusted with the rights, obligations and power of citizens. Women, those supposed creatures of sentiment and emotion, might be fit for wifely comforting, decorous shopping and maternal nurturing, but not much else. Certainly they were not qualified to vote and to hold office in the new revolutionary society. And even those supposedly 'natural' feminine activities should be conducted within the confines of the spaces imagined as 'domestic'.

Today, still, a great deal of research and teaching done by IR specialists – in universities, think tanks, ministries of foreign affairs, ministries of defence, state intelligence agencies, UN departments, international nongovernmental organizations, and in the pages of national newspapers and on radio talk shows – is devoted to past and present, potential, thwarted and successful revolutions, because revolutionary movements usually send shock waves through regional or even global relationships. So it matters what gendered presumptions are held (even if not fully admitted) by both would-be revolutionaries and the people who write and teach about them. Mary Wollstonecraft, however, is rarely required reading for these revolutionary writers, advisers, observers and teachers. Nor are the analyses of Wollstonecraft's feminist successors, whose work includes critiques of the patriarchal flaws running through the Russian revolution and the state legitimized by it, the postrevolutionary Algerian state's attempts to marginalize women and the patriarchal politics of the Nicaraguan Sandinistas in the 1980s (Kampwirth 2004). This centuries-long omission has had serious consequences. Revolutions are described, evaluated and explained *as if* they were only about economic class and nationalized ethnicity, *as if* the power systems dependent on the meanings assigned to masculinity and femininity were irrelevant. This omission, in turn, leaves political specialists declaring a given social movement and its political achievement 'revolutionary', when, more often than not, it has left in place the preexisting system of power which privileges masculinity and most men, leaving most women on the sidelines. Such a system adds up to what feminists label a *patriarchy*.

What is missed when women are ignored?

Feminist investigations by academic and activist researchers have revealed that many forms of public power and private power are dependent for their operation, legitimization and perpetuation on controlling the thoughts and bodies of women and on controlling notions of femininity and masculinity. It follows that if we do not become seriously interested in the conditions and lives of women, we are likely to craft analyses of international power dynamics that are at best incomplete, at worst faulty and unreliable. Women have been left out of the most influential studies of IR because so many investigators have presumed that women are inconsequential in the public arena. Indeed, when we look at photographs of important policy makers assembled at a cabinet meeting, at an international trade organization bargaining session, at a tense peace negotiation, we usually confront a sea of dark suits, ties and short haircuts. So it makes sense to ask, why devote serious intellectual attention to women when the only arena that matters is one in which most women are inconsequential actors (such as wives and secretaries) who have no impact on the decisions made?

Investigators informed by a more expansive and realistic feminist curiosity, however, have challenged this set of assumptions about who and what 'matters' in international politics, who is worthy of serious attention. Feminist-informed investigators ask questions that mainstream thinkers (and policy makers) have written off as 'trivial'. By following this trail they have revealed not that most women have been powerful in the construction and wielding of power but, instead, that women have been deemed significant targets of control. Following this trail of analysis, feminist-informed political researchers have discovered that women have often thwarted efforts to shape their actions and thoughts in ways that served their would-be manipulators. They have continued to marry men outside their own racial or ethnic groups. They have persuaded their sons not to enlist in the government's military. They have gone on strike against low wages and unclean air in their electronics and sneaker factories. They have broken the silence about systematic rapes during wartime. They have insisted that police forces be held responsible for preventing domestic violence. Each of these actions by women, individually and in groups, even when not entirely successful, has sent tremors through the local and international political status quo. Women are not confining themselves to the 'domestic' sphere and on the public sidelines where they are 'supposed' to be playing their support roles.

For example, take the dramatic history of the international political economy of sugar. Feminist British historian Midgeley (1993: 475–88) has conducted innovative research into the late-eighteenth- to early-nineteenth-century British and American transatlantic antis-lavery movement, which ultimately radically altered the globalized trade of sugar and tobacco, as well as basic notions of human rights. Whereas most historians have portrayed the antislavery abolitionist movement as male-led in both its intellectual life and its strategic maneuvers, Midgeley decided to ask, 'Where were the women?' By asking this decept-ively simple question, Midgeley uncovered women's critical roles in both the intellectual and the strategic evolution of this international political movement. First, she discovered that many British women who became active in the antislavery movement led an early international boycott, refusing to allow sugar from slavery-dependent Caribbean colonial plantations to be bought for and used in their households. It turns out, in other words, that by taking seriously women's actions in the supposedly nonpolitical domestic sphere, one uncovers a key to the success of this international boycott. Second, Midgeley found that early-nineteenth-century activist abolitionist women, as they traded ideas with each other, began to make analogies between the enslavement of African women and men, on the one hand, and the constraints forced on white English and American women in their seemingly respectable marriages: to become a wife, according to their evolving theorizing, was to become enslaved. Neither of these actions – women taking a strategic lead in a sugar boycott and extending the arguments against slavery to challenge the state-crafted institution of marriage – was what their male allies in the movement or the majority of British and American men who defended slavery expected nor, in the case of the women activists retheorizing marriage, welcomed.

Consequently, what is deemed 'political', feminist investigators are now convinced, is more wide-ranging than many international commentators have imagined. Look, for instance, at the women from the Philippines who have migrated abroad to work as nannies and maids – in Hong Kong, Malaysia, Israel and Saudi Arabia. The money these Filipinas have been sending home has become crucial to the entire Philippines economy. Or look at the idea of feminine 'beauty'. Beauty turns out to be political. Governments around the world have sponsored beauty queen contestants in order to enhance their own country's prestige (Seager 2003). Women's beauty is often wielded by nationalist or ethnocentric movements' male leaders to create a sense of communal pride and even intercommunal envy and resentment. Women's beauty also has become big global business. If women cannot be persuaded to pursue certain standards of feminine beauty, major cosmetics companies and the governments which rely on their taxes will falter. The international politics of lipstick is no laughing matter. Therefore, we need to constantly reassess what is political and what should be studied for the sake of making better sense of local and global politics.

Where are the men?

Simultaneously, feminist investigators have discovered that the workings of public power and private power cannot be fully described or explained if one does not take seriously how men think about women, about femininity and about masculinity, and what actions flow from those beliefs, worries, hopes and values. Some of the most revealing feminist-informed research being done today on men in IR looks closely at soldiers as international peacekeepers. Is it enough to just think of peacekeepers as peacekeepers – in the Congo, in the Darfur region of Sudan, in Cyprus, Liberia, Haiti and recently in Bosnia, Cambodia and East Timor? Or is it more useful to see them as *male* peacekeepers, since the overwhelming majority of the soldiers sent by their home governments on international peacekeeping missions are, in fact, men? As stories have surfaced about the rise in HIV/AIDS among local women, about the escalation of prostitution and even about international trafficking in girls and women when large peacekeeping operations are launched in a given country, new questions have to be asked about how ideas and policies regarding masculinity undermine international missions intended to create and sustain peace in war-torn regions. Treating peacekeeping soldiers and their civilian superiors as if they were gender free is turning out to have been a misguided research and policy strategy (Whitworth 2004).

Employing a feminist analysis, thus, makes 'men-as-men' visible. In most IR research, men are camouflaged by labels that nonfeminist investigators and policy makers take seriously: diplomats, bankers, generals, presidents, prime ministers, movement leaders, working-class activists, party leaders, miners, voters, insurgents, extremists, terrorists, corporate executives, experts, spies, judges and stock brokers. It is not that these categories are analytically irrelevant. They are useful. But they can be insufficient. To try to make sense, for example, of the peace negotiations between insurgents and state representatives *without* asking which aspects of these negotiations are shaped by the masculinized identities and fears of each may produce a seriously flawed analysis.

Feminisms

Anyone informed by feminist findings and concepts when carrying on their investigations of IR will share with other feminist-informed researchers these understandings: (a) that it is never sufficient to set one's sights only on the arena conventionally thought to be 'public'; (b) that one never knows, until one seriously enquires, whether women will be analytically significant topics in an effort to explain any political dynamic; (c) studying gender (masculinity and femininity) alone without explicitly investigating power is inadequate; and (d) making 'women-as-women' visible will shine useful analytical light on 'men-as-men'.

By the early 2000s, however, many teachers, researchers, activists and writers using feminist questions and methodologies to shed light on the hidden workings of national and international power have come to refer to feminism in the plural: 'feminisms'. What they mean by this plural noun is that, despite these four significant commonalities, they now see feminist theorizing, feminist empirical research and feminist policy interventions as taking several forms. Feminists thus have developed a collective wariness about speaking in universal terms. This wariness about universalizing stems from their intense engagements with each other across complex differences. The international relations of preparing for and engaging in a series of UN international conferences (starting in 1975 and continuing into the early 2000s) have been principal causes of this new consciousness. Here is an instance in which IR has shaped feminist thinking, at the same time as that feminist thinking and organizing has caused IR.

Feminist scholars and activists increasingly avoid referring to a single homogeneous feminism because they have watched women's advocates in so many countries working to build alliances across the politically constructed chasms of class, race, generation, religion, ethnicity, nationality, generation and sexuality. Today there is a realization among feminist political observers that there exist proponents of *liberal feminism* (with its focus on individual rights and equality for women with men), *socialist feminism* (with its focus on the genderings of economic class, as shaped by the dynamics of local and international capitalism), *radical feminism* (highlighting the causes and consequences of patriarchy and misogyny), *poststructural feminism* (paying close attention to identities, images and culture) and *postcolonial feminism* (prioritizing the subtle workings of gendered racialized hierarchies that sustained colonialism and have persisted even long after formal colonial rule has been officially dismantled). Feminist IR thinkers today tend to accept that users of these different feminist political and analytical foci exist simultaneously and thus they seek to enrich the entire feminist intellectual enterprise by ensuring that they engage with one another in their academic course readings, in their conference sessions, in their journal publications and in their activist organizing. These different emphases and explanatory inclinations make for ongoing research and valuable debates among feminists. Feminist IR, therefore, is a field enlivened by continuing discussion and disagreement and the pursuit of new discoveries. That is one sign that it is a genuinely intellectual endeavor.

Feminist curiosity about states and nations

A principal shortcoming in the conventional, nonfeminist approach to international politics, according to feminist students of IR, is its practitioners' tendency to assume that states are the natural actors, coupled with a presumption that states speak for the nations they claim to rule. In contrast, a feminist analysis questions not only the 'naturalness' of states, but that of nations too. Feminist-informed investigations of societies as different as Ireland, Yugoslavia, Canada and Sudan have revealed that both the state and the nation have been constructed out of particular ideas about femininity and masculinity. The building blocks include ideas about femininity that have been wielded in ways to marginalize women in state affairs, as well as in nation-building movements. Where women have become prominent in the decision-making circles of a state or a nationalist movement it is usually because some women have organized to force open those spaces in the masculinized leadership. Thus feminist political analysis takes seriously the ways that ideas about 'motherhood', 'sexual purity', 'the good wife' and 'family stability' shape policy making within nationalist movements, political parties and state institutions.

Most states, feminists have discovered, have sought to entrench (in popular culture and in formal law) particular ideas about women's 'natural home' in the private sphere to legitimize men's allegedly 'natural' place in the public sphere. This feminist finding has helped to explain why officials of states as diverse as sixteenth-century Japan and the contemporary United States are so anxious around challenges to contemporary marriage practices. Virtually every state has taken an intense interest in marriage – to keep working women's wages low, to collect taxes, to enlist young males into armies, to take the census, to promote its own notions of morality and to distinguish itself from rival states.

Since the rise of liberal democratic states in the late eighteenth century, the very idea of the 'citizen' as the elemental and legitimizing member of what became known as the nation-state has been imbued with ideas about manliness. This discovery has prompted feminist scholars to assign importance to movements for women's suffrage. Those suffrage movements have not merely been efforts to gain a single right; suffrage activists are better understood as having launched basic challenges to the very concept of the masculinized state as a powerful web of institutions run by men to protect allegedly maternally privatized, domesticated women. Any woman (such as suffragists Huda Sha'rawi in Egypt, Alice Paul in the United States or Emmeline Pankhurst in Britain) or any man (such as the nineteenth-century reformer John Stuart Mill) who tries to topple this pillar propping up the state can be labeled not merely a 'radical', but a threat to state security, or what is mistakenly called 'national security'.

Similarly, feminist researchers take seriously local and international debates among policy makers about population control. Some state officials today see population growth as the key to their state's international economic and diplomatic stature. Thus French, Russian and Japanese politicians currently express anxiety about their own countries' falling birthrates: if their 'own' women refuse to have larger families, how will they staff their factories and generate tax revenues for workers about to join the pension rolls? By contrast, other policy makers, acting on behalf of international development agencies and governments in Vietnam, China and Nigeria, express alarm at the alleged pressures that population growth imposes on their scarce resources. As dissimilar as these two groups of officials are in their attitudes toward current population trends, they share the belief that women's reproductive capacity is a matter of state and international political concern. Controlling women's bodies, thereby, is transformed into a matter of state security and global stability: the state that fails to ensure that women give birth to, and nurture into healthy maturity, more children is in trouble both in its internal affairs and in its relationships with its neighbours, allies, trading partners and international bankers. Investigating how so many state officials and international agencies come to these positions and act upon them to intervene in women's lives and how women themselves react to those interventions thus has become a serious topic for feminist students of international politics.

Women's rights, patriarchy and 'femocrats'

Out of women's international organizing during the UN 1975–1985 Decade of Women and its successor, the 1995 UN-sponsored international and interstate meeting held in Beijing, came a widespread official and popular discourse on 'women's rights'. These rights, women's activists declared, could not be subsumed under the gender-neutral concept of 'human rights' because the latter was too mired in patriarchal presumptions that the feminized private sphere was separate from the masculinized public sphere, and 'human rights' referred only to those accorded in the public sphere. At international conferences convened throughout the 1990s (held in Vienna, Cairo and Beijing), and into the 2000s, women's advocates asserted that women had the right to be free from violence, whether on the street, in the workplace, in someone else's kitchen or in their bedrooms. Second, they asserted that women had the right to control their own bodies, including their reproductive capacities. Third, they argued that ideological claims that these were private (not political) matters, and diplomatic claims that these were realms for which the sovereign state alone was responsible, were insufficient to keep women from demanding that these rights be actively protected by international law and practice. The outspoken (and even more subtle) resistances mounted by state officials and party politicians to these women activists' claims of rights confirmed what many feminist theorists of the state long had suspected. Not only were state-building and state-maintaining policies rooted in gendered strategies meant to privilege masculinity, but the very principle of state sovereignty – the holy grail of so much IR theory – was itself gendered. That is, the sovereign state is gendered in a way intended to keep most women, regardless of their class or race privilege, politically marginalized.

Patriarchy is a societal system of structures and beliefs that sustains the privileging of masculinity. Feminists do not automatically assume that every state at every stage of its evolution is patriarchal, but they approach every state as problematic. The state is neither natural nor inevitable. Rather, it is a particular sort of social structure held together (often tentatively) by questionable relationships between women and men and by artificial, historically concocted notions about femininity and masculinity. Feminists ask, who inside the state's apparatus and who among those subject to that state's laws and practices do these gendered relationships and gendered ideas privilege? All men? Most men? Some women? This suspicion over patriarchy leaves feminists with an obvious quandary: should any person dedicated to improving the lives of women by reducing masculinity's political privilege even try to pursue those goals by working through or in a given state? The question has profound implications. Should an Israeli battered women's shelter take funds from the Israeli state with it statist strings attached? Should Indian feminists pour their energy and scarce resources into running for parliamentary seats? The risk of co-optation may appear too high.

However, when a liberal political party was in power in Australia during the 1980s, a number of Australian feminists decided to take this risk with their eyes wide open and their monitoring skills at the ready. They coined the term 'femocrats'. These are women intent upon pursuing feminist goals working as civil servants, administrative policy makers inside the state, despite knowing that taking this step is fraught with risk. Today there are feminists working to deprivilege masculinity working inside the European Union, the International Labor Organization, the World Bank, the newly established International Crimes Court and many agencies of the UN. One might think of them as global femocrats. A femocrat, though, does not just work on gender questions. A femocrat is a feminist and thus examines how and why ideas about and practices of gender shape the dynamics of power.

A short history of 'feminist IR'

Feminist theories of and analytical approaches to IR have not come out of the ether. Individual scholars' own innovative, thinking, teaching and writing have been crucial to the development of feminism. But those alone would not have created what by the early 2000s became widely known as (if not always embraced) 'feminist IR' or 'gender and IR'. This intellectual transformation had been generated by a network of women scholars (and some men) working together to reform university curricula and tenure criteria, to change publishers' political science lists, to reimagine professional associations' annual programs and to launch new scholarly journals. This network was created self-consciously across boundaries, not just across the more obvious state boundaries, but also across the more daunting boundaries of race and culture, professional rank and scholarly specialty.

The year 1988 marked an important milestone. At that time the second wave of women's movement activism was at its height in many countries, raising individual conscious-nesses of women, transforming state policies concerning conditions of paid and unpaid work, shining light on the power dynamics inside marriages, political parties, legislatures, courts and peace movements, and converting acts of male violence against women from a private problem into a public issue. The UN Decade of Women, 1975–1985, helped to make these mobilizations more genuinely international. Many women studying for their doctorates and some lucky enough to have academic posts took part in conferences that brought together feminist activists and researchers. By the late 1980s, too, Women's Studies courses were being launched in many universities in Australia, the Philippines, India, Canada, Britain, Germany, Ireland, Scandinavia and the United States, their teachers often overcoming skepticism and direct opposition from their own faculty colleagues, who had cast aspersions on the alleged 'lack of intellectual rigor' of such a new upstart field of inquiry.

By the late 1980s, new Women's Studies journals such as *Signs, Women's Studies International Forum, The Women's Review of Books* and *Feminist Review* had been created, attracting manuscripts from scholars working in history, literature, sociology, art history and anthropology. While some courses in 'Women and Politics' had been created by individual academics as early as the mid-1970s, and while there had been moves by feminist-informed political scientists to organize women's caucuses inside professional groups such as The American Political Science Association, little was being done in the late 1980s to bring feminist ideas into the field of IR, which appeared to be a fortress of intellectual and professional resistance to feminist insights into the workings of power. In this heady atmosphere, the British International Studies Association (BISA) convened its annual gathering at the London School of Economics in the spring of 1988. A small number of women making careers inside academia began collectively to find their voices to insist that women's movement concepts (such as the feminization of unpaid labor, the patriarchal state and marginalization of women) and the wealth of Women's Studies research were relevant for understanding IR.

The BISA, along with the US-based International Studies Association (ISA), had become the institutional arena for determining what would be taken seriously in the scholarly study of IR. Thus not only in the formal panel sessions, but also in the conference's crowded hallways and over beers in the pub after sessions, academics explicitly and implicitly confirmed what was to be 'counted' as 'real IR'. The overwhelming majority of these 1988 program organizers, paper presenters and pub patrons were male, and most of them were white men from Britain, Canada and the United States, although this profile was seemingly so naturalized that very few participants thought it worthy of political analysis. That is, until a handful of women, including Rebecca Grant, Kathleen Newland and Spike Peterson, began to raise questions and began to express a public curiosity about how this distinctive profile of the BISA conference and the larger transatlantic IR academic discipline might be professionally and intellectually distorted by the unquestioned prevalence of unacknowledged masculinist assumptions and practices.

At the same time, a small group of American scholars led by Ann Tickner persuaded the Ford Foundation to sponsor a modest, but intellectually innovative, conference on women, gender and the study of IR. It was held at Wellesley College in Massachusetts. Though a college long renowned for its dedication to women's education, its own political scientists, just like those in scores of political science departments across the United States, taught IR to its undergraduates and graduate students in a fashion that ensured not only that women's lives were invisible, but that 'men-as-men' were deemed analytically irrelevant as well. The lively conversations begun at BISA and at Wellesley set off intellectual sparks. By the early 1990s, several feminist editors inside British and US academic publishing houses began to accept manuscripts that put these emergent feminist ideas about IR into print so that they could be more widely debated, applied and assigned to students; among those early books were *Bananas, Beaches and Bases: Making Feminist Sense of International Politics* (Enloe 1990), *Gender and International Relations* (Grant and Newland 1991) and *Gender in International Relations* (Tickner 1992).

The next step in creating 'feminist IR' was to open up a professional space for feminist IR. A group of academics including Spike Peterson, Ann Tickner, Jindy Pettman, Sandra Whitworth, Christine Sylvester and Anne Sisson Runyan already were active in the ISA. They decided to make it their arena for an ongoing exchange of feminist-informed ideas about IR. That meant persuading the association's officers to open up new panel sessions and to acknowledge that feminist issues could be 'counted' as IR. Fifteen years later, when thousands of academics were preparing for the ISA's 2004 annual conference in Montreal, Quebec, several significant things had been accomplished. First, there was a Women's Caucus, now operating inside the ISA, to monitor and challenge academic sexism in the ISA. Second, the Feminist Theory and Gender Section (FTGS) of the ISA had been institutionalized, helping to mentor younger scholars, encourage participation by feminist-informed scholars in the running of the ISA, sponsor papers and panels at meetings, and to broaden the cultural and geographic profile of feminist IR specialists beyond its largely white and US–British female base. Third, prior to the 2004 ISA conference, 18 full panels were proposed for FTGS sponsorship, while an additional 81 individual papers were proposed on gender, feminism and IR. These numbers suggested the sheer volume of feminist-informed research being conducted in the expanded discipline of IR. By this time, not only were courses on 'Gender and IR', 'IR Feminist Theory', 'Women and Human Rights', 'Gender and International Development', 'Gender and Globalization' and 'Gender and War and Peace' all becoming more commonly offered in universities around the globe, but the professors teaching those courses were more likely to be seen as tenurable by senior faculty at their institutions. In addition, while many members of the IR profession still remained dismissive of feminist theorizing and feminist empirical research – for instance, they rarely incorporated those insights and findings into their own research on trade, security or international organizations – there were increasing numbers of nonfeminist IR faculty who, when they came to design their own 'Introduction to International Relations' undergraduate courses or their graduate seminars on 'IR Theory', now thought it was necessary to devote at least a week or two to feminist approaches and feminist theories. However cursory, such an acknowledgment signaled to young scholars interested in the genderings of power and the patriarchal dynamics of globalized political economy that they did not have to migrate to History or Anthropology. They could pursue their research interests within the academic arena of IR.

In 1999, members of FTGS had also launched a new journal, *The International Feminist Journal of Politics* (*IFPS*). Eight years later, *IFJP*'s international range of contributors, editors, readers and subscribers continues to grow. In the late 1990s, when the journal's founders talked about why they thought the time was ripe for creating such a journal and what values and practices they wanted to inform its operation, they collectively drew on their direct experiences as women, as feminists and as professionals in academia and in the field of IR to craft the new publication. These feminist teachers and scholars furthermore agreed that 'feminist' should be put in the journal's title even though they knew that it might be professionally 'safer' to use the blander term 'gender'. By jointly decided to insert 'feminist' in the title, they agreed that to encourage a scholarly conversation about the workings of constructed femininities and masculinities in local and international affairs – genderings – without explicitly addressing the workings of power, would make the journal less intellectually valuable. The new journal was to serve as a place where the diverse interactions of gender and power would be explored. Furthermore, during the initial discussions about the journal's practices, the founders agreed that not just the content should reflect a feminist investigatory stance, so too should its editorial practices. To these scholars that meant that 'professional' should be disentangled from an institutional culture that was competitive, hierarchical, secretive and exclusivist. They sought to encourage younger scholars to submit articles, to urge external reviewers to conduct their evaluations of manuscripts in a spirit of mentoring and to make transparent the internal processes of the journal.

The feminist IR scholars who founded the *IFJP* also made sure from the start that their discussions were multinational. Canadian, Dutch, Australian, North American and British scholars were already part of the project. Yet they also explicitly made a commitment to move the journal beyond this narrow geographic range by ensuring that the Editorial Advisory Board was more truly international and by inviting feminist scholars in the Global South to submit papers and to serve as manuscript reviewers. Soon they were joined by feminist IR scholars from Japan, Sweden, Norway, Germany, Israel and Turkey. They encouraged men as well as women to submit manuscripts and asked several feminist-informed male scholars to serve on the journal's advisory board. In addition, the journal's founders decided that there should be a three-person senior editorial team, not just a single editor; each of the three core editors would be based in a different geographic region, so as to structurally push the *IFJP* to adopt a genuinely global approach to the creation and distribution of new knowledge. Toward this same end, the founders decided that the operational headquarters of the journal would not be in the United States.

Conclusion

Feminist research and teaching in the newly expanded field of IR remains a work in progress. In its content, as well as its explanations and practices, feminist IR explorations seek to keep the intellectual conversation open and fresh. In 1988, few people understood how paying serious attention to Filipinas scrubbing other people's bathtubs in Hong Kong and Kuwait would make us smarter about the deeply gendered workings of local and international politics. What will surprise us when we look back at the first decade of the new century?

Further reading

Enloe, C. (2004) *The Curious Feminist: Searching for Women in a New Age of Empire*, Berkeley, CA: University of California Press.
Peterson, V.S. (2003) *A Critical Rewriting of Global Political Economy*, London: Routledge.
Pettman, J.J. (1996) *Worlding Women: A Feminist International Politics*, Sydney: Allen and Unwin.

10 Postcolonialism

Rita Abrahamsen

Introduction

In the early 1990s, as postpositivist interventions stimulated a more self-reflective attitude within the discipline of International Relations (IR), the book *Global Voices* (Rosenau 1993) sought to broaden the perspective of IR and begin a dialogue with voices excluded from its traditional purview – such as women, critical theorists, and poststructuralists. Despite the book's inclusive inclinations, there was one notable omission. The absence of any 'Third World' analyst, announced the editor in the introduction to the book, was due to 'space limitations' (Rosenau 1993: xv). Today, the voices of the South are only slightly more audible, and any quick scan of the leading journals and key textbooks will reveal that IR remains a discipline of the rich West, paying scant attention to approximately three quarters of the world's population living in the poorer countries of the South. The 'global voices' in the dialogue of IR are, it seems, not so global after all.

Postcolonial approaches often proceed precisely from a recognition of this Western-centric character of mainstream IR, arguing that the discipline's interpretations of international affairs are profoundly grounded in Western experiences and discursive practices. Placing the South and the subaltern at the center of analyses, postcolonial theory is concerned to 'provincialize Europe' (Chakrabarty 2000) in the sense of both uncovering – and changing – the complex power/knowledge relationships that reproduce the contemporary world order.

Originating in the field of literary and cultural studies, the postcolonial worldview is relatively new to IR. It is also marginal, as indicated either by its total exclusion from most mainstream textbooks or its inclusion at the end, after the other 'peripheral' voices of poststructuralism and feminism. Nevertheless, in recent years postcolonialism has made significant contributions to the study of global politics and has helped to make the South more visible and also to expose some of the Western-centric foundations of conventional approaches. Postcolonial analyses contend that any understanding of contemporary IR requires a careful account of the multiple and diverse power relationships that link the North and the South, both in the colonial past and the postcolonial present. As such, postcolonial theory encourages a refocusing of IR, away from the traditional domain of states, militaries, and diplomacy, toward people, identities, and resistance.

Situating postcolonial theory

Postcolonialism is not a conventional worldview in any traditional academic sense, and some even dispel its classifications as an '-ism' as totally 'bogus' (Spivak 1999). Rather than a unified body of thought, postcolonial theory is multiple, diverse, and eschews any easy definition or generalization. Postcolonial theory also does not have a disciplinary 'home' and cannot be confined to any particular academic department. While originating as an approach to the study of Commonwealth literature in the late 1970s and early 1980s, its focus has broadened to include other aspects of North–South relations and has made an impact in a wide variety of fields, including cultural studies, development studies, anthropology, geography, history, and politics. This open-ended and inclusive character is a defining feature of postcolonial theory, and its multidisciplinary character gives rise to flexible and novel analyses.

Postcolonial approaches to IR stem in large part from its dissatisfaction with mainstream IR and the latter's traditional focus on superpower politics, states, and the balance of power. Born in Europe and currently dominated by US academic influences, the discipline of IR is regarded as the discourse of the powerful, providing a 'worldview' as seen from the West and failing to capture and reflect the concerns and viewpoints of poorer countries and peoples. The universalist, statist, and often elitist character of IR stands in sharp contrast to postcolonialism's focus on the South and marginalized peoples, stressing the importance of specificity and 'differently situated' experiences. Postcolonial writers are also centrally concerned with identity and culture, with race and gender, and with the continued importance of the colonial relationship for an understanding of both the (ex)colonizer and the (de)colonized. A key aim of much postcolonial writing is to expose the extent to which mainstream scholarship and also frequently our 'common sense' understandings of the social world are firmly grounded in a particularly Western perspective, and thus to draw attention to the epistemological bases of Western power. This in turn has led to a focus on discourse and representation, to the way in which the world has been framed and defined, and postcolonial writers argue that these forms of power need to be challenged in order to effect political change.

It is clear from the above that postcolonialism has many affinities with the so-called 'post-positivist' turn in IR, and with poststructuralism and postmodernism more generally. But to reduce or subsume postcolonial theory within any of these approaches, however broadly defined, does not do justice to its originality, heterogeneity, and multiple sources of inspiration. To be sure, thinkers commonly associated with poststructuralism and postmodernism such as Michel Foucault, Jacques Derrida, and Jacques Lacan figure prominently in the pantheon of postcolonialism, but their ideas are frequently applied in novel and eclectic ways. Many postcolonial writers would also argue that their explicit political commitment to the subaltern or the marginalized distinguishes their accounts from what are frequently regarded (rightly or wrongly) as the more relativistic analyses of the other 'post-isms' (Appiah 1997; Paolini 1999; Young 2001). In this respect, postcolonialism is in close dialogue with the Marxist tradition of criticism, as evidenced for example in the widespread use of the Gramscian term 'subaltern'. Again, eclecticism characterizes the use of Marxist-inspired methodologies and theories, combining its traditional materialism with detailed attention to the subjective effects and micro-politics of oppression. Another dialogue is between postcolonial and feminist analyses, both sharing a commitment to ending gendered oppression. As with Marxism, the relationship is ambiguous. While recognizing the oppression of women everywhere, postcolonial writers have pointed to the risk of producing a singular, monolithic 'Third World Woman', where Western women are cast as the normative (liberated) referent and the 'Third World Woman' their binary opposite as poor, victimized, domesticated, and traditional (Mohanty 1993). Postcolonial feminist analyses have thus attempted to draw attention to the differently situated experiences of women in the Third World, while at the same time recognizing the need for solidarity and international links between women's political struggles.

Another important source of inspiration for postcolonial theory is the anticolonial writings of Third World intellectuals like Franz Fanon, Albert Memmi, Amilcar Cabral, Aimé Césaire, and Mahatma Gandhi, to mention a few. Writing in the heat of the struggle for independence, these writers drew attention to the multiple forms of violence entailed in colonial oppression, and exposed its impact on cultures, identities, and forms of resistance. These writers often demonstrated the contradictions and inconsistencies that colonialism entailed for the colonial powers and for their so-called 'civilizing mission'. Césaire's dramatic declaration that 'Europe is indefensible', for example, shows how the practices of colonial oppression undermined the very values of liberty, equality, and respect that Europe claimed to uphold and represent (Césaire 1972: 9). Today, these early voices of the South are often invoked to illustrate the longevity of the relations and structures of power associated with colonialism. Finally, postcolonial theory has important affinities with the subaltern school of Indian historiography, which has been motivated by a desire to retell history from the counter-hegemonic standpoints of the colonized. Starting from the observation that history, and imperial history in particular, has been the story of the powerful, the subaltern school has sought to offer an alternative history centered on the experiences and resistance of the colonized, or the subaltern (Guha 1997; Prakash 1990), and similar motivations drive many postcolonial scholars within the field of global politics.

Recognizing the diversity of postcolonialism's intellectual antecedents is important not only because it demonstrates the richness of the approach and the inherent difficulties in defining it as one unified school of thought, but also because critics have often dismissed it as a predominantly 'Western discipline' (Dirlik 1994; Williams 1997). According to such criticisms, postcolonial theory is associated with privileged diasporic Third World intellectuals attempting to come to terms with their own conditions within the Western academe and thus reflects the concerns of the rich and well-educated rather than the poor and marginalized. Dirlik thus dates the beginning of the postcolonial to the arrival of the Third World intellectual in the First World academe, regarding 'postcoloniality as the condition of the intelligentsia of global capitalism' (Dirlik 1994: 56). While it is the case that many of its most well known exponents, such as Gayatri Spivak and Homi Bhabha, are based in Anglophone universities, the interpretation of postcolonial theory as 'Western' ignores the substantial influence of many thinkers from the former colonies. Moreover, to pose the question of postcolonialism's geographical identity pursues the wrong line of inquiry, as a central aim of the approach is precisely to abandon such strict boundaries and classifications in favor of a focus on mutually constitutive relations. This crucial aspect is perhaps best illustrated through a discussion of the 'post' in postcolonial theory.

The 'post' in postcolonial theory

The 'post' in postcolonial theory makes for an inherently fuzzy and ambiguous term, and a long-standing debate concerns its precise meaning and time frame. Critics charge that it indicates the end of colonialism, and hence of oppression and exploitation, and that the focus on the colonial invariable privileges the colonial experience and relies on a sharp dichotomy between the colonial and the postcolonial. By starting their inquiry with the colonial encounter, postcolonial writers are perceived to continue the Eurocentric attitude of much conventional social science where the so-called 'emerging areas' are presented as 'people without history' (Wolf 1982). The 'post' in postcolonialism, however, should not be taken as a straightforward temporal marker, but indicates instead a different vision of history. While the 'post' can be seen to signify the end of colonialism as direct domination at least in most parts of the world, it does not imply a period 'after imperialism' as a global system of hegemonic power (Young 2001). Thus, Spivak (1990: 166) has no hesitation in maintaining that 'we live in a post-colonial, neocolonized world' while Bhabha (1994: 6) argues that postcoloniality is 'a salutary reminder of the persistent "neocolonial" relations within the "new" world order and the multi-national division of labour'. In this way, despite recognizing that colonialism as conventionally defined in terms of formal settlement and control of other peoples' land and goods has (with few exceptions) come to an end, many postcolonial writers stress the continued relevance of its structures and relations of power. The 'post' in postcolonialism is not a clearly dividing temporal marker, but rather an indication of continuity. The term is accordingly best approached as an attempt to transcend strict chronological and dichotomous thinking where history is clearly delineated and the social world neatly categorized into separate boxes, and seeks instead to capture the continuities and complexities of any historical period. In the words of Prakash (1996: 188), postcolonialism 'sidesteps the language of beginnings and ends'.

That said, the colonial experience is accorded a special status and is regarded as indispensable to an understanding of contemporary IR. By the 1930s, colonies and ex-colonies covered more than four fifths of the land surface of the globe (Loomba 1996), and colonialism formed a key transformative encounter for both the colonizer and the colonized. Colonial power not only changed the ways of imposing and maintaining rule in the colonial territories, but also transformed the terrain and discourses within which colonized people could respond to domination. For example, the terrain of the nation-state and the discourse of nationalism came to occupy an increasingly hegemonic status as the basis for effective resistance (Chatterjee 1986). The global reach of Western imperial power also brought new peoples and places into the world capitalist economy, and compelled them to remain, even after their formal independence, within this economic system. The colonial encounter thus marks a crucial reordering of the world, and many postcolonial writers argue that the return to a pristine, unspoilt precolonial culture is impossible and have warned against such nostalgia for lost origins (Appiah 1991; Spivak 1988: 211–313). Crucially, however, this does not mean that the colonial era came to an abrupt end, but rather the present is regarded as a complex mix and continuation of different cultures and temporalities.

The connections between the past and the present, the colonial and the postcolonial, the North and the South thus emerge as a key focus of postcolonial investigations. Rather than pointing to fixed temporal and geographical periods and spaces, postcolonial theory draws attention to continuities, fluidity, and interconnectedness, economically, politically, and culturally. The constitutive relationship of the North and the South and the way in which the two produce and reinforce the identity of each other both in the colonial past and in the postcolonial present are key insights and concerns of postcolonial thinking. Approached from this perspective, the meaning of common terms like 'the West' or 'Africa' can only emerge from recognition of their relationship to the other. During colonialism, for example, the claims of 'civilization' came to rest on the deficiencies of 'barbarism', with the description of 'savages' reinforcing the 'civilized' character of Europeans and legitimizing the authoritarian nature of colonial rule. This constitutive relationship continues today, with Achille Mbembe observing that 'Africa still constitutes one of the metaphors through which the West represents the origins of its own norms, develops a self-image, and integrates this image into the set of signifiers asserting what is supposed to be its identity'

(Mbembe 2001: 2). By the same token, the identity of Africa, and the South more broadly, is constituted and produced in interaction and dialogue with 'the West'.

Power/knowledge and politics of representation

Despite the diversity that characterizes postcolonial theory, it is possible to identify certain common themes and concerns that figure prominently in the writing of many key thinkers. The centrality of power in postcolonial theory is the first point of commonality to note. Postcolonial analyses have engaged extensively with the role of power in the formation of identity and subjectivity, as well as the relationship between power, knowledge, and political practices. While mainstream IR and political science tend to conceive of power as located primarily in the state and as associated with economic and military might, postcolonial approaches employ a more complex and multifaceted understanding of power.

Drawing on poststructuralist theory and in particular the thinking of Foucault (1970, 1977, 1980, 1991), power is no longer perceived as only repressive, nor is it understood in purely material or institutional terms. Instead, power is a relational force that is productive and creative of subjects. It is also intimately linked to knowledge, not in the strict instrumental sense that knowledge is always in the service of the powerful, but in terms of the production of truth and rationality. Truth, in the Foucauldian sense, is a thing of this world, produced through discourses that establish dominant or hegemonic ways of understanding and representing social reality. Discourses then are practices that systematically form the objects of which they speak, that have acquired the position to shape the manner in which a particular aspect of social reality is imagined and acted upon; that is, discourses are practices that have material effects. Seen in this light, the social sciences do not merely describe the world as they find it, but instead they construct and create the manner in which it is perceived and understood. Any object of scientific investigation is simultaneously its effect, and drawing on these insights, postcolonial analyses seek to establish how certain ways of understanding and representing the world became dominant, and to demystify and politicize their truths.

Much postcolonial scholarship is informed, in one way or another, by this understanding of power and this in turn explains the considerable attention to discourse and representational practices. The importance assigned to the power/knowledge nexus in postcolonial studies can be traced back to Edward Said's *Orientalism* (1979), often regarded as the founding text of postcolonial studies. Arguing that there is 'no such thing as a delivered presence; there is only a re-presence, or representation' (1979: 21), Said shows how in the case of the Orient knowledge and power went hand in hand, undermining the possibility of an innocent, objective academic standpoint. Said's central contention is that Orientalism was a 'systematic discipline by which European culture was able to manage – and even produced – the Orient politically, sociologically, militarily, ideologically, scientifically, and imaginatively during the post-Enlightenment period' (1979: 3). For Said, the Orient was ultimately a political vision whose structure promoted a binary opposition between the familiar (the West/us) and the strange (the Orient/them). In this way, the Orient is revealed as central to European self-understanding and identity, while knowledge, representation and the ability to interpret social reality emerge as a form of power that shape identities and ways of life. The observation is relevant not only to the invention of the Orient, but also to colonial power more broadly. As Comaroff and Comaroff note, the 'essence of colonization inheres less in political overrule than in seizing and transforming "others" by the very act of conceptualizing, inscribing, and interacting with them on terms not of their own choosing; in making them into the pliant objects and silenced subjects of our scripts and scenarios; in assuming the capacity to "represent" them' (1991: 15).

The power of Western discourses to create 'regimes of truth' that marginalize or silence other discourses and ways of being is not limited to the colonial period. On the contrary, as Grovugui (2004: 33) observes, 'the representations of "international reality" and "international existence" have remained grounded in Western institutional and discursive practices so as to reflect and affirm parochial structures of power, interest and identity'. A contemporary illustration can be found in the discourse and practice of development, which from a postcolonial perspective can be seen to continue many of the structures and relations of colonialism (Escobar 1995). Rather than focusing on the stated aims of development policies, a postcolonial approach seeks to discover its effects and to question and destabilize the taken-for-granted character of key concepts and categories. Thus, 'development' and 'underdevelopment' are not accepted as self-evident or preordained categories. Instead they are discursive constructs; particular ways of seeing and acting upon the world that reflect not only the conditions they describe but also the constellations of social, economic, and political forces at the time of their emergence. With the problematization of 'underdevelopment', social reality became ordered into new categories such as underdeveloped, malnourished, and illiterate. This ordering of the world not only shapes and influences the identities of people and countries, but also establishes Third World countries as objects of intervention, and normalizes the right of the North to intervene and control, adapt and reshape the structures, practices, and ways of life of the South. The ability of the rich industrialized countries to set standards for what constitutes development conditions the choices and identities available to poor countries, and in this way development discourse helps legitimize interventions in poor countries in order to remodel them according to Western norms of progress, growth, and efficiency. Seen from this perspective, development is a form of power in international politics, and through its interventions the underdeveloped subject becomes known, categorized, incorporated into statistics, models, and graphs, which in turn legitimate practices and facilitate the emergence of the developed, disciplined subject. Importantly, for most postcolonial analysts this does not entail a denial of the material condition of poverty or the disparities between rich and poor, but poses instead a challenge to their conceptualization and the political practices that they make possible.

A further illustration of the continuing relevance and importance of the power/knowledge nexus in North–South relations can be found in current IR and policy discourses on the so-called 'failed state'. In uncanny echoes of colonial discourses, failed and failing states are framed as childlike and chaotic, descending helplessly and inevitably into anarchy and violence (Helman and Ratner 1993; Kaplan 1994; Rotberg 2004). Helman and Ratner, for example, use the analogy of 'serious mental or physical illness' and a 'hapless individual' to describe these states, arguing for the reinstatement of Western protectorates (1993: 12). Similarly, the former British Foreign Secretary Straw (2002) refers to the West as 'the doctor' able to 'prevent' and 'cure' the condition of 'state failure'.

The replay of colonial imagery establishes failed states as deficient, abnormal, and lacking, and thereby reinforces the identity of the West as democratic, rational, and morally superior. It also serves to absolve the West from responsibility for the conditions associated with state failure, as the perceived chaos and failure is presented as an expression of otherness. The numerous ways in which international politics, including decades of development policies advocating economic liberalization and state curtailment, have contributed to the weakening of the capacities, and integrity of these states thus disappear from view. The West remains the 'doctor' able to 'prevent' and 'cure'. It is the solution rather than part of the problem (Abrahamsen 2001). Following the events of 11 September 2001, the discourses on the failed state have taken on a new urgency, as poor states in the periphery have come to be regarded not primarily as pernicious obstacles to the well-being of their own populations, but as 'breeding grounds for terrorism' and hence direct threats to international security (Straw 2002). From a postcolonial perspective, the politics of representation in the 'war on terrorism' is thus of crucial importance, as the 'truth' about failed states also determines actions toward them and their peoples (Abrahamsen 2005).

Identity, hybridity and authenticity

The importance of identity is another key theme in postcolonial theory, and again this is linked to the understanding of power as productive of subjects and identities through various micro-technologies and relations. Identities and subjectivities were profoundly influenced and reshaped by the colonial experience, and accordingly colonialism finds continued expression in a multiplicity of practices, philosophies, and cultures imparted to and adopted by the colonized in more or less hybrid, or mixed, forms. The notion of hybridity, as Young (2001) points out, was first placed at the heart of postcolonial studies by Ashis Nandy's *The Intimate Enemy: Loss and Recovery of Self under Colonialism* (1983). Nandy's starting point is the observation that 'colonialism is first of all a matter of consciousness and needs to be defeated ultimately in the minds of men' (1983: 63). The psychological and cultural impacts of colonialism, rather than the political or economic, are thus placed at the center of analysis, drawing attention to the continuity and longevity of colonial power as embedded in the postcolonial self. While anticolonial writers like Fanon (1986), Memmi (1990), and Césaire (1972) lament the violent impact of colonial power on local cultures and the often concomitant destruction of pride and self-confidence, they mostly recognize, as do contemporary postcolonial writers, that there can be no return to an unsullied, pure position of cultural authenticity. The colonial encounter may have resulted in what Fanon (1986) refers to as an 'inferiority complex', but this does not mean that the recovery of 'self' is to be found in a return to ancient cultural practices and symbols, or that hybridity is inherently bad.

Identities and cultures inevitably negotiate the past, and the notion of hybridity encapsulates the way in which the colonizer and the colonized are forged in relationship with each other, an observation which is powerfully expressed by Franz Fanon's statement that 'the Negro is not. Any more than the white man' (Fanon 1986: 231). According to Fanon, the white man's self-perception as moral, rational, and civilized required the image of the Negro as barbaric and uncivilized. The notion of hybridity helps to break down this essentialized, binary opposition between the colonized and the colonizer, between black and white, between self and other. Hybridity also signifies the failure of colonial power to fully dominate its subjects, and shows their creativity and resilience. Particularly in the interpretation of Bhabha (1994), the notion of hybridity marks the failure of colonial power in the sense that the colonized was never fully dominated, never completely the same as the colonizer. Thus, where Said's *Orientalism* at times seems to exaggerate the ability of the West to produce the Orient, Bhabha's treatment of hybridity shows that the colonized were not passive victims whose identities were narrated in a one-way process by colonial authority. The ambivalence of hybrid cultures and practices, the way in which they are 'almost the same, but not quite', is for Bhabha a sign of the agency of the colonized and their ability to resist domination.

In this way, hybridity is a potential site of resistance and subversion, as it breaks down the symmetry of the self/other distinction. While the exercise of colonial authority requires the production of differentiation between the white man as more civilized than the black, for example – hybridity disrupts this differentiation. Hybridity rules out recognition, as the differences that were relied upon to justify colonial power are no longer immediately observable. Mastery is constantly asserted, but always incomplete, always slipping (Bhabha 1994). Herein lies the menace of hybridity and mimicry; it discloses the ambivalence at the heart of colonial discourse and has the potential to disrupt its authority. From the 'in-between', hybrid identities can engender new forms of being that can unsettle and subvert colonial authority. The interpretation also has contemporary relevance, and more recently the notion of hybridity has been invoked as a measure of local agency in the face of globalization. Hybridity or, as it is sometimes called, 'creolization' is seen to signify the creative adaptation, interpretation and transformation of Western cultural symbols and practices, and shows that the peoples of the South are not simply passive victims in the face of an all-powerful Western culture (Ashcroft 2001; Hannerz 1996).

At this point it is important to highlight a certain tension in postcolonial theory. On the one hand, it celebrates hybrid identities, while, on the other, its explicit commitment to the subaltern frequently leads to a privileging of local cultures and identities and a concern for the survival of the ways of life of marginalized peoples encountering powerful global forces. In terms of political choices, the notion of hybridity serves to refute political and cultural positions that advocate a return to origin or tradition. This view, for example, underpins Said's (1993) incisive critique of the philosophy of negritude, which he regards not only as reinforcing the imperial hierarchies between the colonized and the colonizer, but also as proposing an essentialized identity or 'Africanness' that is not only impossible, but also politically potentially dangerous and damaging as narratives of purity can justify a range of actions from the expulsion of migrants to ethnic cleansing. Said accordingly suggests that there is much to be gained from not remaining trapped in such emotional celebrations of one's own identity, and in this way postcolonialism's focus on hybridity can be regarded as a warning against the violence of essentialist, exclusionary discourses.

Others, however, fear that to abandon the belief and pursuit of 'authenticity' is simultaneously to undermine the possibility for resistance and opposition (Paolini 1999). In the same manner as the anticolonial struggles gained much of their force from an appeal to a traditional, 'national' identity different from that of the colonial power, so contemporary political and cultural struggles might need unifying essentialist identity discourses. The Tibetan struggle is a case in point. As Anand has commented, while it might be comfortable for some diasporas to speak of the failings of their nation-states, for the Tibetan diaspora this is 'a luxury they can hardly afford' (2004: 211). Giving up on the idea and discourse of a unified, essential Tibetan identity could erode the capacity for an effective campaign against Chinese occupation, leaving the exiled Tibetans with few means to argue their case.

This is a crucial issue for postcolonial writers, as it relates specifically to how this mode of analysis can be applied to political criticism and activism. Writing with reference to African-Americans, Hooks (1993) observes that 'it's easy to give up identity, when you got one'. Recognizing the dangers of essentialism, she nevertheless warns us to be 'suspicious of postmodern critiques of the "subject" when they surface at a historical moment when many subjugated people feel themselves coming to voice for the first time' (Hooks 1993: 425). Despite her critical reflections, Hooks is clear that there can be no return to essentialized identities and political discourses. A critique of essentialism, she argues, offers the possibility to affirm multiple black identities, and thus represents a challenge to paradigms that represent 'blackness one-dimensionally in ways that reinforce white supremacy' (1993: 425). At the same time, what she calls the 'authority of experience' must be recognized, so that the image of a black essence is replaced by recognition of the way in which black identity is specifically constituted in the experience of exile and struggle (1993: 426). In response to similar dilemmas, Spivak (1985) has argued for what she calls a 'strategic essentialism' that allows for some form of essentialized identity in order to facilitate resistance, while at the same time recognizing that there can be no pure identities. Applied to the case of Tibet, this would entail recognition of the constructed character of these collective identity claims, while simultaneously recognizing their strategic and tactical importance in political struggles (Anand 2004).

The postcolonial focus on hybridity and the constructed character of identity thus serves as a warning that the local voice, once heard, does not create its own forms of violence, silencing and oppressing of new minorities and subalterns. It is a recognition that local identities are not exhaustive and that appeals to fixed identities (even if national or local) can contain their own dangers and an effort to advocate a more generous and pluralistic vision of the world, where the possibilities for oppressive identity claims are minimized. In the words of Said, by drawing attention to the fluid and constructed character of all identities it offers the 'possibility of discovering a world not constructed out of warring essences' (Said 1993: 277).

Resistance

Resistance is another recurring theme in postcolonial theory. Hybridity, for example, is seen as intimately linked to resistance, as it signifies the creativity and adaptability of the subaltern in the face of power and demonstrates that the colonial encounter as well as contemporary North–South relations cannot be understood in terms of a one-way relationship of domination. The stated aim of many postcolonial writers is to give voice and make visible those who are not normally heard or seen, and their commitment to the marginalized, or the subaltern, is frequently invoked to differentiate postcolonialism from postmodernism. In this regard, postcolonial approaches have much in common with the Subaltern Studies Group of Indian historiography. Arguing that a conventional historical account of India's colonial experience and independence struggle is a history of the elite, these historians have sought to retell history from the perspective of the subaltern. By bringing the agency and the resistance of the subaltern to the forefront, the Subaltern Studies Group has painted more complex picture of the colonial relationship, demonstrating that the subaltern were not passive victims of imperial power (Guha 1997).

Postcolonial approaches share much with this revisionist Indian project, and many writers seek to recover the subject positions of the marginalized or retell history from counter-hegemonic standpoints. This is not so much an attempt to speak on behalf of the subaltern as an effort to mark the space of the silenced in conventional imperial history and contemporary accounts of world politics, history, and culture. The process of reinterpretation and recovery of previously marginalized or silenced voices is seen as an act of resistance and subversion, as a way of breaking the hegemony of dominant discourses. Again, Said's *Orientalism* is an important inspiration. By drawing attention to the intimacy of power and knowledge, he made the first steps toward challenging the hegemonic narratives of the West. As the 'empire writes back' to the metropolis, telling its own stories, it challenges and disrupts the familiar narratives of Western historiography. This act of reinterpretation and retelling is simultaneously an act of resistance and a form of empowerment. In other words, effective resistance and the possibility of alternative ways of being and acting require a reconfiguration of the conceptual space in which we understand and act upon the world.

The understanding of power as productive and ubiquitous has clear implications for post-colonial analyses of resistance. As seen in the interpretation of hybridity and ambivalence, resistance is often much more subtle than in mainstream political analyses in that it is not necessarily overt or in a direct relationship of opposition and polarity (colonized/colonizer, white/black). As such, postcolonial theory illustrates the inadequacy of conventional binary oppositions between domination and resistance, and shows how resistance cannot be ideal-ized as pure opposition to the order it opposes, but operates instead inside a structure of power that it both challenges and helps sustain (Mbembe 2001). Nationalist struggles for independence serve as a useful example. While the demand for nationalist independence effectively utilized Western discourses against Empire, the endorsement of the nation-state simultaneously ensured the survival of the colonial redrawing of the world map and enshrined the importance of the nation-state in the international system.

Following Foucault's insight that power works through micro-processes and relations and should therefore be investigated from the 'ground up', postcolonial investigations of resistance tend to focus on everyday forms of behavior rather than the conventional preoccupation of political science with revolutions, armed struggles, or large-scale political opposition. The subaltern, even in conditions of extreme domination, is found to have multiple ways of resisting and avoiding power, including mockery and ridicule. James Scott's explorations of everyday forms of resistance, for example, demonstrate how the subaltern frequently avoids and mocks power through what he calls 'hidden transcripts' and veiled forms of practical resistance (Scott 1985, 1990). In postcolonial Africa, Mbembe similarly shows how ordinary people mock state power through vernacular rewritings of party slogans, gossip, and popular cartoons, and how these forms of resistance go someway toward making the state 'lose its might' (Mbembe 2001). Dominance, in other words, is never total, and the subaltern always has her own agency and subjectivity. Given the postcolonial skepticism of meta-narratives and universal truths, it should be noted that such local, micro struggles against the dominant order take on a particular importance.

By drawing attention to the epistemic aspects of colonial and postcolonial power and violence, postcolonial writers have also problematized the target of resistance. The solution is no longer to be found simply in seizing state power or the means of production. Instead, postcolonialism's project can be described as material, cultural, and epistemological in that it entails a recognition that changing economic and political structures of domination and inequality requires a parallel and profound change in their epistemological and psycholo-gical underpinnings and effects. This is the insight of Nandy's (1983: 63) statement that 'colonialism is first of all a matter of consciousness and needs to be defeated ultimately in the minds of men'. Critics of postcolonial theory have often been particularly scathing on this issue, arguing that the focus on discourse and epistemic power has led to a neglect of the structural inequalities of power and wealth between the North and the South. According to the critics, representations and discourses are largely irrelevant to the everyday struggles of the poor and marginalized, and reflect instead the concerns of the academic 'ivory towers' (Dirlik 1994; Williams 1997). What, such critics ask, have postcolonial approaches got to say about the exploitation of poor countries by transnational capital, about the debt crisis, or about Western trade protectionism? The ability to mock power or retell history may well demonstrate the agency of the subaltern, but according to the critics this does little to actually change the distribution of resources domestically or globally. Hence, the poor continue to suffer, despite the counter-hegemonic narratives of postcolonial writers.

Against such dismissals, it can be said that the postcolonial project is primarily one of critique and that its strengths derive precisely from its location outside of the immediate policy community. As such, Fanon's plea at the end of *Black Skin, White Masks* could stand as the axiom of many postcolonial approaches; 'make of me always a man who questions' (Fanon 1986: 232). More importantly, perhaps, this type of rebuff frequently ignores or misstates the understanding of power that underpins the critical project of postcolonialism. From a postcolonial perspective, effective resistance of any kind requires the simultaneous disruption and transformation of our epistemic and discursive universes. The focus on representation is thus a way of making explicit the forms of truth and rationality that underpin 'common sense' and 'expert' knowledges and practices, and in this way exposing the contingency of current social and political order. These are not 'ivory tower' critiques, far removed from the realities of everyday survival. On the contrary, the very maintenance and reproduction of the current social and political order depend precisely on these knowledges and discursive practices. As such postcolonial critiques can help generate possibilities for the transformation of social and political condition, even when their analyses do not appear as immediately policy relevant.

It is also important to recognize that postcolonial writers have more recently began exploring and engaging with more contemporary political issues, dealing more directly with material and structural inequalities. In part this reflects the journey of postcolonial theory from departments of Literature and Cultural Studies to departments of Politics and IR, and in part it is a response to an ongoing internal debate about 'the political necessity of taking a stand', as Said expressed it (Krishna 1993: 389). Thus, a recent collection on postcolonialism and IR includes essays on the Asian financial crisis, child labor, and the sex trade, hardly issues to be dismissed as the esoteric concerns of the distant intellectual (Chowdhry and Nair 2004). In another recent contribution, Dunn (2003) insightfully shows how an understanding of the contemporary conflict in the Democratic Republic of Congo (DRC) requires an appreciation of how, since colonial times, Western discourses of a 'chaotic' and 'barbaric' Congo have influenced actions and policies toward Congo/Zaire/DRC. These discourses and images have in turn shaped the identity and politics of contemporary DRC, so much so that without attention to the 'imagining of the Congo' it is impossible to fully understand the ongoing conflict in the DRC, which to date has claimed more than 100,000 lives.

Numerous other examples could be given, but the crucial point is that postcolonial theory is increasingly being applied to contemporary political issues. To a significant extent, then, postcolonialism has begun to answer the challenge to move away from a politics of theory toward a new theory of politics where 'the accent is on political rather than cultural criticism' (Scott 1999: 19). This of course does not mean that postcolonial perspectives have abandoned the attention to the past or to the power of representation or that they can be subsumed under one uniform banner, espousing the same theories and the same politics of resistance. The heterogeneity of postcolonialism remains its key distinguishing feature, but its political edges are perhaps becoming more discernible as authors increasingly turn to contemporary issues and challenges.

Conclusion

Postcolonial theory is a relatively new entrant to IR, but in the space of a few years writers working within this mode of analysis have both challenged conventional perceptions and made considerable contributions to our understanding of contemporary IR. In particular, postcolonial approaches have helped make the countries and peoples of the South more visible in IR, drawing attention to the inadequacies and silences of Western-centric forms of analyses. By critiquing the state-centric foundations of much IR theory, postcolonial investigations have stressed the interconnectedness of the North and the South and the continued importance and political relevance of their mutually constitutive relationships. As such, they have gone some way toward expanding the dialogue in IR and including previously excluded Third World perspectives 'among the global voices clamouring to be heard in a discipline in flux' (Rosenau 1993: xv).

Nevertheless, postcolonial theory remains on the margins of IR. As a heterogeneous, critical perspective questioning dominant interpretations and focusing primarily on the powerless, it is unlikely to command the same kind of influence and status as perspectives concerned with the interests and actions of core states. The focus on culture, identity and complex patterns of power and resistance fits ill with a discipline so long dominated by a preoccupation with states and military and economic might. Nonetheless, to understand world politics in an increasingly globalized, hybrid, and interdependent, yet vastly unequal, world, postcolonial theory offers crucial and invaluable insights. As such, postcolonial analyses do not only pose a theoretical challenge to the discipline of IR, deconstructing its 'common sense' and revealing its complicity with power, but can also contribute to political challenges to the contemporary world order.

Further reading

Ashcroft, B. (2001) *Post-Colonial Transformations*, London: Routledge.
Spivak, G.C. (1999) *A Critique of Postcolonial Reason*, Cambridge, MA: Harvard University Press.
Young, R. (2003) *Postcolonialism*, Oxford: Oxford University Press.

11 Theories of state formation

Heather Rae

Introduction

Despite arguments that the effects of globalization may be undermining the authority of the sovereign state, states remain important actors in contemporary global politics. If scholars of International Relations (IR) are to fully understand the sort of changes states and the states system may be undergoing, the problems states face and, indeed, the problems that this form of political organization may create, it is vital to further our understanding of how this institutional form, which has come to dominate the globe, developed. States have formed in different geographical areas, in different historical periods and under very different conditions. The early development of the modern state occurred in Western Europe, and this was followed by later episodes of state formation in the nineteenth century culminating in a number of new states gaining recognition after World War I, during the period of decolonization following World War II and, more recently, following the end of the Cold War. Thus, while an understanding of the general processes involved in state formation is important we should also be attentive to the particularities of different epochs and, within these epochs, the differences as well as similarities between states. Having said that, most work on state formation with which IR scholars are familiar focuses on early modern-state building in Western Europe and the discipline would benefit from a wider focus. Nonetheless, this chapter begins with Western Europe. It then provides a brief account of the successive phases of state formation, an overview of contending approaches to the study of state formation, and consideration of the possibilities for further research in this area.

The development of the modern state was a gradual process in which rulers in core areas of Western Europe slowly gained centralized control over the means of violence and the means of revenue collection, resulting in the formation of the early 'core' states of Spain, England and France. The first of these two interconnected processes began with monarchs wresting secular authority from the Catholic Church and the Holy Roman Empire and disarming the nobility (Elias 1982). In time this consolidation of control of the means of violence would lead to the development of standing national armies, rather than the earlier reliance on mercenaries. As monarchs extended their rule, they were able to better organize the second aspect of control, the routine extraction of funds from their populations. This was something that they needed to do in order to fund the wars in which they were often engaged and it also played an important role in the economic development of states as feudalism gave way to capitalism (Braudel 1972; Tilly 1985; Wallerstein 1974).

Thus the classic definition of the modern state is of a centralized political authority that claims legitimate control over the means of violence within a clearly demarcated physical territory and over a defined population, though exactly how this population has been defined has differed over time (Anderson 1991; Rae 2002). While the territorial sovereign state has undergone many changes and challenges, the claim that it is the state, and the state alone, that legitimately controls and uses the means of violence – that it is not legitimate for nonstate actors to use violent means without state sanction – remains central to the legitimacy claims made by contemporary states.

Phases of state formation

There is much debate over exactly when the processes of early modern state formation started, with some scholars looking as far back as the eighth or tenth century (Teschke 2003; Tilly 1990). Others cite the early fifteenth century, with the convening of the Council of Constance of 1414–1418 (Wight 1977: 129–52), treaties agreed upon at the Peace of Westphalia in 1648 (see Teschke 2003 for a trenchant critique of this view), or the eighteenth century (Hinsley 1963) as the most significant dates in the development of the modern state.

Taking a middle path I begin this discussion with the fourteenth century, a time when Europe was wracked by conflict. The crisis caused by conflict was made worse by economic recession, plague, widespread crop failures and famine (Braudel 1972). In a short period the population was decimated. Labor became very scarce and those who sought to sell their labor began to move more freely as feudal authority structures lost much of their legitimacy. In short, this was a time of social and political fragmentation and conflict.

Nonetheless, arising out of this devastation, a number of monarchs managed to consolidate their authority in a surprisingly short time, with Spain, England and France emerging as the front-runners. Importantly, these rulers would not have seen themselves as state builders, but they were intent on restoring order in their realms and expanding the reach of their authority. To do this they embarked on programs of centralizing authority and pacification within their 'proto-states' and engaged in war in order to either extend their imperial reach or protect their realms from the imperial ambitions of others (Wallerstein 1974). In so doing they created the foundations of the territorial sovereign state and, at the same time, began to more clearly define the hitherto amorphous boundary between what we now take for granted as the domestic and the international realms. As Tilly (1990: 69–70) notes, as monarchs armed against external threats,

> the state's expansion of its own armed force began to overshadow the weaponry available to any of its domestic rivals. The distinction between 'internal' and 'external' politics, once quite unclear, became sharp and fateful. The link between war-making and state structure strengthened.

Other scholars stress the ideational aspects as well as the material aspects of this transformation. For example, Ruggie (1993) argues that the shift to the modern state was part of a broader transformation in which developments in science and the arts during the Renaissance heralded the development of a uniquely modern, individualistic form of human subjectivity and the spread of private property rights. In this transformation, he argues, the way in which the social world, including dominant forms of political authority, was conceptualized underwent an epochal change, laying the foundations for the 'parcelization' of sovereign possessions into putatively unitary, discrete, bounded territories.

Despite the many differences between scholars over what were the most important factors in this change, there is no doubt that early modern state builders unwittingly played a central role in the transition to a new institutional form, which would be imitated as it proved its viability over time. That the form was imitated does not mean that it did not undergo significant change as the principles of legitimacy underpinning territorial sovereignty changed, as the transformation from the absolutist state to the national and democratic state demonstrates. However, as Spruyt (2002) argues, a certain institutional logic held sway as the *claim* to – and mutual recognition of – a single, sovereign and territorially defined authority as legitimate continued even as the content of that legitimacy changed (Bukovansky 2002; Reus-Smit 1999; Wight 1977: 153–73). By the end of the twentieth century this institutional form – the territorial, sovereign state – would be the first form of political authority in history to be genuinely global in its reach.

State formation in the twentieth century

Central to the globalization of the sovereign state were the processes of imperial collapse and decolonization. The early states were also colonial powers that did not entertain any conception of the rights of colonial peoples to independence. However, by the nineteenth century and into the early twentieth century national sentiment was stirring within many colonial possessions, even if these claims would not come to fruition until after 1945. In the nineteenth century both Italy and Germany became unified national states, and nationalist sentiment was on the rise within the Habsburg, Russian and Ottoman Empires. Greece gained independence from the latter in the 1820s, and Serbia, Romania and Bulgaria followed suit later in the century. World War I dealt the final blow to these Empires. As the conflict drew to a close, a number of groups claimed independent statehood, including Czechoslovakia, Yugoslavia and Poland. Others such as Hungary and Turkey, which had been at the core of Empires were also recognized as sovereign states within newly demarcated boundaries. The tasks faced by state builders varied, but all faced the problem of building a cohesive, legitimate, central authority as well as a unitary national identity. This was not as easy as nationalists might have assumed or hoped. Despite shared ethnolinguistic characteristics, in many cases there were very different histories to be overcome by those that came together in new states. In Yugoslavia, for example, Croatia and Slovenia had been part of the Hapsburg Empire while Serbia, Montenegro and Bosnia had been part of the Ottoman Empire.

Despite these often very different histories, the right to national self-determination that was widely acknowledged after 1918 was based on a racial and ethnic conception of national identity. However, as the populations were extremely heterogeneous, no matter how boundaries were drawn, it was inevitable that a number of minorities would exist within each new state, something that did not 'fit' with nationalist ideology, particularly as these minorities were likely to have loyalties to neighbouring states. This was a distinct possibility when many Germans, Austrians, Russians and Hungarians found themselves outside their 'home' states, giving rise to the fear of irredentism (a territorial claim made by one state to areas under the sovereign authority of another state). At the international level there was much concern that minorities would be vulnerable to discrimination and ill-treatment. For the first time this was seen as an issue for which the international community should take some responsibility. The League of Nations Minorities Treaties were an attempt to set standards for the appropriate treatment of such minorities (Jones 1994). However, the new states that came under the provision of the treaties system saw the treaties as discriminatory, and they were ineffective in protecting minority rights. Furthermore, Germany, regarded as a 'civilized state', did not come under the treaties' system, yet it was here that the Holocaust took the lives of an estimated six million Jews during World War II, as well as those of other minority groups. Thus when formerly colonial possessions gained independence after 1945 the international community shied away from racial or ethnic definitions of the national communities that were to gain independent statehood, referring instead to the existing colonial boundaries as the legitimate boundaries of the new states (Moore 1998; Sellers 1996).

Just as World War I brought the European and Ottoman Empires to an end, so too World War II contributed to the collapse of colonial Empires in Asia and Africa. Claims by non-Western peoples to the right to self-determination were rejected after World War I, but after 1945 they pressed their claims more vigorously. Though some colonial powers (e.g. the Dutch in what was to become Indonesia) resisted these claims, the legitimacy of this form of rule no longer held (Jackson 1993). Since 1945, when the United Nations (UN) had 50 member states at its inception, there are now 192 members, many of which are postcolonial states. So what then was the process of state building that took place in postcolonial states? Under the Declaration of the Granting of Independence to Colonial Countries and Peoples (UN General Assembly 1960), it was asserted that all peoples have the right to independence and that this should take effect immediately without reference to whether or not a country was 'ready' in social, political or economic terms. Cast in terms of a human rights claim (Reus-Smit 2001a), the declaration emphasized the injustices suffered under colonial rule and thus legitimated immediate sovereign independence.

While it is hard to generalize about such a large number of states, these state builders faced a number of different tasks under very different conditions to those faced by early state builders. They inherited domestic institutions that were often inappropriate and were faced with having to govern states that existed territorially and legally but which, once the euphoria of independence had passed, faced problems of maintaining a legitimate central authority and, often, a lack of state capacity (Jackson 1990). They also came into existence in the context of the Cold War which engendered regional instability as the so-called 'proxy wars' were fought while the superpowers maintained a bipolar balance of power (Ayoob 1995). And they were also in many cases faced with the task of creating national identities out of great diversity, as the new boundaries enclosed many different ethnic groups (or in some cases cut across communities). The simultaneous tasks of state building and nation building have been undertaken in different ways but, as Martin Wight foresaw in his prescient discussion of the vulnerability of minorities under the 'majoritarian principle' of legitimacy heralded by this understanding of self-determination (Wight 1977: 168–72), the potential for the ill-treatment of minorities was not allayed by the rejection of race or ethnic identity as the basis of international recognition of the right to self-determination. This vulnerability was demonstrated by the many cases of discrimination and attacks on minorities that were often accompanied by descent into civil war. Aside from this issue, many newly independent states soon suffered instability, elite corruption and the emergence of authoritarian regimes, many of which received arms from superpower patrons during the Cold War. Access to modern weaponry served to buttress the resistance of such regimes to domestic constraints on their authority.

As Tilly (1990) and Spruyt (1994) point out, the institutional structures that came to characterize Western European states developed over a number of centuries as rulers gradually conceded authority to their subjects and refrained from overt coercion, recognizing that this would undermine their legitimacy. States that came into existence in the twentieth century arrived into a very different environment, where external military support could mitigate against claims for democratic government and the need to maintain legitimacy.

As the current processes of democratization in many states, fragile and contested as they are, demonstrate, institutional development on the scale of states takes time, and there is no guarantee that democratic, representative institutions will be the outcome everywhere.

In the post-Cold War era the world witnessed yet another phase of state formation as the Soviet Union collapsed, followed by the violent disintegration of the former Yugoslavia and the peaceful 'velvet divorce' of the Czech Republic and Slovakia. War in the former Yugoslavia witnessed the return of the 'ethnic principle' of state formation in the claims made by nationalists who embarked on programs of ethnic cleansing in attempts to create homogeneous national states. While on one level this was not accepted as legitimate by the international community, in practice conflicting signals were given to the contending parties as concern with maintaining order and stability, based on the recognition of new sovereign states, took precedence over humanitarian concerns (Rae 2002). There have also been conflicts in parts of the former Soviet Union, as struggles over what form the state should take are still being played out in the Central Asia and the Caucasus.

From this brief overview it is clear that more recent state formation has taken place under very different conditions to those of the first phase. The early state makers not only 'made' their states, as they jostled for position against one another they contributed to the creation of the international realm into which later states entered at independence. Thus, as we have seen, in the early, mid-, and late twentieth century new states arrived into an increasingly more institutionalized international environment and were constituted according to dominant norms within this system. Such norms can of course be challenged or revised, as the story of the changing content of self-determination in the wake of the two World Wars and the delegitimation of colonialism demonstrates (Jackson 1993). What this should alert us to is that while we may identify many similarities between states at the international level, we should also be sensitive to the different conditions under which they were constituted and what this means for their current functioning, both domestic and international. This is not an evolutionary argument that there is a single path that all states must pass through. On the contrary, it is a call to recognize that legal recognition as a state (or juridical sovereignty) is an important part of the story. However, states have different histories and varying capacities for empirical sovereignty, for the capacity to function effectively at the domestic as well as the international level. Understanding the relationship between states and their societies becomes important in this context as well (Migdal 2001). The issue that highlights many of these problems is contemporary state breakdown and various forms of humanitarian intervention, which are, however, beyond the purview of this chapter. Leaving this aside, we now turn now to a brief overview of different approaches to state formation.

Contending approaches to state formation

Mainstream theories of IR explicitly bracket off processes of state formation. For example, neorealist scholars such as Kenneth Waltz focus on the anarchic structure of the international system and how it forces states to undertake 'self-help' in the absence of any overarching authority (Mearsheimer 2001; Waltz 1979). Thus, what happens inside states or how states came to exist in the first place is not relevant to such accounts. As long as the basic functions of statehood are performed – a central government that has control over the means of violence, over a defined population and over a defined territory – we do not need to inquire any further into the nature of the state in order to study IR. Other mainstream theories, such as neoliberalism, argue that states do not only operate in terms of self-help but can act cooperatively for mutual gain. Despite this they have shared neorealism's basic assumption that the state can be assumed to be a rational, unitary actor. More recently there is growing recognition of the role that beliefs and norms can play in constituting what is seen as rational both within states and in the international domain (Keohane 2002: 245–71).

The view of the state as a rational, unitary actor was first challenged in the 1980s by critical theorists who argued that rather than regarding states as presocial 'facts' scholars of IR should investigate the way in which states, and the states system of which they are part, are constituted through economic, social, political and cultural practices. Critical theorists argued that there is nothing inevitable about the dominance of the modern state as an institutional form and it should not be taken for granted. Understanding how it had become so dominant would also allow insight into possible changes and challenges to this institutional form. This work drew on the scholarship of sociologists at this time who were concerned that the state had been ignored in their discipline (Evans *et al.* 1985). Nonetheless, most critical theorists were not working specifically on state formation so much as challenging the reification of dominant ideas such as sovereignty and territoriality as well as critiquing the epistemological bases of mainstream theories. I now turn to look at some important contributions specifically concerned with understanding state formation.

Immanuel Wallerstein's materialist account

Materialist accounts, such as that of Wallerstein (1974), explain the development of states and the states system as a function of the world economy, assuming the interests of state builders to be purely economic. While Wallerstein characterizes the disorder of the fourteenth century as the outcome of economic pressures, the fifteenth-century construction of what was to become a new order – involving neither the total collapse of the world economy nor its transformation into a world empire – is understood as a prerequisite of economic resurgence. Thus he argues that the capitalist world economy needed and assisted the centralization of authority within a number of core states such as Spain, France, England and, later, the Netherlands. According to this view 'strong states' were necessary for economic development and so we see their emergence and the development of statism, the claim that states should legitimately be the holders of centralized power, as the prevailing ideology of the world economy. In this account economic factors are clearly seen to determine political outcomes. States were formed in response to the needs of the world economy and they, in turn, were structured differently according to the needs of the world economy. This view has been criticized for being economically reductionist and for failing to account for the more complex relationship between the political, economic and indeed the cultural aspects of state formation. Critics argue that it is not adequate to see states and the states system as merely the political superstructure of the capitalist world economy. For example, in an early critique that gave greater importance to political factors, Zolberg (1981) argued that it was the development of the modern state that allowed the formation and expansion of the capitalist system (for a more recent historical materialist account rejecting the assumption that the development of states and the states system was driven by the 'logic of capital', see Teschke 2003).

Institutional accounts

Institutional accounts also take the economic motivation of actors as a given, though from a position of methodological individualism rather than being driven by the logic of the capitalist system as such. This means that events can be explained as outcomes of the rational choices made by important individual actors, thus assigning importance to the concept of human agency, despite the fact that agents are always constrained by existing institutions. As noted above, even within the same phases of state formation, there were differences between states, and institutional accounts have much to tell us about the choices that state builders made with regard to property rights and the sort of states that resulted from their choices. For example, North and Thomas (1973) argue that the modern state became the most viable form of political and economic organization because it was the most efficient provider of private property rights.

Granted, in the earliest phases of state formation coercion was the most salient means of consolidating power. However, as rulers engaged in internal pacification and external expansion *via* war and dynastic marriages, they needed increased revenue in order to maintain themselves and they chose different options to do this. According to this view, the key to the different paths of development in early modern Europe is the variety of deals that rulers struck in order to raise revenue: the concessions they made, who they made them to and how they made them. Thus the institution of private property rights developed out of the trading of privileges for revenue that occurred between rulers and their subjects, particularly the nobility and the rising merchant class. Those rulers who instituted and enforced private property rights allowed economic efficiency and growth and provided a model of success, while those who continued to support monopoly rights, as in Spain, blocked innovation, efficiency and growth. Thus England and the United Provinces (the Netherlands) became successful capitalist states while Spain, an earlier front-runner, declined.

Despite the emphasis here on institutional choices this could, nonetheless, lead us to assume that the dominance of the institutional form of the modern state was inevitable and that whoever made the most efficient choices within that form dictated which states would be most economically successful. In his account of state formation Spruyt (1994, 2002) argues that the success of the institutional form of the sovereign state against competitors that developed in late medieval and early modern Europe, namely city-states and city leagues, needs to be explained rather than taken for granted. What then made the sovereign state so successful? According to Spruyt, what became the nation-state outlasted its competitors because it could meet both the internal needs of centralized authority and administration, and the external need to be recognized as a legitimate actor that could make and keep agreements in the long term. At the center of these capacities is the concept of territorial sovereignty. The territorial demarcation of the fixed boundaries of the political authority meant that the reciprocal recognition of states as legitimate political actors was possible. Because states were compatible in this way, they could make and keep long-term agreements, and the success of this institutional form meant that others copied it or defected to it.

Spruyt accepts the important role of warfare in state-making but asks why the state was better than its competitors at waging war. Size and military capacity alone cannot explain this, he argues, as at times city-states and city leagues outstripped states on these criteria. What was crucial, in his view, was institutional efficiency, and the key to effective institutional organization was the presence of 'clear sovereign authority'. It is the presence or absence of such authority that, he argues, accounts for 'variation between units'. If we look at the competitors to the sovereign state we see a great many differences. City leagues had no internal borders, no hierarchy, no agreements on weights or currency, and diverse legal codes. Sovereign actors benefited from the leagues' lack of unity. Importantly, lack of a clearly defined sovereign authority made it hard for the leagues to *credibly* commit to international agreements. Like city leagues, city-states had no internal hierarchy, lacked internal unity and made no moves toward the rationalization of economic practices or the unification of legal codes. However, they did survive for quite some time. Spruyt argues that this was possible because the city-states were represented by dominant cities and were thus able to behave like sovereign states – that is, as unitary actors, despite their internal differences – in their external actions, and were thus considered legitimate actors in the international system.

Institutional accounts give important insights into the variation in institutional forms and the bargaining within states between rulers and subjects, mediated by those very institutions. However, it can be argued that the focus on the rational choices made by individuals, which does bring human agency back into the picture, still takes the rational, economically motivated actor as a given, discounting other factors, such as the desire for power or how different identities may lead actors to understand their interests in a number of different ways. In the next section, I discuss the view that it is the desire for power that drove early modern-state building, before concluding this overview with a discussion of constructivist accounts.

Power and state building

There are a number of power-based explanations of state building, which in different ways emphasize the role of violence in the development of sovereign states. Elias (1982) traces the process by which monarchs gained control over the means of violence and taxation, both of which were necessary to further war-making. An important part of this process was the 'taming' of the nobility, which occurred over a long period. The means by which absolutist rulers gained ascendancy, by manipulating the balance of power between the nobility and the bourgeois, is exemplified, Elias argues, by Louis XIV's France. Through this 'royal mechanism', Louis successfully maintained his own position by controlling and manipulating the tensions between these competing groups. According to Giddens (1985: 104–10), two factors drove the development of the state: changes in military technology, and the pressure of the states system as a primary 'source' and 'condition' of state formation. This means he gives priority to the international system as the structure that shapes states as agents. This is despite his avowed interest in providing a theory of structuration that takes into account the dual nature of social structures as both the medium and the outcome of social action. Thus, he emphasizes how military interaction is driven by new technologies, and how the system shapes and defines states as actors. Like Giddens, Mann (1993) emphasizes the military capacity of the modern state. He also identifies three other sources of social power – the economic, political and ideological – and acknowledges the important role that religion played in early modern or 'proto-national' states. However, in his view it is military capacity, aligned with political power, which is crucial in the development of the modern state.

Tilly (1985, 1990) offers a nuanced power-based explanation of state formation that takes into account institutional developments and economic factors. He argues that war and coercion were the driving force behind the formation and early development of states, although, like institutionalists, he acknowledges that as states stabilized and grew they became less coercive as institutions developed and capital and rulers struck bargains with one another. Yet, unlike institutionalists, Tilly rejects the idea that processes of state-building were the outcome of rational choices. Nor does he reduce these processes to a by-product of the development of the capitalist world economy. In his view, states emerged as the contingent outcome of the struggle for power which pushed rulers to consolidate their realms in order to fight wars.

Tilly (1985) identifies how the process of internal consolidation was concomitant with the differentiation of the internal and external aspects of the state. In the early modern period, states had to deal externally with the impact of other states and the pressure from the system of states as it began to take shape. These processes were inextricably bound up with the struggles over centralization, pacification and the construction of single, sovereign identities, all of which were internal to states.As they armed against external threats, states gained an internal monopoly over the means of violence, and the boundary between the internal and the external aspects of states sharpened. Thus, Tilly argues, states made war and war made states.

Tilly was among the first scholars to ask important questions about the contemporary ramifications of the different conditions under which more recently independent states have come into existence. Early modern states might have begun as a form of 'protection racket' whereby state rulers offered protection from threats that they themselves played an important role in creating but, as institutionalists also show us, as Western European states stabilized over time they became less coercive as institutions developed which allowed the mediation of relations between rulers and ruled, or, more lately, national, representative governments and the citizens they are meant to represent. Thus Tilly asks questions about the very different processes that more recent states went through as they formed and what the consequences might be of weak institutional development and the tendency of the means of violence to rest in the hands of the few.

Constructivist accounts

While not discounting the factors discussed above, constructivists pay sustained attention to the importance of normative or ideational structures as well as material structures in the development of states and the states system. Rather than beginning with assumptions about the initiating and structuring effects of the capitalist world economy (Wallerstein), the development of 'efficient' institutions as an outcome of rational choice (institutionalists) or the driving force of the desire for power, they assert that 'identities constitute interests and actions' and that agents and structures are mutually constituted (Price and Reus-Smit 1998: 266–7). They are more likely to ask questions about how the logic of the capitalist system came to be so dominant, the conditions under which certain choices came to be understood as rational, and how power has been understood in different contexts and the consequences of this understanding for how power has been pursued. Thus, to the constructivist

> social realities are as influential as material realities in determining behaviour. Indeed, they are what endow material realities with meaning and purpose. In political terms, it is these social realities that provide us with ends to which power and wealth can be used.
>
> (Finnemore 1996: 128)

From a constructivist perspective, understanding the construction of identities and interests is the key to understanding political action and change in the international system. Thus constructivists seek to trace how intersubjectively constituted identities at both the domestic and the international levels translate into political action. Having said this, there is debate among constructivists as to which level of analysis is most appropriate. For example, Wendt (1994) sidelines the construction of the 'corporate' (i.e. domestic) identity of the state, echoing structural realism, while other scholars emphasize the mutually constitutive relationship between the domestic and the international aspects of state formation (for an overview see Reus-Smit 2005). Leaving to one side Wendt's exclusive focus on the 'social' (i.e. international) identity of the state, in general, constructivists would agree that the development of the new institutional form of the territorial sovereign state was accompanied by the development of new forms of collective political identity and normative structures both within states (Hall 1999; Philpott 2001; Rae 2002) and internationally, as demonstrated in the shift from the dominance of absolutist norms of legitimate statehood to liberal democratic ones (Reus-Smit 1999).

An important early contribution to constructivism is Ruggie's (1993) argument, noted earlier, that the changes that brought about the modern states system represent an epochal shift into a new spatial configuration of political authority – the territorially bounded sovereign state – and into a new 'social episteme' in which the way the world is conceived also radically changed. Like many other scholars, Ruggie's interest in the development of the early modern state, and the entry in the modern epoch that it accompanied, arises from the desire to correct the ahistorical view of the international system held by neorealists, which entails understanding contemporary conditions in historical context. In this case he is interested in whether we are once again seeing an epochal shift toward a new form of sovereign authority, heralded by more diffuse concepts of sovereignty operating in Europe. As a preliminary to examining whether we are currently undergoing epochal change Ruggie returns to what he sees as an earlier ephocal shift, the shift to modern territorial rule.

It is this form of rule, Ruggie (1993: 151) argues, that expresses the 'consolidation of all parcelized and personalized authority into one public realm. This consolidation entailed two fundamental spatial demarcations: one drawn between the public and private realms and another drawn between the internal and external realms.' Ruggie captures the beginnings of the transformation from the medieval to the modern worldview, a process in which ideas of political community were rearticulated from universal Church and Empire to territorially defined sovereign states. However, while the form of the territorial state is indeed one of the hallmarks of modernity, there was an intervening absolutist period in which a hierarchical and dynastic form of authority remained dominant for some time, with competing claims between absolutist rulers who attempted to assert their precedence over one another. With this in mind the political entities that Ruggie describes may be better cast as 'early modern' rather than fully modern. These changes are discussed by constructivist scholars such as Reus-Smit (1999).

Constructivist accounts are open to a number of criticisms that are pertinent to understanding state formation. Although constructivists acknowledge that material factors are as important as ideational ones, much constructivist scholarship to date has, perhaps not surprisingly, tended to focus on the latter and leave the former underspecified. Likewise, if notions of power are socially constructed rather than simply driven by material factors (the greater possession of which allows A to make B do as A wishes), as realists argue, more needs to be done to trace such constructions, both historically and in the contemporary system. In a recent attempt to overcome this lacuna, Barnett and Duvall (2005: 41) argue that because rival accounts to realism, including constructivism, have 'juxtaposed their arguments to realism's emphasis on power, they have neglected to develop how power is conceptualized and operates within their theories'. This does not need to be the case, they argue, and they go on to develop a framework that allows for multiple conceptions of power. From this brief discussion of constructivist scholarship we can see how scholars taking this approach have made an important contribution to understanding the social construction of states and the states system. Nonetheless, further work remains to be done that incorporates analyses of the interaction of ideational and material factors and concepts of power into constructivist accounts of world politics.

Conclusions

The preceding discussion has given an overview of a number of different approaches to the study of state formation in IR and more generally in the field of politics. With this in mind, what conclusions can we draw about studying the state today and, more broadly, about the possibilities for dialogue and synthesis in IR as an academic field of study? At first glance, some of the different approaches discussed here are more amenable to dialogue and possibly synthesis (understood as a combination of different approaches) than others. For example, there is a strand of constructivist scholarship which aligns itself more closely with rational choice approaches, seeing an unproblematic 'division of labour' between approaches that focus on 'interest formation' and 'interest satisfaction' (Reus-Smit 2005: 203). However, this is not always a simple matter as a number of constructivists reject this as resulting in a hollowed-out form of constructivism that has a very narrow focus on interest formation alone, leaving aside questions about how these interests are put into practice (Reus-Smit 2005: 203). Further, this division is underpinned by very different views on the nature of what constitutes valid social science (Kratochwil 2003; Moravcsik 2003) and what this means for how we should go about studying IR. This division echoes the earlier debate between rationalist and critical scholars, highlighting the difficulties, though not the impossibility, of dialogue across epistemological and methodological boundaries (see the debate replayed in various contributions to Hellman 2003).

   The study of the state demands, in my view, an approach that is pluralist and 'question driven'. As Kratochwil (2003: 127) argues, good research arises when scholars identify interesting and important problems and then consider the best ways to go about answering the questions they have, rather than trying to find a problem or question that fits some predetermined template that flies under a particular 'flag' (Katzenstein 1995) or which must adhere to narrowly defined definitions of valid knowledge. If we are concerned with finding important and interesting questions, then Katzenstein's (1995: 14) remark, intended to apply to the study of politics broadly understood, is illuminating: 'Rethinking the past in light of the present and conversely rethinking the present in light of the past are productive ways of searching for important and intriguing questions.' So what then are the questions that might animate the study of the state and processes of state formation today? As noted, states claim not only the right to control the means of violence (and it is both the *claim* to legitimacy and the intersubjectively perceived *legitimacy* of the claim that are important here) but also a monopoly on the right to define identity (Linklater 1990: 149) as well as a monopoly on the right to control the legitimate movement of people (Torpey 1998). If we are looking for important and interesting questions that might animate the further study of the state and state formation, we can ask, what are the principles of legitimacy that hold sway in today's system? What are the legitimacy claims that are made by state builders and are they contested? If so, by whom and how are they contested? Even if they are contested how do they continue: how are they supported both domestically and internationally? What are the implications of answers to these questions for the processes of state building that are still underway in many parts of the world and, in turn, the impact that these processes may have on the states system itself? As we have seen, most accounts of state formation that are on the 'radar screens' of scholars of IR have taken the development of the Western state as their template. Perhaps it is now time to build on the work done so far by looking at non-Western states on their own terms and in terms of the impact that the contested notions of sovereignty or, more accurately, the principles of legitimacy that underpin sovereignty may be having on such states.

As we have seen, the twentieth century saw the globalization of the form of the territorial, sovereign nation-state as part of what Ruggie (1993: 168) describes as 'the spatial and temporal implosion of the globe; the integration of separate and coexisting world systems, each enjoying a relatively autonomous social facticity and expressing its own laws of historicity, into a singular post-Columbian world system'. However, non-Europeans were not just passive subjects of this process and, as Ruggie notes, although the post-Columbian system may be dominant, other social forms coexist with the dominant one. Important areas of further research include investigation of the impact of the particular historical conditions of state formation on the current Islamic fundamentalist challenge to the legitimacy of the international system. Another area of research is suggested by an article in which Acharya (2004) focuses on the potential for normative change in the contemporary Southeast Asian regional system. Beginning with an account of the way in which 'norm takers' in premodern Southeast Asia adapted Buddhism to indigenous societies in practices of norm 'localization', Acharya then investigates two contemporary attempts at norm localization, one of which (the development of the ASEAN Regional Forum) was relatively successful while the other (the Association of Southeast Asian Nations' rejection of the concept of 'flexible engagement') was strongly resisted. Acharya argues that the former was more acceptable as it fits with regionally dominant ideas of territorial sovereignty. The dominance of a more 'absolute' form of sovereign identity in this region can be traced directly to the fight for independence and the legitimating principle of national self-determination. While this is work that is being done at the level of the region, more work needs to be done at the level of state formation and identity construction within relatively recently independent states (including those in Eastern Europe and the former Soviet Union) and exploring what this means for regional politics as well as at the global level. This needs to be work that brings together the sort of empirical accounts seen in much of the work on European state formation, discussed above, with theoretical work on the states system and broader debates about how we should understand the state today.

In this chapter we have reviewed a number of different accounts of state formation which emphasize material, institutional, or power-based factors, with more recent constructivist accounts investigating the social construction of collective identities. While a number of scholars have investigated early state formation in order to better understand contemporary states, IR scholarship would now benefit from more sustained attention to the conditions under which states have formed in the twentieth century and the ramifications of these processes for the contemporary system of states.

Further reading

Jackson, R.H. (1990) *Quasi-States: Sovereignty, International Relations and The Third World*, Cambridge: Cambridge University Press.

Rae, H. (2002) *State Identities and The Homogenisation of Peoples*, Cambridge: Cambridge University Press.

Tilly, C. (1990) *Coercion, Capital and European States, AD 990–1990*, Oxford: Basil Blackwell.

12 International political economy

Tom Conley

Introduction

International Political Economy (IPE) is a relatively new field of inquiry, albeit one with an old pedigree. It emerged in the late 1960s and early 1970s, partly as a result of the inadequacy of the discipline of International Relations (IR) in dealing with global economic changes in that era, but its antecedents can be traced back to the classical political economy of Adam Smith (1723–1790), David Ricardo (1772–1823) and Karl Marx (1818–1883). These great figures considered themselves to be political economists, although the analysis of Smith and Ricardo about the nature of an economy as a 'self-regulating market' led, ironically, to the separation of political economy into two distinct disciplines – political science and economics (Caporaso and Levine 1992: 3). The retreat of economics from politics was formalized by Alfred Marshall's late-nineteenth-century study *The Principles of Economics* (1890). During the twentieth century, economics and political science were consolidated as autonomous areas in the academy, and each expressed little interest in the subject matter of the other. This process had a negative impact on the utility of both disciplines, and the division extended into the international realm. The IR, which emerged as an academic discipline after World War I, pejoratively referred to foreign economic policy concerns as 'low' politics. In a seminal article in the 1970s entitled 'International Economics and International Relations: A Case of Mutual Neglect', Strange (1970: 307) argued that '[i]nstead of developing as a modern study of international political economy, [IR] is allowing the gulf between international economics and international politics to grow yearly wider and deeper and more unbridgeable than ever' (for a mid-1990s reassessment see Strange 1995a). Undoubtedly, IPE has had a far greater impact on those who study politics and IR than it has on those studying economics. This is not surprising given the nature of economics as a discipline and its more rigid methodologies.

This chapter outlines some of the main ways that political and economic factors and forces in both the domestic and the global domains interact, and the way that IPE attempts to understand the complexities and outcomes of these interactions. My central argument is that IPE should retain its propensity to utilize the insights of a wide range of disciplines within the social sciences. In particular, it should retain its focus on the interaction of political and economic variables and resist colonization by economics in terms of subject matter and methodology. Attempts to delineate 'appropriate' topic areas or impose particular methodologies will lead to the same problems that developed over the twentieth century with the distinct separation of political science and economics and the separation of IR into 'high' and 'low' politics. In recent years, the possibility of economism has been reinforced by the dominance of constructions of economic globalization. The process of globalization and the way it is commonly understood provides a significant challenge to the IPE agenda. Arguments about the 'limits of politics' and the 'decline of the state' pose the possibility that political factors will once again be downgraded in the discussion of 'economic' developments and analyses of the 'economy'. The chapter contends, therefore, that a focus on the state as the mediator between the domestic and the world political economies should remain an essential, but not exclusive, component of IPE. Indeed, this is because of, not despite, contentions about a new era of globalization. The chapter also maintains that analytical distinctions between politics and economics, and between the global and the domestic, remain essential to understanding the world, despite pleas to remove dualisms or dichotomies in IPE and the assertion that such distinctions are now meaningless in light of globalization. I argue that the task of international *political* economy remains the investigation of these complex interrelationships and to maintain a focus on the significance of political action.

Defining political economy

Scholars in IPE have varying views on the appropriate subject matter of their discipline. To make some sense of efforts to define IPE, it will be useful to begin by defining 'political economy'. Caporaso and Levine (1992: 7) argue that 'when we say that economics and politics are separate, we mean only that they are analytically distinct'. Such a conception requires a further digression to define what is meant by 'politics' and 'economics'. Politics can be identified with government and governing, with what is public, or with the *authoritative* allocation of values. In contrast, the term 'economic' originates from the ancient Greek language, in which it refers to the management of the household. Today, most economists equate economic activity with the market, and see the market as the best mechanism for producing and distributing goods and services, both domestically and internationally. Hence

> economics and politics are alternative ways of making allocations regarding scarce resources. Politics refers not to the formal structures of government but to a distinctive way of making decisions about producing and distributing resources. Unlike economics, which emphasizes juridically voluntary exchange, the system of political allocation involves authority.
>
> (Caporaso and Levine 1992: 16)

When considering economics and politics as alternative ways to allocate values (and thus separating them analytically), it is necessary to consider the ways that economic factors shape political factors, and vice versa. If we consider politics as the authoritative allocation of values and economics as involving voluntary exchange, it is essential to note that politics shapes the structures within which 'free' exchange takes place and that power derived from free exchange in turn affects the political process. In other words, the two domains of activity are analytically separable but inextricably intertwined. Each is shaped by continuing interaction with the other.

It is also important to note that this definition of politics is a broad one, extending beyond association with what governments or states do. Politics defined as 'what governments do' often contributes to its negative image in public discourse. 'Politics' is often seen as a fundamental impediment to 'the free market', rather than its essential prerequisite. Electoral pressures and excessive societal expectations, many economists argue, impede governments from making 'sound' policy decisions by forcing politicians to make promises and enact policies that are economically suboptimal (for classic statements of this position see Brittan 1975; King 1975). This view has led many to argue that the policy discretion of elected governments should be restricted by constitutional devices at the national and international levels, including independent central banks, balanced budget amendments and liberal international economic governance structures (Gill 1992). Some commentators even argue that one of the major benefits of economic globalization is that it restricts political discretion (Wriston 1992). In this sense, a restrictive definition of politics helps to reinforce the arguments of those aiming to limit the role of government (and political action) in shaping social outcomes that represent alternatives to the outcomes resulting from giving freer reign to economic or market power. Such attempts to limit the role of politics should, of course, be seen as political interventions.

Politics, therefore, is best seen expansively. According to Held and Leftwich (Hay and Marsh 1999: 13) 'politics is about power; about the forces which influence and reflect its distribution and use; and about the effect of this on resource use and distribution'. Economic agents 'act' politically, often attempting to influence and shape the policy process and the distribution of national resources. In certain circumstances, no overt action is even necessary as policy makers realize the potential power of major economic actors to augment or impede their ability to create the conditions for economic growth. Wealth generates potential power and provides the wherewithal for substantive influence on formal policy processes. As a corollary to this, accounts of IPE that focus rigidly on the methodology of economics will only reinforce the problems associated with the separation of politics and economics and culminate in the dominance of economic concerns over political ones. Fundamental to the explanatory power of IPE, therefore, is its catholic character. As Stilwell (2002: 4) points out, '[r]eal world phenomena do not fit neatly into boxes'. Most practitioners of IPE agree that its fundamental strength is that it starts from the assumption of the intertwined nature of politics and economics and the global and the domestic. This does not mean that scholars cannot retain a *normative* preference for, or criticism of, markets, since the various perspectives in IPE (and more widely in IR) have both analytic and normative elements.

The value of theoretical eclecticism

The IPE often describes both a field of study and its subject matter. We can distinguish between them by describing the 'thing being studied' as the world political economy and the 'subdiscipline' as IPE. Within IPE there is significant disagreement about how the world should be viewed or understood. This is as it should be. According to the late Strange (1991), IPE should adopt an eclectic approach to its subject matter. Scholars should also acknowledge and examine the 'basic values which human beings seek to provide through social organization, that is wealth, security, freedom and justice' (Strange 2003: 17). She argued that different systems of political economy vary in the priorities they give to these basic values, which can be illustrated by comparing the political economies of East Asia, Western Europe and the United States. We can learn a great deal about particular societies by considering what values prevail and who gets to decide which values predominate. Gilpin (2001: 24) also argues that the purpose of economic activity is a fundamental issue for IPE: 'Is the purpose of economic activity to benefit individual consumers, to promote certain social welfare goals, or to maximize national power?...The answer is a political matter that society must determine.'

One of the consequences of globalization as both a material phenomenon and an increasingly dominant set of ideas has been the view that questions about values are less important today because of the dominance of economics over politics and the ascendancy of the global over the domestic. In other words, values are now decided by the market or powerful economic actors and, as a corollary, are increasingly irrelevant because they are incapable of being shaped by actions through the formal political process. The idea of political or democratic choice is seen as less relevant in a world where 'there (really) is no alternative' if a country wants to maintain its international competitiveness and living standards. To ask questions about values and to investigate more thoroughly the relationship between politics and economics allows us to think about the way the way the world political economy and individual domestic political economies are structured. It also allows us to question existing arrangements and to interrogate commonsense understandings of the way things (supposedly) are.

According to Stilwell (2002: 4), the most important questions are, 'What is happening? Why? Who gains, Who loses? Does it matter? If so, what can be done about it, and by whom?' A theoretically eclectic IPE helps us to answer these questions by allowing us seek answers from a wide range of sources. The utility of these questions is best illustrated with an example. A pertinent one today concerns the implications of China's rise as a great power.

To answer the question 'what is happening?' we need to consider a range of statistics and analyses of outcomes: China's growth rates, the expansion of trade and investment, the rise of an entrepreneurial class and class divisions, massive environmental damage and much else. Analysts, of course, disagree about what is happening in China. Breslin (2005) argues that interpretations of Chinese power depend in part on whether China is analysed from the 'outside in' or the 'inside out'. The 'outside in' view sees China as increasingly powerful, with the growth of the Chinese economy having a significant impact on particular countries, regional political economies and ultimately the world. In contrast, an 'inside out' view sees China beset by problems and probably unable, over the long term, to maintain the economic dynamism that is the source of its growing political power. Answering the 'why' question is equally difficult. Is China's economic success due to the far-reaching reforms of the late 1970s that ended its isolation from the world economy, or the ability of an authoritarian regime to direct and mobilize resources on a massive scale, or the power of the free market to generate economic dynamism despite the actions of the state? Is there some Chinese or Asian cultural propensity toward economic success which explains why Asian countries in general have been more economically successful than developing countries in other regions of the world?

In relation to 'who benefits', there are a range of approaches that one can adopt. As with all fundamental and rapid changes, there are winners and losers in China. Some people have become very rich in China, whilst many others, especially those who live in rural areas, have benefited less. There has been a reduction in aggregate absolute poverty, whilst at the same time there has been a large increase in inequality. It also might be the case that rising inequality will eventually be ameliorated by state redistribution. The restructuring of the state-owned sector of the economy has also led to problems for many former employees, while party officials have often maintained or enhanced their positions. Obviously, whom we focus on matters enormously for our perceptions of success and failure. Economists generally see what is happening in China as a story of amazing growth, whereas environmentalists see what is happening as a story of devastating environmental damage. Such relative and uncertain processes make the *cui bono* question difficult to answer.

The rise of China matters enormously, not just for those who live in China but for the rest of the Asian region and the wider IPE. Southeast Asian countries have been particularly concerned that the rise of China will divert foreign investment away from them and that they will lose export markets to Chinese competition. At the same time they have seen the possibility that they could be further integrated into an East Asian production structure based on Japan and China. Many in the United States fear that China's cheap labor will have a devastating effect on their employment and wages. A China that can sustain its current rate of economic growth will have the economic clout to become a world power capable of challenging American hegemony. In other words, there are both international political (security) and global economic (distributional) consequences for China's rise, as well as domestic implications within China. The last question, 'what can be done?', assumes that the rise of China will cause problems or at least changes that will need to be dealt with by other countries. What, for example, will (or should) be the reaction of the United States to the possibility of a China capable of challenging its primacy in East Asia and elsewhere? Will the United States 'contain' or 'engage' China and what will be the consequences of the choice? Similarly, how will (or should) the rest of Asia react? Will other states react to China's rise by increasing their economic competitiveness, bolstering their own security or developing regional institutions under China's leadership? These reactions will, in turn, affect the way that China develops.

The wide range of questions that can be addressed *via* an IPE approach are more difficult to answer in the fluid international environment of the early twenty-first century, in marked contrast to much of the Cold War era. During the Cold War, security concerns were predominant in the minds of many policy makers and IR specialists. With the demise of the Soviet Union in 1991, some scholars continued to argue for the fundamental importance of security considerations, focusing on the possibilities for disorder in the post-Cold War world (Ikenberry 1996; Mearsheimer 1990a). They argued that, although there was much anxiety about nuclear war during the Cold War, the prospect of mutually assured destruction led to stability, at least in the developed world (Gaddis 1986; Mearsheimer 1990b). Notwithstanding these debates, it is undoubted that the prime focus of IR as practice and discipline in the West had ended, opening up possibilities for alternative analyses. Fukuyama (1992) believed that the end of the Cold War signaled the unequivocal triumph of liberal democratic capitalism. This 'End of History' analysis was heavily criticized, but reflected a wider belief in the West that liberal capitalism had prevailed over communism and that there really was no better system than that embodied by the United States and the wider West. Fukuyama's thesis stated baldly what many other commentators were thinking – that fundamental political questions had been settled and that what was important for the former socialist world and the wider developing world was to embrace capitalism and gradually develop more democratic forms of government.

At the time of the First Gulf War in 1991, President George H. Bush talked about a New World Order 'where diverse nations are drawn together in common cause to achieve the universal aspirations of mankind: peace, security, freedom and the rule of law' (Crockatt 2003: 110). Bill Clinton, Bush's successor in the White House, argued that precedence had to be given to the economic underpinnings of US power. Despite winning the First Gulf War, George Bush Senior was defeated by Clinton, whose economic focus was immortalized by the phrase 'it's the economy, stupid'. Clinton believed in the opportunities of globalization, and that the United States should use its power to engineer a more favorable environment for US firms. Clinton resisted calls for increased protectionism and argued that, despite the challenges of global capitalism and the negative social effects of economic restructuring, the United States was a net beneficiary of the globalization process. The call was for the United States and other Western countries to 'compete, not retreat' in the face of economic competition. The response of most Western policy makers was to liberalize their economies (although, not in all areas) and to demand that other countries do the same. Particularly important were the lowering of trade barriers and the freeing up of financial and investment regulations. This political reaction to the opportunities and constraints of the world political economy greatly accelerated the process of economic globalization (Conley 2002a).

In the 1990s, 'globalization' became the most important concept in the social sciences, and economic issues appeared to gain precedence over security concerns. Globalization was seen as an inevitable and irreversible phenomenon as countries around the world liberalized their economies and worked to attract investment and increase exports. States, it was argued, would become less important than markets and multinational corporations. According to Luttwak (1993), geopolitics had been replaced by 'geoeconomics'. Ideas about the increasing importance of economic issues, however, while increasing the attractiveness of IPE, accelerated the trend toward economic determinism.

Since 9/11, terrorism and the return to war in Afghanistan and Iraq have undermined the confident assertions of a New World Order and have given renewed credence to realist assertions that, in the final analysis, security is the fundamental issue for states. However, globalization has not been seen to be less important because of terrorism. Indeed, the rise of terrorism has often been seen as a response to globalization (Cronin 2002/03). Confusingly, we now have two dominant phenomena – globalization and terrorism – existing side by side as markers of the twenty-first century.

States, markets and IPE

Related to concerns about the relative importance of, and relationship between, political and economic factors in IPE is the contested analysis of states and markets in the field. What is the relationship between states and markets? Is it complementary or conflictual? Most scholars in the field recognize that the state has been fundamental to the intensifying globalization of the world political economy. As Sassen (1996: 42, 45–6) points out, there has been 'a growing consensus among states to further the growth and strength of the global economy'. The view that states and international economic actors are inextricably opposed entities, both seeking dominance in the world political economy, provides an inadequate understanding of the relationship between states and markets, politics and economics. Unfortunately, this view is promoted by many economic liberals who see the state as 'the problem', impeding the proper functioning of the market. From a different perspective, it has also been encouraged by the social democratic view that state power should be used to maintain the policy structures of the postwar Keynesian welfare state in the developed world.

For Strange (2003: 13–14), what is necessary for an IPE analysis is to 'synthesize politics and economics by means of structural analysis of the effects of states – or more properly of any kind of political authority on markets' and vice versa. Underhill (2000: 821) argues that states and markets 'are not separate *things* as such' and that they should be seen as part of 'an integrated ensemble of governance, a state market *condominium*'. Nevertheless, it is necessary to note that the power resources used by political and economic actors are different. While both can exercise authority, the forms of authority can and should be distinguished. Political actors can more easily call on notions of legitimacy than can economic actors. Care also needs to be taken to avoid under-theorizing the political in political economy.

Nowhere is it as important to emphasize the role of politics as in the description of IPE's broad subject matter. In its widest meaning, the world economy refers to the sum total of economic transactions (both domestic and international), but what is often referred to as the world economy is really a world *political* economy, in which states and other forms of political authority continuously shape economic activity and vice versa. Some economists think of the economy as a separate, self-regulating, entity wherein governments and regulatory authorities play a supporting role that frequently becomes too extensive. The global 'market', however, does not exist independently of politics. Underpinning market transactions is a complex set of political, legal and cultural factors that may be obscured by rhetoric about free markets and *laissez faire*. In his classic work *The Great Transformation* (1944), Polanyi turned the standard liberal version of the relationship between politics and markets on its head. He argued (1957 [1944]: 141) that '[w]hile laissez-faire economy was the product of deliberate state action, subsequent restrictions on laissez-faire started in a spontaneous way. Laissez-faire was planned; planning was not'.

Thus the world political economy is a complex array of economic transactions and politically constructed institutional structures that support these transactions. My use of the term 'world' is deliberate. For some scholars, globalization means that we have moved from an *international* to a *global* world. Over the last couple of decades there has been increasing use of the term 'global' (and globalization) and a shift away from the term 'international' (and internationalization) to describe developments in the world political economy. The distinction implies a qualitative change to a new economic system with international(ization) no longer adequately explaining the extent or quality of economic interactions (Hirst and Thompson 1996; Strange 1994). Dicken (1992: 1), for example, stresses that

> 'Internationalization' refers simply to the increasing geographical spread of economic activities across national boundaries; as such it is not a new phenomenon. 'Globalization' of economic activity is qualitatively different. It is a more advanced and complex form of internationalization which implies a degree of functional integration between internationally dispersed economic activities.

Certainly, it is important to distinguish between different components of the world political economy. Today, financial, particularly currency, markets are highly globalized and trade and production much less so. It is also important to recognize the continuing importance of national economies as conceptual and statistical entities and as sites of political legitimacy. Some writers argue that globalization has made the distinction between the internal (the domestic political economy) and the external (the world political economy) completely irrelevant. Rosow (1994: 473) argues that 'the "world economy" is as much inside the "national" economy as outside, if this distinction continues to make much sense at all'. Such arguments, however, need to note that most economic activity continues to take place wholly within the boundaries of states and most of that which does not is still designated as 'foreign'. Trade, international production and even most financial flows would need to progress much further to make the distinction between the internal and the external meaningless (Conley 2002a). States continue to have considerably more influence over national economic actors than foreign ones and are still able, despite constraints caused by financial and trade liberalization, to utilize macroeconomic and microeconomic policy to influence economic conditions within countries. States also retain the ability to regulate the activities of foreign economic actors operating within their borders, albeit imperfectly, as has always been the case. While the connections between the internal and the external are increasingly intimate and integrated, the continuing articulation of distinct spheres remains valid. State institutions and national regulations still matter and continue to shape the impact of global economic processes on the domestic economic actors and populations. In sum, even though global economic processes and international governance structures moderate the autonomy of the state (to varying degrees), the continuing division of the world into separate territories and formally sovereign states, the strength of conceptions of national identity and culture, and 'national' democratic legitimacy ensure that the distinction between the internal and the external remains highly significant.

Complex interactions: A continuing focus on the state

Despite the contentions of many that IPE needs to move beyond an international focus and state-centrism, it is still essential for students of IPE to focus on the state and the way that states adapt to internal and external forces. This would still be the case, even if the state were 'in retreat' as Strange (1996) and others assert (Friedman 1999; O'Brien 1992; Ohmae 1995; Van Creveld 1999). States are situated between domestic and international society, and governments must manage the constraints imposed by both domains and develop the state's autonomy wherever possible. The state continues to be the preeminent focus for studies of IPE because it is the state that continues to organize adjustment by mediating between politics and economics and between the international and the domestic. As Evans *et al.* note, states are 'janus-faced, standing at the intersection of transnational and domestic processes' (Evans *et al.* 1985: 350). Focusing on the state does not require underestimating the importance of nonstate actors and international organizations, or economic actors such as multinational corporations and financial market actors.

The danger of an increased focus on economic globalization is that it may make the effects of the world political economy appear overwhelming. Just as extensive economic interconnections between countries are a long-standing phenomenon, so is the dilemma facing states in deciding how to adjust to developments in the world political economy. Recent debate about the impact of economic globalization is only the most recent installment in a long-running debate about the effect of the outside world on the inner workings of the nation-state. While external developments have long constrained state actions, states have also long been constrained by their ability to raise revenue and maintain stability – societal factors that have shaped their ability to sustain or strengthen their position in the world political economy. Governments leading state apparatuses in democracies continue to face the constraint of periodic judgment by citizens. Even authoritarian governments must face up to judgments by their societies over time. An understanding of the way that states manage the often-competing pressures emergent from the internal and external domains is integral to understanding the impact of globalization on policy change. Gourevitch's (1978: 911) plea for the continuing importance of politics is perhaps even more relevant 30 years later:

> However compelling external pressures may be, they are unlikely to be fully determining, save for the case of outright occupation. Some leeway of response to pressure is always possible, at least conceptually. The choice of response therefore requires explanation. Such an explanation necessarily entails an examination of politics; the struggle

among competing responses. The interpenetrated quality of international relations and domestic politics seems as old as the existence of states.

Held and McGrew (1993: 265) make an important distinction between sovereignty – 'the political authority within a community' – and autonomy – 'the state's capacity to act independently'. Accordingly, 'sovereignty is only eroded when it is displaced by forms of "higher" and/or independent authority which curtail the rightful basis of decision-making within a national polity'. States continue to be the locus of authoritative, but not necessarily effective, decision-making, developing institutional structures that both mediate and shape the effects of the world political economy (Pauly 1995). Thus the story of financial discipline is much more complex than the more breathless accounts of financial globalization would suggest. For example, financial market discipline from global markets, it is often argued, will force governments to curb their spending. However, the ratio of rich-country government debt to GDP has expanded enormously during the supposed era of financial discipline. Increased financial market discipline on the expansion of public debt in OECD countries has not taken place overnight.

Even in economic liberal arguments, the notion of an unequivocal reduction in the role of the state is misleading. Those advocating a reduction in the role of the state do not advocate a reduction in *all* of the state's functions or of state power. Instead, the focus is usually on decreasing the state's redistributive functions. Those arguing for welfare state retrenchment often (at the same time) generally support an increase in the state's policing and security roles. There is now an extensive literature countering the view that globalization weakens the state (Conley 2002b). Unfortunately, it is also the case that the more nuanced academic debate about globalization continues to be ignored by many in the public arena (Hay and Rosamond 2002; Mosley 2005; Rosamond 2003).

Arguments about the effect of globalization on the state also need to take into consideration the enormous expansion of the state over the twentieth century, particularly after World War II. As Dunn (1994: 3–4) argues, each of the three pivotal events of the twentieth century, the two World Wars and the collapse of Communism, 'drastically extended the nation-state as a political format and strongly reinforced it as an ideological option'. The 'crisis of the state' in an era of globalization is more accurately understood as a crisis of continuing societal expectation about what the state should do (Dunn 1994: 12; Waltz 1999). Governments have not yet been able to extricate themselves from managing the deleterious effects of market processes, but through efforts at public persuasion and through coercive policy changes, policy makers have worked on reversing expectations about the state's protective and redistributive functions. As Ikenberry (1995) contends, the advanced capitalist states have tried to reduce the public's expectations about what national governments are responsible for doing and achieving. The goal is to reduce some of the state's perceived responsibility for social and economic well-being, and thereby remove it as an object of blame and resentment. The gradual shift to more liberal economic policies since the breakdown of the postwar international economic order and the economic woes of the 1970s and 1980s needs to be seen as both an *economic strategy* to reinvigorate economic growth as well as a *political project* that has aimed to establish market governance and reshape public expectations about the role of the state. Pressured by both external and internal developments and forces, states have attempted to offset the challenges to external autonomy by shifting adjustment onto domestic society (Conley 2002b).

Finally, it is important to note that when using a generic term like 'the state' we do not assume that all states are the same. Important differences exist among the 192 members of the United Nations. To be sure, during the twentieth century and particularly since the end of the Cold War there has been a considerable increase in the number of democratic states, but vast differences remain between political regimes. There are also fundamental differences in terms of power and wealth. Some countries have states only in the weakest sense, unable to effectively rule their territories. At a more refined level of abstraction and theory building, generalizations about a generic 'state' are problematic. This is an important reason why IPE analyses need to be melded with those from comparative political economy. There are also important differences between large and small states. Major powers can shape the way the world works, influencing the structures within which all states and societies must operate. It is unlikely that small states will be able to change the way the world economy 'works', so the brunt of adjustment for them must be borne domestically. This may be achieved by protection, compensation or liberalization (or, most likely, a combination of all three). Some domestic factors cannot be adjusted, at least not in the short term, but others *are* manipulable. Adjustment strategies will, in the main, be a product of domestic political struggles that are influenced by economic forces and international developments. Many different forms of adjustment are possible. Who and what is 'adjusted' is the pertinent question. Choices of adjustment strategies will be heavily influenced by the political process and the strength of particular interests and their ability to form coalitions (Ikenberry 1986a). In examining such choices across societies, the *autonomy* of the state and its *capacity* to adapt are crucial concerns. With policy makers aiming to open economies more fully to globalization and move to more market-based regulatory structures, capacity is the ability of a state, in Cox's (1992: 31–2) words, to 'adjust national economic practices and policies to the perceived exigencies of the world political economy' (Cox 1987). Increasingly from the 1980s, the political outcome that has been sought by policy makers is to adapt to international and domestic pressures by reducing the state's direct control over, and responsibility for, economic outcomes. Halliday (1994: 81) argues that 'participation in the international realm enhances and strengthens states' and 'enables them to act more independently of the societies they rule'. But it is not society as a whole from which states seek independence or autonomy, only particular sections of it. Governments have increasingly sought to adjust to the challenges of globalization by enhancing state autonomy from domestic opponents of the globalization project. While many states have undoubtedly succeeded in globalizing their economies, they have been significantly less successful in removing themselves from responsibility for economic outcomes.

Conclusion

In many ways, this chapter is an analytical and normative plea to maintain the role of political analysis in our understanding of the world political economy. The IPE needs to be wary of colonization by economics, particularly given the dominance of globalization as a frame of reference. Even if it were true that globalization had weakened the state and downgraded the importance of politics – defined as the ability of individuals and groups within societies to shape their destinies through electoral choices, pressure and persuasion – this would not reduce the importance of a *political* economy analysis. It would still be necessary to consider the political factors – defined in terms of power – that had led to this situation. In other words, it would still be essential to attempt to answer who and what has structured this outcome. In a world where economics takes center stage, the power of politics to shape outcomes may only be evident in the aftermath of traumatic and destabilizing events. Politics should never be underestimated.

Further reading

Gilpin, R. (2001) *Global Political Economy: Understanding the International Economic Order*, Princeton, NJ: Princeton University Press.

Philips, N. (2005) *Globalizing International Political Economy*, Basingstoke: Palgrave Macmillan.

Scholte, J. (2005) *Globalization*, 2nd edn, Basingstoke: Palgrave Macmillan.

13 Worldviews and international political theory

Anthony J. Langlois

Introduction

Thousands of children die each day of mostly resolvable poverty-related causes. Millions of displaced persons live on contested borders and in refugee camps – for many of these people, such camps are the only 'home' they have known. In other parts of the world, the 'camps' resemble another form of lost freedom, where multinational corporations (MNCs) provide employment at rock-bottom wage rates, complete with mandatory and highly restrictive accommodation systems and private militias for security. Within the Global South, the so-called 'failing states' have lost all but notional sovereignty over their populations and territory. In addition, the twenty-first century has witnessed the return to prominence of religion on the international stage (Carlson and Owens 2003; Norris and Inglehart 2004; Petito and Hatzopolous 2003). Religion was, of course, a significant factor in the creation of the modern international system (Philpott 2001). The Treaty of Westphalia (1648) was in large part a response to wars that were caused by religious difference, and the Westphalian resolution subsequently subordinated religion to reason of state as a legitimate justification for war. The 9/11 and subsequent events have signaled a need to again engage with the question of religious violence in the international system. The religious fundamentalism that motivates and supports contemporary terrorism has complex roots. It has been argued that this particular clash, often billed as a 'clash of civilizations' between the West and Islam, will form the ideological structures that will shape International Relations (IR) for the foreseeable future (Huntington 1997).

Religious terrorism is condemned as a violation of the human rights of those who are terrorized. But, in one of the ironies of political life, some of the measures that have been put in place in and between states since the 11 September 2001 attacks have also demonstrated a lack of regard for human rights – the human rights of regular law-abiding citizens, along with those of people either suspected of or shown to have been involved with terrorism. In the name of security, civil liberties have been forgone, fundamental political principles have been overturned, and egregious breaches of protocol have been sustained. Both in the pursuit of terror suspects and in the provision of new regulative and legislative frameworks for security within and between states, governments have undermined many of the principles that – by virtue of being nonarbitrary and accountable regulators of the exercise of power in the pursuit of justice – set orderly government apart from the behavior of terrorists. The 'war on terror' falls into incoherence and internal contradiction if it is initiated and waged on any other basis than respect for human rights. This observation takes us back to one of the most influential traditions of thought about war within the field of IR, the just war tradition (Walzer 2000, 2004). For a war to be just, two sets of criteria must be met: those that deal with the justice of the initiation of a war; and those which deal with the justice of the prosecution of the war. On this basis, the war against terror will not be a just war if it is waged in a manner that undermines the rights of those whom it seeks to protect or, of those whom it seeks to protect us against (Bellamy 2005).

The necessity of international political theory

These introductory observations about our world raise many questions. The debates with which we engage in an attempt to provide answers to these questions are debates within international political theory. Before elaborating on the nature and development of this academic discipline, let us look again at the examples that I have given and probe them again, observing the ways in which they set before us problems which cannot be interpreted and understood, let alone resolved, without drawing on complex intellectual traditions within political theory.

First is the issue of poverty-related morbidity for children (on world poverty more generally, see Pogge 2002). The statistics regarding child morbidity are horrifying. And, given the likelihood of this strong emotional response, they are useful statistics to use when urging change in IR. The danger, however, along with many statistics of this nature, is that they cause a 'we must do something' reflex, which can lead to counterproductive measures (Kennedy 2004). There are two issues here. First, why is it that we *must* do something? Second, if we must, how should we proceed in our attempt to ameliorate the problem? The first question is about political and moral responsibility – the sense that something must be done flows from deeply held commitments, for example, to the equality of all persons, and thus to the conclusion that it is wrong for one to live in luxury while children die for want of food in a world of plenty (Singer 2002). But where do such ideas come from, and why should we think them justified? These questions may disturb us when applied to our responses to the facts of child morbidity, but they are more obviously necessary when – having agreed that we must do something about the problem – we ask, 'what shall we do?' Is it legitimate, for example, to raise a tax on financial market transactions, and to then give the money to these children and their communities? It is all very well to speak of raising taxes, but who shall do it? Individual states? The United Nations? What are the grounds upon which one should be preferred to the other? To generalize from this specific problem, is it better for global issues to be managed by states operating autonomously or in concert, or for states to be managed by global authorities? Is the latter option realistic? Can we expect states to cede much of their authority to global authorities, and at what cost?

Further questions along these lines arise from my second example concerning displaced peoples and failing states. In the traditional story of IR, the state is the primary political agent, and all people are assigned to a particular state that 'acts' on behalf of its citizens. This assumption is clearly difficult to uphold under contemporary circumstances, raising the question of whether other states or the United Nations should intervene in the so-called 'failed states'. Contemporary debates over the ethics and politics of humanitarian intervention require us to attend to our basic assumptions and presuppositions about the nature of international political community.

The same is the case for the question of our responses to terrorism and religious violence in international affairs. There are many questions that have been thrown up for scrutiny in the wake of 11 September 2001. One of the most fundamental is the question of the proper relationship between religion and politics. Western liberal democracies have, since the Enlightenment, proceeded on the basis of an institutionally entrenched separation between church and state. This is a separation that some would argue has no analogue in the Islamic religious tradition, thus complicating the pursuit of clear and legitimate lines of authority and responsibility for the prevention of terrorist activity. Furthermore, the manner in which the 'coalition of the willing' led by the United States has promulgated the 'war on terror' has caused further confusion regarding due process. As noted above, great confusion has been stirred about the just nature of the war because of the apparent inconsistency between the ways in which different constituencies have been treated. Universal human rights have been granted selectively, if at all, to those in the path of the military juggernaut. This poses in acute form one of the oldest questions for international political theory. Does might make right? If we are committed to the normative position that might does not make right then, among other things, international political theory is about setting out and defending alternative accounts of the nature of justice.

These reflections on the state of the world involve different accounts of the nature of justice and its application in political life, both at the level of the individual, the group and the state, and in the international arena. A common interpretation of the traditional realist position is that justice is irrelevant in the international world of *realpolitik*: might alone makes right (see, however, Lebow 2003 for a different reading of realism). At the other end of the spectrum are those who argue for the fundamental salience of justice by linking it to the well-being of each individual human person, frequently using the language of human rights (Tan 2004).

At whatever point one begins on this continuum, however, international political theory *is* being done: claims are being made about the nature (or absence) of political association, the nature of community, the prerogatives (or limitations) of sovereignty, what is due to the individual, and the legitimacy of different kinds of action (or inaction). This is equally true whether one is a realist or a liberal internationalist. The evident necessity of international political theory to these different worldviews makes it all the more strange that, for most of the twentieth century, the discipline of IR routinely set itself apart from other disciplines within the field of politics, claiming – among other things – that there was no room for ethics, normative theory or political philosophy within its remit (Boucher 1997: 193–213). The key point of my argument, however, is that the worldviews that we use for our evaluation of IR will always and inescapably have normative or evaluative dimensions built into them (Frost 1996, 1998). Consequently, our worldviews themselves are political. By claiming variously to observe, create, monitor and evaluate the world in which we live, they become part of a larger political landscape in which they also are a feature. They do not and cannot function merely as the tool or instrument by which we see the landscape; they are inevitably themselves a part of that landscape (Walker 1993).

International relations and international political theory

Why has discipline expressed so much skepticism about the role of ethics, the legitimacy of normative theory and the salience of political philosophy to the study of IR? There are three main reasons. The first is historical, deeply related to events of the twentieth century, both within the subject matter of our discipline as well as within the discipline itself, shaping the ways in which it has pictured itself including its incorporation of particular forms of knowledge (Lawson 2002). Second, there is a set of ideological reasons. The IR has long been dominated by realism, which contains a distinctive set of views regarding the pertinence of ethical matters. Third, there is a set of epistemological reasons. North

American IR in particular identified itself within the academy as one of the social sciences, and a key legitimating factor for its claim to such status was its association with positivism.

The Treaty of Westphalia in 1648 is of great significance for students of international affairs because it allegedly marks the commencement of the modern interstate system, or the Westphalian system. Following Westphalia, we see the progressive codification of a system of governance that has subsequently spread over the globe. Perhaps the most crucial factor of the Westphalian settlement for our purposes is the role that it plays in the telling of disciplinary history. Westphalia marks the point, it is often assumed, at which IR became something different to the study of politics in general. The consolidation of the modern state system – with its characteristic anarchical structure, balances and concerts of power and, crucially, its alleged autonomy from the political activity that took place *within* the state – is taken by many twentieth-century commentators to have signaled the need for the creation of a new academic discipline. Among other things, this discipline should be intellectually structured by modes of study appropriate to its object (Hutchings 1999: 21). Consequently, as this story is told in the twentieth century, the influence of realism and positivism meant that many of the theoretical resources used in the study of politics more generally were deemed inappropriate to the study of this autonomous disciplinary arena.

It is important to stress this latter point, for while the Westphalian consolidation is dated from 1648, it is only in the twentieth century that the study of IR becomes so critically self-conscious, and self-confident, that it intellectually and institutionally isolates itself from the broader study of politics, economics, history, law and philosophy. Right up until the interwar years of the twentieth century, the subject matter of IR was studied within these broader disciplines, and it is only with the end of World War II that the study of IR became the academic discipline of IR – furthermore, a discipline that saw its subject matter, and therefore its modes of study, as *sui generis*. International relations were claimed to be different from all other social relations. The corollary claim was that they needed distinctive forms of academic discourse (Brown 2002: 2).

Westphalia may have marked the consolidation of the modern international system. It is alongside two other historical events of the twentieth century, however, that the discipline of IR as a *sui generis* discipline developed. These were the great wars of the twentieth century (Knutson 1992: 184–212). The horror of World War I precipitated the creation of a wide range of university chairs in IR in Britain and the United States, which became the institutional hubs for the creation of a whole new generation of scholars with a principled commitment to the new discipline. The significance of the Wars, however, cannot be limited to these institutional innovations – these in themselves were a response to something far more fundamental: a ground-level shift in the *zeitgeist*, an intense and deeply emotional reevaluation of how IR should be considered.

Despite the signs of looming conflict prior to 1914, the intellectual tenor of early-twentieth-century Europe was optimistic and idealistic. The general belief was that European civilization had outgrown its violent and irrational past. This belief was shown by the 1914–1918 war to be a serious error of judgment that needed to be rectified by the application of scientific thought to the questions of human social and political arrangements (Brown 2002: 60). Consequently, a sustained critique of various forms of liberal thought regarding IR developed during the interwar period. These critiques were to be reinforced by the coming of World War II. By the time we get to the end of World War II, in English-speaking countries a new institutional network is in place for the study of IR. From the outside world a series of cataclysmic events undermined the liberal predispositions of an earlier era and provided a foundation for a new pessimism about international affairs. These developments coalesced to reinforce the *sui generis* conception of the study of IR, and reinforced the marginalization of what came to be called 'normative concerns' within the new academic discipline.

As noted, the end of World War I precipitated a significant intellectual critique of liberalism. Prominent among the critics were a number of thinkers who proved to be seminal influences in the newly emerging discipline of IR. Ironically, it was the United States' last great public theologian who shaped the moral sensibilities of a generation or more of IR scholars (Lovin 1995). Reinhold Niebuhr (1892–1971) engaged with both the intelligent layman and the academic in his elaboration of the human condition, an elaboration that was deeply rooted in the theological pessimism of the Augustinian tradition about what it was possible for human community to create by way of salvation on earth. Individual persons have moral capacities, and should use these in the best way they know how in their thought and action; but these capacities are limited, finite – in theological language, human beings are 'fallen' and subject to original sin. Our capacity to find security in collective action is thus highly circumscribed, as is well expressed in the title of one of his key texts, *Moral Man and Immoral Society* (Niebuhr 2002 [1932]).

Two other key texts of the period are worth noting: *The 20 Years Crisis* by Carr (1946) and *Politics Among Nations* by Morgenthau 2005[1948]. While Morgenthau's work builds on the general framework laid out by Niebuhr, Carr's argument provided a justification for the new discipline which was to prove enduring – and which would also prove deeply unsympathetic toward an understanding of international politics that would prefer to see no fault line between it and the categories used for the analysis of politics in general. In particular, Carr gave the discipline a strong theoretical dichotomy as its basic working principle, that between 'realists' and 'idealists' or 'utopians' (Hutchings 1999: 15–16). As did Niebuhr, Carr and Morgenthau argued that liberalism's insistence that the common interests of peoples were achievable through cooperation overlooked certain realities in IR. For Carr, these realities were interpreted via a quasi-Marxist intellectual framework, and had to do with the nature of scarcity and the predilection of the rich to use rough means to keep what they have – wealth, status, power and control of world affairs. Liberal politics had failed to appreciate this reality. Its goals and objectives were, therefore, idealistic and utopian. For all the sophistication of Carr's analysis, his generalized legacy in the discipline was a tendency to dismiss any other approach as one which did not deal with the real world, but with a world which – however desirable – was nonetheless a liberal fiction, the world as the utopians wished it to be.

These theorists set the tone of IR scholarship throughout the twentieth century until the end of the Cold War, and it was a tone that sat comfortably with both historical events and the Western intellectual milieu more broadly. Putting these two together, we may identify five characteristics that came to predominate the newly emerging discipline. First, it was skeptical with regard to all claims to do with values, ethics or normative concerns. Following on from the perceived failure of liberal ideals to generate collective security and a measure of international harmony, realism settled for a generalized moral skepticism, which in turn was based upon an egoism that saw only varieties of self interest at the heart of human behavior. The state acted in its interests to retain its power and ensure its survival. Any other 'norm' would prove to be an elaboration of these prior interests, or mere window dressing. Second, in an anarchic world there were no moral laws beyond the sovereign law of the state. The state's sovereignty could not be abrogated by appeals to supra-state authority of any sort (legal, moral, religious, metaphysical). Third, and by corollary, realism was universal. It applied at all times and in all places. Fourth, this was a factual – realist – account of the way the world is; it was not another ideology or set of normative preferences. Finally, and as a further implication of realism's universalism, it was ahistorical. Realism did not conceive of itself as an expression of the mood of its day, as a consequence of a particular set of historical circumstances or as an analytical or policy approach that may only be temporarily relevant. It was the final word on the nature of things in IR.

This last conclusion was significantly fostered by the rise of the new social sciences within the academy and, in particular, with the adoption of positivism as their epistemological guide. As is well known, it was a widespread ambition of the new social sciences as they emerged in the twentieth century to be for the study of the social world what the so-called 'hard sciences' were for the study of the physical world. Central to this ambition was the idea of science as a unified field of knowledge (Smith *et al.* 1996: 11–44).

The key distinguishing feature of positivism is its reliance on empirical validation or falsification as the hallmark of any legitimate scientific inquiry (Smith *et al.* 1996: 15). Knowledge was derived, and was only to be derived, from the observation of regularities – the familiar ideal here is the test-tube experiment: a scientific experiment that is observable, repeatable and falsifiable. Such observation is the only ground for justified belief. The overwhelming salience of the rise of positivism and its centrality to the new social sciences for our present purposes is the way in which it combined with the historical events of the twentieth century and the ideological consequences of realism to produce a profound and lasting skepticism regarding the application of ethics, normative theory and political philosophy within the international arena (Frost 1996). Because of the empirical validation criterion that positivism imposes for anything to count as knowledge and because of the dichotomous fact/value distinction that this criterion creates, most if not all of the substance of those academic disciplines out of which the study of IR was traditionally done was disqualified from the status of 'real knowledge'. Philosophy, ethics, history, political theory, law and economics – these were not disciplines that, as classically practiced, could develop knowledge that counted under the strictures of positivism. These disciplines, along with others in the humanities, were considered speculative, or 'soft'. Their knowledge was considered to be subjective, because it was not able to be tested and verified using the strict methods of a verificationist empiricist epistemology (Smith *et al.* 1996: 15). Knowledge that was subjective was not real knowledge. At best it could be said that it had an inner mythical truth for the person concerned – such as the truth of a particular interpretation of a poem, or the truth of one's personal identification with a religious image or a certain set of moral norms. But it was not the kind of truth that was required for science (Brown 1992: 82–106).

Fortunately, it is increasingly acknowledged that the social sciences cannot do without the theoretical and philosophical disciplines that provide the values and norms upon which social science rests. Much of this argument is encapsulated in the phrase 'the theory laden nature of scientific method'. Norms inevitably have a place in our social scientific investigations. This is because 'facts' do not exist, as they were portrayed under the light of positivism's fact/value dichotomy, where facts were given autonomous freestanding objective status, apparently unalloyed with the subjective and therefore unscientific stuff of human values and norms. Rather, postpositivists recognize that while of course there are facts (sometimes called 'brute facts'), these do not stand freely and independently within human knowledge. They are not, as it were, self-interpreting (Smith *et al.* 1996: 20).

Our recognition of facts as facts, our understanding of them and our capacity to know what to do with them, how to treat them, how to note, measure, monitor, report or evaluate them – all these capacities require more than positivism routinely asserts that we need in the way of untrammeled access to the way the world is through our direct observations. Indeed, some postpositivists argue that there is no direct observation of facts (Frost 1998). Our very capacity to observe facts is governed by the conceptions we have regarding what facts are and what facts there might be. These conceptions are the consequence of theories that we carry with us about what is in the world (ontology) and how to know things in the world (epistemology). Such theories are always and fundamentally normative and evaluative in character.

In some parts of the academy, particularly those broadly classified as the humanities, the claims of positivism have often been treated with a great deal of skepticism, while the role of theoretical and philosophical thought in mediating and shaping human knowledge has never been questioned. What we see in IR through the last two decades or so of the twentieth century is a growing openness to, and an increased intellectual self awareness of, the role that considerations variously described as philosophical, normative and ethical inescapably play in the way in which the subject matter of the discipline is approached and engaged.

A greater self-reflective awareness about the role that theories play in IR is very important from the point of view of the ethical possibilities that are opened to us as a consequence of different ways of doing IR. A useful analogy here is to think of worldviews of IR as frames through which we see and understand the world. As frames, worldviews are crucial, because they circumscribe what we can see, and thus they give grounds for a particular interpretation of international politics. The crucial role that a frame plays with a work of visual art is to highlight the outer limits of that which is depicted. The implication of this way of looking at the matter is that there is material there in the world that is not included in the picture because of the frame. The frame sets the picture. There are contested interpretations of works of art where the point of contestation centers around the relationship between what is in the picture, and 'something' that – for example – the person in the picture may be responding to. But we cannot see this 'something', so we do not know what is really going on. Worldviews of IR are often in the same situation: they are necessarily limited, both by the intellectual milieu out of which they spring, their historical time and place, and by our finitude as human beings. One key issue that arises here is the way in which ethical possibilities will then be constrained by our worldviews. Those that deny the possibility of change, or which insist on the inevitability of violence or which relegate certain classes of agents to a permanent backseat in international affairs – these theories will necessarily be blind to ethical possibilities of progress (Crawford 2002).

Another way of pushing this argument even further would be to change the analogy slightly from picture frames, in the context of art, to the idea of 'being framed'. Here it is a person who is framed, in the sense of being falsely accused, or 'set up'. The point is to think about the ways in which our worldviews might 'set up' the 'realities' of IR. A key example here may be the question of agency in IR (Wendt 1999). Worldviews have very sophisticated accounts of who may or may not be an agent in IR. Realism, for example, is commonly characterized as granting almost sole agency to the state. All other actors are seen as peripheral to the role that the state plays. Such a strong vision of the role of the state goes along with a very constrained set of ethical possibilities within IR – a set of possibilities that might be augmented by admitting other agents and actors. Much criticism of realism has been over this issue, which is a clear example of how the epistemological and ontological assumptions of our worldviews constrain us to 'see' only a certain range of outcomes, which in turn constrain the possibility of ethical intervention. If, however, the theory is limited, or inadequate, then the 'realities' and ethical possibilities of IR have indeed been 'framed' – in the sense of being set up and unnecessarily limited.

Proponents of international political theory would argue that it is precisely because of the way in which worldviews in IR have 'set up' or framed both the subject matter of the discipline and the way in which the discipline itself has been understood that there has been such a marginalization of ethics, normative theory and political philosophy within the discipline. The postpositivist recognition that worldviews provide frameworks within which we work, and through which we apprehend the realities of international politics, and that these worldviews are necessarily predicated on evaluative and normative assumptions and presuppositions has opened once again a space within the discipline for overt discussion of the political theory which lies behind our interpretations of IR. In what follows, I will give an indication of some of the key issues that are presently on the agenda for discussion within this space.

The one and the many

As Brown (2002: 76) rightly suggests, it is possible to argue that there is only one central problem at stake in all the discussions about international political theory. This is the question of how, in the context of any specific issue, we find the right relationship or balance between universalism and particularism. Universalism provides us with general laws, norms or principles, which have application in all situations and purport to cover all contingencies. Particularism, by contrast, points up the individual nature of those contingencies, and is the basis for the argument that since individual cases are never exactly alike, they should never be treated exactly alike. Thus universalism gives us a general blanket account of matters, whereas particularism urges us toward a 'case by case' approach. The tension between universalism and particularism is the creative tension at the heart of international political theory.

This tension is most fundamentally exemplified in the original terms of the Westphalian system itself. There we have the creation of a universal system of modern nation-states in which each nation-state is granted the maximum degree of particularist autonomy possible within a universal system. This was done, as is well known, by giving each state complete responsibility for the nature of the political community that was to exist within its borders. It was facilitated too by a world in which it was possible to maintain the view that interdependence with others was contained by borders. Today, the norms of the Westphalian system – with pride of place given to the particularism and autonomy of individual states – are the principal norms of international affairs exemplified in the doctrine of state sovereignty (Jackson 1990).

Nonetheless, increasingly we see the development of additional universal norms, besides those of the minimalist framework of sovereignty provided by the Westphalian system. The development and implementation of human rights norms over the last half century or so has been the key development here, and one of crucial significance (Dunne and Wheeler 1999). This is because the claim of universal human rights is that they trump state sovereignty. For states to retain their political legitimacy they must operate within the framework of human rights. This represents a broad shift from the rights of states within IR, to the rights of individuals, a shift that is central to many of the key issues on the international political theory agenda. For example, not only in discussions of human rights themselves, but also in debates over humanitarian intervention, poverty, refugees, cultural identity and diversity, the movement from a world in which sovereign states may do what they like, providing only that they respect the rights of other states, to a world in which states are to be constrained (by themselves or by other mechanisms) fundamentally on the basis of how they treat individual human beings is the key movement which animates contemporary discussions. To take one particularly pertinent question today, how do we find the right balance between universalism and particularism in the case of humanitarian intervention? What is at play here in the movement from a world denominated in states' rights to a world denominated in human rights? At its broadest level the debate on this topic goes to the heart of what it means to be humane or indeed to the question of who truly qualifies as being human. And even at this fundamental level there is a fundamental balance to be struck between respect for autonomy and paternalistic engagement. A respect for autonomy can indicate equal regard, a regard which may allow people or states to damage themselves without hindrance within the context of nonintervention; whereas a paternalistic engagement may allow states to intervene in a manner which has humanitarian results, but which is predicated upon unequal regard – a regard which does not recognize equal rights or standing within the community. These ambiguities haunt the history of humanitarian intervention.

Earlier I noted that the Westphalian system has come to be a global universal structure for international affairs. It was not always so. Those European states which formed the core of Westphalia also had humanitarian concerns about the rest of the world, but these concerns operated within a context where the rest of the world did not have the rights of European states. Humanitarianism was expressed in a context replete with European ethnocentrism, racism and imperialism. In this context, we might argue, being humane was a form of charity; humane interventions were not mandated by justice and equality but by a volunteerist conscience (if not merely a self-serving interest). This was because, at a basic level, the articulation of what it meant to be human was to be European – or, at least, Christian. Thus, what we have seen fulfilled since the end of World War II is the universalization of the Westphalian system beyond Europe. In turn, it has expanded the categories of other human beings about whom we should be interested for humane reasons from those with whom we have ethno–religious links. The major development in IR that now under-girds our discussions of international justice is the emergence after World War II of the international human rights regime. The touchstone for the human rights regime is the Universal Declaration of Human Rights, promulgated by the United Nations in 1948. This document, along with the human rights law instrumentalities that have followed in its wake, has collectively provided the international community with an aspirational ethical constitution. The various human rights declarations and instrumentalities put forward standards of behavior below which no person or state should fall in their treatment of another. Needless to say, international politics continues to be a field in which such standards are frequently breached; but their development, and their affirmation even by those who offend against them most egregiously, is a significant milestone for international ethical cooperation (Langlois 2001).

While the development of the international human rights regime is often taken to be a boon, especially for those concerned with the many issues listed above, the regime is no panacea (Benhabib 2004). Indeed, it is a paradigm case of Brown's claim that there is only one central issue in international political theory: the question of how we find the appropriate balance between particularism and universalism.

This question dominates contemporary debates about human rights. On the one hand, the moral claims of the human rights regime are universal ones. In contrast, within the Westphalian system, states were granted complete autonomy with regard to the nature of the political community which pertained within their borders, providing they met only a very few requirements regarding how they related externally to other states. Putatively, that has all changed with the adoption of the Universal Declaration on Human Rights. The adoption of this document and the regime that has followed in its wake makes it a requirement that the internal workings of states meet certain minimal standards, which are routinely scrutinized. Needless to say, this is an ideal account of how the system might work; but even given the vastly incomplete application of the human rights regime, what we have is a fundamental change in the balance between particularism and universalism within the international arena.

On the other hand, although the human rights regime may declare itself to be universal, as a set of political and ethical norms and ideals it has a very concrete provenance (Herbert 2003). The discourse of human rights emerges out of the Western intellectual tradition, and in its modern form it is the crowning achievement of political liberalism. This historical fact is not necessarily a handicap. A good idea is a good idea wherever it comes from. However, within the debate about the legitimacy of political ideas, one of the key points of contestation is the criteria we use to judge an idea to be a good one. The debate over the universalism and particularism of human rights, the appropriateness of human rights for all people of the earth, has been a debate about precisely this question: in what ways and to what extent can we say that a set of moral and ethical norms created from one political tradition should be applied to, or in conjunction with, all others? This debate raged in Asia in the 1990s over the issue of 'Asian values', and has analogues in many other regions (Langlois 2001). It will long remain one of the key points of contestation among international political theorists.

Conclusion

As I have argued in this chapter, for much of its brief existence as an academic discipline, IR has thought of itself as *sui generis* – a 'stand alone' discipline in no need of the traditional ways of thinking of the disciplines out of which it emerged: history, classics, philosophy, law, economics and diplomacy. The influence of positivism as an epistemological guide for the social sciences and of realism as a dominant worldview meant that IR went its own way for much of the twentieth century. It was claimed by proponents and critics alike that there was no room for ethics, normative theory or political philosophy within the discipline; the structure of the world of international affairs (realism) and the manner in which that world was most appropriately known (positivism) ruled out such concerns, which, if they were to have any pertinence to politics, only achieved traction within the domestic affairs of sovereign states. The right and the good could be pursued within the state; outside it those nurtured by the idealistic fantasies of achieving a good world would find themselves crushed by the stark realities of a state of nature world.

Over the closing decades of the twentieth century, however, all of the intellectual and empirical grounds upon which these arguments were mounted have come into question. The hubristic self-separation of the discipline of IR has been challenged as intellectually untenable. The judgment that realism is the only natural and objective account of the nature of political affairs in the international arena has been undone. Positivism's role as the only legitimate epistemology within the discipline has been overturned, and a new generation of scholars have begun anew the task of engaging with the philosophical questions that lay long neglected at the heart of the discipline. International political theory is one of the ways of doing IR that allows us to engage with these fundamental philosophical questions;

it is crucially important as an intellectual tool that prevents us from being complacent about the 'status quo' answers to those questions. It is indeed the claim of much international political theory that the acceptance of the status quo is in large measure a consequence of the acceptance of intellectual approaches such as realism that have persuaded us that, in Margaret Thatcher's famous phrase, 'there is no alternative'. International political theory is the space, within the broader church of IR, to test the claims of our worldviews at the level of their philosophical foundations and to work up from those foundations to the conclusions that we draw about the events around us.

Further reading

Brown, C. (2002) *Sovereignty, Rights and Justice*, Cambridge: Polity Press.
Rawls, J. (2001) *The Law of Peoples*, Harvard, MA: Harvard University Press.
Tan, K.-C. (2000) *Toleration, Diversity and Global Justice*, Princeton, NJ: Princeton University Press.

Bibliography

Abrahamsen, R. (2001) 'Development policy and the democratic peace in Sub-Saharan Africa,' *Conflict, Security & Development* 1: 79–103.
—— (2005) 'Blair's Africa: the politics of securitization and fear,' *Alternatives* 30: 55–80.
Acharya, A. (2004) 'How ideas spread: whose norms matter? Norm localization and institutional change in Asian regionalism,' *International Organization* 58: 239–75.
Adamson, F.B. (2005) 'Globalisation, transnational political mobilisation, and networks of violence,' *Cambridge Review of International Affairs* 18: 31–49.
Adler, E. (2005) 'Barry Buzan's use of constructivism to reconstruct the English School: not "all the way down",' *Millennium: Journal of International Studies* 34: 170–82.
Adorno, T. (1983) *Negative Dialectics*, New York: Continuum.
—— (2000) *Problems of Moral Philosophy*, Cambridge: Cambridge University Press.
Agamben, G. (1998) *Homo Sacer: Sovereign Power and Bare Life*, Stanford, CA: Stanford University Press.
Almond, G.A. (1989) 'The international-national connection,' *British Journal of Political Science* 19: 237–59.
Anand, D. (2004) 'A story to be told: IR, postcolonialism, and the discourse of Tibetan (trans) national identity,' in G. Chowdhry and S. Nair (eds), *Power, Postcolonialism and International Relations*, London: Routledge.
Anderson, B. (1991) *Imagined Communities: Reflections on the Origin and Spread of Nationalism*, 2nd edn, London: Verso.
Angell, N. (1913) *The Great Illusion*, London: William Heinemann.
Appiah, K.A. (1991) 'Out of Africa: topologies of nativism,' in D. LaCapra (ed.), *The Bounds of Race: Perspectives on Hegemony and Resistance*, Ithaca, NY: Cornell University Press.
—— (1997) 'Is the "post" in post-colonial the "post" in postmodern?' in A. Mclintock, *et al.* (eds), *Dangerous Liaisons: Gender, National and Postcolonial Perspectives*, Minneapolis, MN: Minnesota University Press.
Armstrong, D. (1995) 'Why is there too much international theory?' *Australian Journal of Political Science* 30: 356–63.
Ashcroft, B. (2001) *Post-Colonial Transformations*, London: Routledge.
Ashley, R. (1984) 'The poverty of neorealism,' *International Organization* 38: 225–61.
—— (1988) 'Untying the sovereign state: a double reading of the anarchy problematique,' *Millennium: Journal of International Studies* 17: 227–62.
—— (1991) 'The state of the discipline,' in R. Higgott and J. Richardson (eds) *International Relations: Global and Australian Perspectives on an Evolving Discipline*, Canberra: The Australian National University Press.
Ashley, R.K. (1982) 'Political realism and human interests,' *International Studies Quarterly* 25: 204–36.
Ayoob, M. (1995) *The Third World Security Predicament: State Making, Regional Conflict and the International System*, Boulder, CO: Lynne Rienner.

Badran, Margot (1996) *Feminists, Islam and Nation: Gender and the Making of Modern Egypt*, Princeton, NJ: Princeton University Press.

Bagby, L.J. (1994) 'The use and abuse of Thucydides in international relations,' *International Organization* 48: 131–53.

Baldwin, D.A. (ed.) (1993) *Neorealism and Neoliberalism: The Contemporary Debate*, New York: Columbia University Press.

Banks, M. (ed.) (1984) *Conflict in World Society*, Brighton: Wheatsheaf.

Barkin, S. (2003) 'Realist constructivism,' *International Studies Review* 5: 325–42.

Barnett, M. and Duvall, R. (2005) 'Power in international politics,' *International Organization* 59: 39–75.

Barry, B. (1995) *Justice as Impartiality*, Oxford: Oxford University Press.

Bartelson, J. (1995) *A Genealogy of Sovereignty*, Cambridge: Cambridge University Press.

Beitz, C. (1979) *Political Theory and International Relations*, Princeton, NJ: Princeton University Press.

Bellamy, A.J. (2003) 'International law and the war in Iraq,' *Melbourne Journal of International Law* 4: 497–520.

—— (2005) 'Is the war on terror just?' *International Relations* 19: 275–96.

—— (2006) *Just Wars*, Cambridge: Polity.

—— and Williams, P.D. (2005) 'Who's keeping the peace? Regionalization and contemporary peace operations,' *International Security* 29: 157–95.

Benhabib, S. (2004) *The Rights of Others*, Cambridge: Cambridge University Press.

——, Bonss, W. and McCole, J. (eds) (1993) *On Max Horkheimer: New Perspectives*, Cambridge, MA: Harvard University Press.

Bennett, J. and Chaloupka, W. (eds) (1993) *In the Nature of Things: Language, Politics and the Environment*, Minneapolis, MN: University of Minnesota Press.

Bernstein, J.M. (2001) *Adorno: Disenchantment and Ethics*, Cambridge: Cambridge University Press.

Bhabha, H. (1994) *The Location of Culture*, London: Routledge.

Bleiker, R. (2000) *Popular Dissent, Human Agency and Global Politics*, Cambridge: Cambridge University Press.

—— (2005) 'Order and disorder in world politics,' in A.J. Bellamy (ed.), *International Society and its Critics*, Oxford: Oxford University Press.

Block, F. (1987) *Revising State Theory: Essays in Politics and Postindustrialism*, Philadelphia, PA: Temple University Press.

—— (1990) *Postindustrial Possibilities*, Berkeley, CA: University of California Press.

Bogner, A. (1987) 'Elias and the Frankfurt School,' *Theory, Culture and Society* 4: 249–85.

Booth, K. (1991) 'Security and emancipation,' *Review of International Studies* 17: 313–26.

—— (ed.) (2005) *Critical Security Studies and World Politics*, Boulder, CO: Lynne Rienner.

Borradori, G. (2004) 'Fundamentalism and terror: a dialogue with Jurgen Habermas,' in G. Borradori (ed.), *Philosophy in a Time of Terror: Dialogues With Jurgen Habermas and Jacques Derrida*, Chicago, IL: University of Chicago Press.

Bottomore, T. (1984) *The Frankfurt School*, Chichester: Tavistock.

Boucher, D (1997) 'Political theory, international theory, and the political theory of international relations,' in A. Vincent (ed.), *Political Theory: Tradition and Diversity*, Cambridge: Cambridge University Press.

Bowker, J. (1975) *Problems of Suffering in Religions of the World*, Cambridge: Cambridge University Press.

Boyer, R. and Drache, D. (1996) (eds), *States Against Markets: The Limits of Globalization*, London: Routledge.

Braudel, F. (1972) *The Mediterranean and the Mediterranean World in the Age of Philip 11*, New York: Harper & Row.

Breslin, S. (2005) 'Power and production: rethinking China's global economic role,' *Review of International Studies* 31: 735–53.

Brewer, A. (1991) *Marxist Theories of Imperialism*, London: Routledge.

Brittan, S. (1975) 'The economic contradictions of democracy,' *British Journal of Political Science* 5: 129–59.

Bronner, S.E. (1994) *Of Critical Theory and its Theorists*, Oxford: Oxford University Press.

Brooks, S.G. and Wohlforth, W.C. (2000) 'Power, globalization, and the end of the cold war,' *International Security* 25: 5–53.

Brown, C. (1992) *International Relations Theory: New Normative Approaches*, New York: Columbia University Press.

—— (1997) *Understanding International Relations*, New York: St Martin's Press.

—— (2002) *Sovereignty, Rights and Justice*, Cambridge: Polity Press.

Buchanan, C. (2005) *Missing Pieces*, Geneva: Humanitarian Dialogue.

Bukovansky, M. (2002) *Legitimacy and Power Politics: The American and French Revolutions in International Political Culture*, Princeton, NJ: Princeton University Press.

Bull, H. (1966a) 'International theory: the case for a classical approach,' *World Politics* 42: 361–77.

—— (1966b) 'The Grotian conception of international society,' in M. Wight and H. Butterfield (eds), *Diplomatic Investigations*, London: Allen and Unwin.

—— (1977) *The Anarchical Society*, Basingstoke: Macmillan.

—— (1984a) *Justice in International Relations*, Ontario: University of Waterloo.

—— (1984b) 'The revolt against the west,' in H. Bull and A. Watson (eds), *The Expansion of International Society*, Oxford: Clarendon Press.

Butler, J. (1990) *Gender Trouble: Gender and the Subversion of Identity*, London: Routledge.

—— (2003) *Precarious Life: The Powers of Mourning and Violence*, London: Verso.

Butterfield, H. (1951) *History and Human Relations*, London: Collins.

—— (1953) *Christianity, Diplomacy and War*, London: Epworth Press.

—— (1966) 'The balance of power,' in H. Butterfield and M. Wight (eds), *Diplomatic Investigations*, Cambridge, MA: Harvard University Press.

Buzan, B. (1993) 'From international system to international society: structural realism and regime theory meet the English School,' *International Organization* 47: 327–52.

—— (2001) 'The English School: an underexploited resource in IR,' *Review of International Studies* 27: 471–88.

—— (2004) *From International to World Society? English School Theory and the Social Structure of Globalisation*, Cambridge: Cambridge University Press.

—— (2005a) 'International political economy and globalization,' in A.J. Bellamy (ed.), *International Society and its Critics*, Oxford: Oxford University Press.

—— (2005b) 'Not hanging separately: responses to Dunne and Adler,' *Millennium: Journal of International Studies* 34: 183–94.

—— and Little, R. (2001) 'The "English patient" strikes back: a response to Hall's mis-diagnoses,' *International Affairs* 77: 943–6.

Byers, M. (2004) 'Agreeing to disagree: security council resolution 1441 and intentional ambiguity,' *Global Governance* 10: 165–86.

—— (2005) *War Law: International Law and Armed Conflict*, London: Atlantic Books.

Campbell, D. (1992) *Writing Security*, Manchester: Manchester University Press.

—— (1994) 'The deterritorialization of Responsibility: Levinas, Derrida, and ethics after the end of philosophy,' *Alternatives* 19: 455–84.

—— (1998) *National Deconstruction: Violence, Identity and Justice in Bosnia*, Minneapolis, MN: University of Minnesota Press.

—— and Shapiro, M.J. (1999) *Moral Spaces: Rethinking Ethics and World Politics*, Minneapolis, MN: University of Minnesota Press.

—— (1992) *Truth and Historicity*, Oxford: Clarendon Press.

Caney, S. (1997) 'Human rights and the rights of states: Terry Nardin on non-intervention,' *International Political Science Review* 18: 27–37.

Caporaso, J.A. and Levine, D.P. (1992) *Theories of Political Economy*, New York: Cambridge University Press.

Caputo, J.D. (ed.) (1997) *Deconstruction in a Nutshell*, New York: Fordham University Press.

Carlson, J.D. and Owens, E.C. (eds) (2003) *The Sacred and the Sovereign: Religion and International Politics*, Washington, DC: Georgetown University Press.

Carr, E.H. (1946) *The 20 Years Crisis 1919–1939*, London: Macmillan.

Carver, T. (2004) *Men in Political Theory*, Manchester: Manchester University Press.

Cerny, P.G. (2000) 'Political agency in a globalizing world: towards a structurationist approach,' *European Journal of International Relations* 6: 435–63.

Césaire, A. (1972) *Discourse on Colonialism*, New York: Monthly Review Press.

Chakrabarty, D. (2000) *Provincialising Europe: Postcolonial Thought and Historical Difference*, Princeton, NJ: Princeton University Press.

Chatterjee, P. (1986) *Nationalist Thought and the Colonial World*, London: Zed Books.

Chowdhry, G. and Nair, S. (eds) (2004) *Power, Postcolonialism and International Relations*, London: Routledge.

Christensen, T.J. (1996) *Useful Adversaries: Grand Strategy, Domestic Mobilization, and the Sino–American conflict, 1947–58*, Princeton, NJ: Princeton University Press.

—— and Snyder, J. (1990) 'Chain gangs and passed bucks: predicting alliance patterns in multipolarity,' *International Organization* 44: 137–68.

Cockburn, C. (2004) *The Line: Women, Partition and the Gender Order in Cyprus*, London: Zed Books.

Cohn, C. (1987) 'Sex and death in the rational world of defense intellectuals,' *Signs: Journal of Women in Culture and Society* 12: 687–718.

Collins, A. (1997) *The Security Dilemma and the End of the Cold War*, New York: St Martin's Press.

Comaroff, J. and Comaroff, J. (1991) *Of Revelation and Revolution: Christianity, Colonialism, and Consciousness in South Africa (Volume One)*, Chicago, IL: University of Chicago Press.

Commission on Global Governance (1995) *Our Global Neighbourhood*, Oxford: Oxford University Press.

Conley, T. (2002a) 'The state of globalisation and the globalisation of the state,' *Australian Journal of International Affairs* 56: 447–71.

—— (2002b) 'Globalisation as constraint and opportunity: the restructuring of the Australian political economy,' *Global Society* 16: 377–99.

Connolly, W.E. (1991) *Identity/Difference: Democratic Negotiations of Political Paradox*, Ithaca, NY: Cornell University Press.

Cooper, R.N. (1980) *The Economics of Interdependence*, New York: Columbia University Press

Copeland, D.C. (2001) *The Origins of Major War*, Ithaca, NY: Cornell University Press.

—— (2003) 'A realist critique of the English School,' *Review of International Studies* 29: 427–41.

Cox, M. (2003) 'The empire's back in town – or America's imperial temptation – again,' *Millennium: Journal of International Studies* 32: 1–27.

Cox, R. (1996) 'A perspective on globalization,' in J.H. Mittelman (ed.), *Globalization: Critical Reflections*, Westview, CO: Lynne Rienner.

Cox, R.W. (1981) 'Social forces, states and world orders: beyond international relations theory,' *Millennium: Journal of International Studies* 10: 126–55.

—— (1983) 'Gramsci, hegemony and international relations: an essay in method,' *Millennium: Journal of International Studies* 12: 162–75.

—— (1987) *Production, Power, and World Order*, New York: Columbia University Press.

—— (1992) 'Global Perestroika,' in R. Miliband and L. Panitch (eds), *The Socialist Register 1992*, London: Merlin Press.

—— and Schlechter, M.G. (2002) *The Political Economy of a Plural World: Critical Reflections on Power, Morals and Civilization*, London: Taylor and Francis.

—— and Sinclair, T.J. (1996) *Approaches to World Order*, Cambridge: Cambridge University Press.

Crawford, N.C. (2002) *Argument and Change in World Politics: Ethics, Decolonization, and Humanitarian Intervention*, Cambridge: Cambridge University Press.

Crockatt, R. (2003) *America Embattled: September 11, Anti-Americanism and the Global Order*, London and New York: Routledge.

Cronin, A.K. (2002/03) 'Behind the curve: globalization and international terrorism,' *International Security* 27: 30–58.

Cruikshank, B. (1999) *The Will to Empower*, Ithaca: Cornell University Press.

Dalby, S. (1990) *Creating the Second Cold War*, London: Pinter.

—— (2002) *Environmental Security*, Minneapolis, MN: Minnesota University Press.

Darby, P. (ed.) (1997) *At the Edge of International Relations: Postcolonialism, Gender and Dependency*, London: Pinter.

De Goede, M. (2005) *Virtue, Fortune and Faith*, Minneapolis, MN: University of Minnesota Press.

De Saussure, F. (1966) *Course in General Linguistics*, New York: McGraw Hill.

Debrix, F. (1999) *Re-Envisioning Peacekeeping: the United Nations and the Mobilization of Ideology*, Minneapolis, MN: University of Minnesota Press.

Deleuze, G. (1990) *The Logic of Sense*, trans. M. Lester, London: Athlone.

—— and Guattari, F. (1983) *Anti-Oedipus: Capitalism and Schizophrenia*, trans. R. Hurley, M. Seem and H.R. Lane, London: Athlone Press.

Der Derian, J. (1992) *Antidiplomacy: Spies, Terror, Speed and War*, Cambridge, MA: Blackwell.

—— and Shapiro, M.J. (1989) *International/Intertextual Relations*, New York: Lexington Books.

Derrida, J. (1976) *Of Grammatology*, trans. G.C. Spivak, Baltimore: Johns Hopkins.

—— (1987) *Positions*, London: Athlone Press.

—— (1988) *Limited Inc*, Evanston, IL: Northwestern University Press.

—— (1992) 'The force of law and the mystical foundations of authority,' in D.G. Carlson, *et al.* (eds), *Deconstruction and the Possibility of Justice*, New York: Routledge.

—— (1994) *Specters of Marx*, New York: Routledge.

Desch, M.C. (1998) 'Culture clash – assessing the importance of ideas in security studies,' *International Security* 23: 141–70.

Dessler, D. (1989) 'What's at stake in the agent-structure debate?' *International Organization* 43: 441–74.

Deutsch, K. and Singer, D.J. (1964) 'Multipolar power systems and international stability,' *World Politics* 16: 390–406.

Devetak, R. (2005) 'Postmodernism,' in S. Burchill *et al.* (eds), *Theories of International Relations*, Basingstoke: Palgrave Macmillan.

DiCicco, J.M. and Levy, J.S. (1999) 'Power shifts and problem shifts: the evolution of the power transition research program,' *Journal of Conflict Resolution* 43: 675–704.

—— (2003) 'The power transition research program: a Lakatosian analysis,' in C. Elman and M.F. Elman (eds), *Progress in International Relations Theory: Appraising the Field*, Cambridge, MA: MIT Press.

Dick, K. and Kofman, A.Z. (2002) *Derrida*, Jane Doe Films Inc. USA, 85 mins.

Dicken, P. (1992) *Global Shift: The Internationalization of Economic Activity*, New York: Guilford Press.

Diez, T. and Steans, J. (2005) 'Forum on Habermas,' *Review of International Studies* 31: 127–40.

Dillon, M. (1996) *The Politics of Security*, London: Routledge.

Dirlik, A. (1994) 'The postcolonial aura: third world criticism in the age of global capitalism,' *Critical Inquiry* 20: 228–56.

Donnelly, J. (1995) 'Realism and international relations,' in J. Farr, *et al.* (eds), *Political Science in History: Research Programs and Political Traditions*, New York: Cambridge University Press.

—— (2000) *Realism and International Relations*, Cambridge: Cambridge University Press.

Doran, C.F. (1989) 'Systemic disequilibrium, foreign policy role, and the power cycle: challenges for research design,' *The Journal of Conflict Resolution* 33: 371–401.

—— (2000) 'Confronting the principles of the power cycle: changing systems structure, expectations, and war,' in M.I. Midlarsky (ed.), *Handbook of War Studies II*, Ann Arbor, MI: University of Michigan Press.

—— and Parsons, W. (1980) 'War and the cycle of relative power,' *The American Political Science Review* 74: 947–65.

Doty, R.L. (1996) *Imperial Encounters*, Minneapolis, MN: University of Minnesota Press.

Doyle, M. (1990) 'Thucydidean realism,' *Review of International Studies* 16: 223–37.

Drucker, P. (1989) *The New Realities*, Oxford: Heinemann.

Dunn, J. (1994) 'Introduction: crisis of the nation-state?' *Political Studies* 42: 3–15.

Dunn, K.C. (2003) *Imagining the Congo*, London: Palgrave Macmillan.

Dunne, T. (1995) 'The social construction of international society,' *European Journal of International Relations* 1: 367–89.

—— (1998) *Inventing International Society*, London: Palgrave.

—— (2003) 'Society and hierarchy in international relations,' *International Relations* 17: 303–20.

—— (2005a) 'The new agenda,' in A.J. Bellamy (ed.), *International Society and its Critics*, Oxford: Oxford University Press.

—— (2005b) 'System, state and society: how does it all hang together?' *Millennium: Journal of International Studies* 34: 157–69.

—— and Wheeler, N.J. (eds) (1999) *Human Rights in Global Politics*, Cambridge: Cambridge University Press.

——, Kurki, M. and Smith, S. (eds) (2007) *International Relations Theories: Discipline and Diversity*, Oxford: Oxford University Press.

Edkins, J. (1999) *Poststructuralism and International Relations*, Boulder, CO: Lynne Rienner.

—— (2000) *Whose Hunger?* Minneapolis, MN: University of Minnesota Press.

—— (2003) *Trauma and the Memory of Politics*, Cambridge: Cambridge University Press.

Elias, N. (1982) *The Civilizing Process, State Formation and Civilization* (Volume Two), Oxford: Blackwell.

Elman, C. (1996a) 'Horses for courses: why *not* neorealist theories of foreign policy?' *Security Studies* 6: 7–53.

—— (1996b) 'Cause, effect, and consistency: a response to Kenneth Waltz,' *Security Studies* 6: 58–61.

—— (2001) 'History, theory and the democratic peace,' *The International History Review* 23: 757–66.

—— (2003) 'Introduction: appraising balance of power theory,' in J.A. Vasquez and C. Elman (eds), *Realism and the Balancing of Power: A New Debate*, Upper Saddle River, NJ: Prentice Hall.

—— and Elman, M.F. (1995) 'Correspondence: history vs. neo-realism: a second look,' *International Security* 20: 182–93.

—— (2002) 'How not to be Lakatos intolerant: appraising progress in IR research,' *International Studies Quarterly* 46: 231–62.

—— (eds) (2003) *Progress in International Relations Theory*, Cambridge: MIT Press.

Enloe, C. (1990) *Bananas, Beaches and Bases: Making Feminist Sense of International Politics*, Berkeley and London: University of California Press.

—— (1998) 'All the men are in the militias, all the women are victims – the politics of masculinity and femininity in nationalist wars,' in L.A. Lorentzen and J.E. Turpin (eds), *The Women and War Reader*, New York: New York University Press.

—— (2004) *The Curious Feminist: Searching for Women in a New Age of Empire*, Berkeley, CA: University of California Press.

Escobar, A. (1995) *Encountering Development: The Making and Unmaking of the Third World*, Princeton, NJ: Princeton University Press.

Evangelista, M. (1999) *Unarmed Forces: The Transnational Movement to End the Cold War*, Ithaca, NY: Cornell University Press.

Evans, G. and Sahnoun, M. (2002) 'The responsibility to protect,' *Foreign Affairs* 81: 99–107.

——, Rueschemeyer, D. and Skocpol, T. (1985) 'On the road toward a more adequate understanding of the state,' in P.B. Evans, *et al.* (eds), *Bringing the State Back In*, Cambridge: Cambridge University Press.

Falk, R. (1995) *On Humane Governance*, Cambridge: Polity.

—— (2005) '(Re)imagining the governance of globalization,' in A.J. Bellamy (ed.) *International Society and its Critics*, Oxford: Oxford University Press.

Fanon, F. (1986) *Black Skin, White Masks*, London: Pluto Press.

Fearon, J. (1998) 'Domestic politics, foreign policy and theories of international relations,' *Annual Review of Political Science* 1: 289–313.

Feaver, P.D., Hellman, G., Schweller, R. Taliaferro, J., Wohlforth, W., Legro, J., and Moravcsik, A. (2000) 'Correspondence: brother, can you spare a paradigm?' *International Security* 25: 165–9.

Feinstein, L. and Slaughter, A.-M. (2004) 'A duty to prevent,' *Foreign Affairs* 83: 136–46.

Ferguson, J. (1994) *The Anti-Politics Machine*, Minneapolis, MN: University of Minnesota Press.

Fierke, K.M. (2002) 'Meaning, method and practice: assessing the changing security agenda,' in S. Lawson (ed.), *The New Agenda for International Relations*, Cambridge: Polity.

Finnemore, M. (1996) *National Interests in International Society*, Ithaca, NY: Cornell University Press.

—— (2001) 'Exporting the English School?' *Review of International Studies* 27: 509–13.

—— and Sikkink, K. (2001) 'Taking stock: the constructivist research program in international relations and comparative politics,' *Annual Review of Political Science* 4: 391–416.

Fishel, K.L. (2002) 'Challenging the Hegemon: Al Qaeda's elevation of assymetric insurgent warfare onto the global arena,' *Low Intensity Conflict and Law Enforcement* 2: 285–98.

Foot, R., Gaddis, J.L. and Hurrell, A. (eds) (2003) *Order and Justice in International Relations*, Oxford: Oxford University Press.

Forde, S. (1992) 'Varieties of realism: Thucydides and Machiavelli,' *The Journal of Politics* 54: 372–93.

—— (1995) 'International realism and the science of politics: Thucydides, Machiavelli and neorealism,' *International Studies Quarterly* 39: 141–60.

Forsythe, D.P. (2000) *Human Rights in International Relations*, Cambridge: Cambridge University Press.

Foucault, M. (1970) *The Order of Things: An Archaeology of the Human Sciences*, London: Tavistock.

—— (1977) *Discipline and Punish: The Birth of the Prison*, London: Allen Lane.

—— (1980) *Power/Knowledge: Selected Interviews and Other Writings*, London: Harvester Wheatsheaf.

—— (1991) *Discipline and Punish: The Birth of the Prison*, London: Allen Lane.

—— (1998) 'Nietzsche, geneaology, history,' in P. Rabinow (ed.), *Essential Works of Foucault 1954–1984, Aesthetics, Methods, and Epistemology* (Volume Two), New York: The New Press.

——(2000) *Power: Essential Works of Foucault 1954–1984*, New York: The New Press.

—— (2003) *Society Must be Defended: Lectures at the College de France, 1975–76*, London: Allen Lane.

Franck, T.M. (2002) *Recourse to Force: State Action Against Threats and Armed Attacks*, Cambridge: Cambridge University Press.

Freud, S. (1991) *The Interpretation of Dreams*, Harmondsworth: Penguin.

Friedman, T. (1999) *The Lexus and the Olive Tree: Understanding Globalisation*, New York: Farrar, Strauss, Giroux.

Frost, M. (1996) *Ethics in International Theory: A Constitutive Theory*, Cambridge: Cambridge University Press.

—— (1998) 'A turn not taken: ethics in IR at the millennium,' *Review of International Studies*, Special Issue 24: 119–32.

—— (2003) 'Tragedy, ethics and international relations,' *International Relations* 17: 477–95.

Fukuyama, F. (1989) 'The end of history?' *The National Interest* 16: 3–18.

—— (1992) *The End of History and the Last Man*, London: Penguin.

—— (2004) *State-Building: Governance and World Order in the 21st Century*, Ithaca, NY: Cornell University Press.

Gaddis, J.L. (1986) 'The long peace: elements of stability in the postwar international system,' *International Security* 10: 99–142.

Garst, D. (1989) 'Thucydides and neorealism,' *International Studies Quarterly* 33: 3–27.

George, L.N. (2002) 'The pharmacotic war on terrorism: cure or poison for the US body politic?,' *Theory Culture and Society* 19: 161–86.

Gibney, M.J. (ed.) (2003) *Globalizing Rights*, Oxford: Oxford University Press.

Giddens, A. (1985) *The Nation-State and Violence: Volume Two of a Contemporary Critique of Historical Materialism*, Cambridge: Polity Press.

Gill, S. (1992) 'Economic globalization and the internationalization of authority: limits and contradictions,' *Geoforum* 22: 269–83.

—— and Law, D. (1988) *The Global Political Economy: Perspectives, Problems and Policies*, Baltimore: The John Hopkins University Press.

Gilpin, R. (1981) *War and Change in World Politics*, Cambridge: Cambridge University Press.

—— (1988) 'The theory of hegemonic war,' *Journal of Interdisciplinary History* 18: 591–613.

—— (2001) *Global Political Economy: Understanding the International Economic Order*, Princeton, NJ: Princeton University Press.

Glaser, C.L. (1994/95) 'Realists as optimists: cooperation as self-help,' *International Security* 19: 50–90.

—— (1997) 'The security dilemma revisited,' *World Politics* 50: 171–210.

—— (2003) 'The necessary and natural evolution of structural realism,' in J.A. Vasquez and C. Elman (eds), *Realism and the Balancing of Power: A New Debate*, Upper Saddle River, NJ: Prentice Hall.

Gourevitch, P. (1978) 'The second image reversed: the international sources of domestic politics,' *International Organization* 32: 881–912.

Grader, S. (1988) 'The English School of International Relations: evidence and evaluation,' *Review of International Studies* 14: 29–44.

Gramsci, A. (1971) *Selections from Prison Notebooks*, London: Lawrence and Wishart.

Grant, R. and Newland, K. (1991) *Gender and International Relations*, London: Open University Press and Bloomington: Indiana University Press.

Grieco, J.M. (1988) 'Anarchy and the limits of cooperation: a realist critique of the newest liberal institutionalism,' *International Organization* 42: 485–508.

—— (1993) 'The relative-gains problem for international cooperation,' *American Political Science Review* 87: 729–43.

—— and Ikenberry, G.J. (2003) *State Power and World Markets*, New York: Norton.

Griffiths, M. (ed.) (2005) *Routledge Encyclopedia of International Relations and Global Politics*, New York: Routledge.

Grovugui, S.N. (2004) 'Postcolonial criticism: international reality and modes of inquiry,' in G. Chowdhry and S. Nair (eds), *Power, Postcolonialism and International Relations*, London: Routledge.

Guha, R. (1997) *Dominance without Hegemony*, Cambridge, MA: Harvard University Press.

Gunaratna, R. (2003) 'Sri Lanka: feeding the Tamil Tigers,' in K. Ballentine and J. Sherman (eds), *The Political Economy of Armed Conflict – Beyond Greed and Grievance*, Boulder, CO: Lynne Rienner.

Gunnell, J. (1987) 'In search of the political object,' in J. Nelson (ed.), *What Should Political Theory Be Now?* New York: University of New York Press.

Gunnell, J.G. (1975) *Philosophy, Science and Political Inquiry*, New Jersey: General Learning Press.

Habermas, J. (1979) *Communication and the Evolution of Society*, London: Polity.

—— (1990) *Moral Consciousness and Communicative Action*, Cambridge: Polity Press.

—— (1997) 'Kant's idea of perpetual peace, with the benefit of two hundred years' hindsight,' in J. Bohman and M. Lutz-Bachmann (eds), *Perpetual Peace: Essays on Kant's Cosmopolitan Ideal*, London: MIT Press.

—— (1998) 'Paradigms of Law,' in M. Rosenfeld and A. Arato (eds), *Habermas on Law and Democracy*, London: University of California Press.

Hacke, J. (2005) 'The Frankfurt School and international relations: on the centrality of recognition,' *Review of International Studies* 31: 181–94.

Hall, I. (2001) 'Still the English Patient? Closures and inventions in the English School,' *International Affairs* 77: 931–42.

Hall, R.B. (1999) *National Collective Identity*, New York: Columbia University Press.

Hall, S. (1992) 'The question of cultural identity,' in S. Hall, *et al.* (eds), *Modernity and Its Futures*, London: Polity.

Halliday, F. (1994) *Rethinking International Relations*, Vancouver: British Columbia Press.
—— (2002) 'The pertinence of imperialism,' in M. Rupert and H. Smith (eds), *Historical Materialism and Globalization*, London: Routledge.
Hannerz, U. (1996) *Transnational Connections*, London: Routledge.
Hardt, M. and Negri, A. (2000) *Empire*, Cambridge, MA: Harvard University Press.
Haslam, J. (2002) *No Virtue Like Necessity*, New Haven, CT: Yale University Press.
Hay, C. and Marsh, D. (1999) 'Introduction: towards a new (international) political economy,' *New Political Economy* 4: 5–22.
—— and Rosamond, B. (2002) 'Globalization, European integration and the discursive construction of economic imperatives,' *Journal of European Public Policy* 9: 147–67.
Held, D. (1995) *Democracy and the Global Order*, Cambridge: Polity.
—— and McGrew, A. (1993) 'Globalization and the liberal democratic state,' *Government and Opposition* 28: 261–88.
Hellman, G. (ed.) (2003) 'Are dialogue and synthesis possible in international relations?' *International Studies Review* 5: 123–53.
Helman, G.B. and Ratner, S.R. (1993) 'Saving failed states,' *Foreign Policy* 89: 3–20.
Herbert, G.B. (2003) *A Philosophical History of Rights*, New Brunswick: Transaction Publishers.
Herz, J.H. (1950) 'Idealist internationalism and the security dilemma,' *World Politics* 2: 157–80.
—— (1957) 'The rise and demise of the territorial state,' *World Politics* 9: 473–93.
Higgins, R. (1994) *Problems and Process: International Law and How We Use It*, Oxford: Oxford University Press.
Higgott, R. (2002) 'Taming economics, emboldening international relations: the theory and practice of international political economy in an era of globalization,' in S. Lawson (ed.), *The New Agenda in International Relations*, Cambridge: Polity Press.
Hindess, B. (1996) *Discourses of Power: From Hobbes to Foucault*, Oxford: Blackwell.
Hinsley, F.H. (1963) *Power and the Pursuit of Peace*, Cambridge: Cambridge University Press.
Hirst, P. and Thompson, G. (1996) *Globalization in Question*, Cambridge: Polity Press.
Hobbes, T. (1962) *Leviathan*, New York: Macmillan.
Hobson, J.M. (2002) 'What's at stake in bringing historical sociology *back* into international relations?' in S. Hobden and J.M. Hobson (eds), *Historical Sociology of International Relations*, Cambridge: Cambridge University Press.
Holsti, J. (2001) 'Along the road of international theory in the next millennium: four travelogues,' in R. Crawford and D. Jarvis (eds), *International Relations: Still an American Social Science?* New York: State University of New York Press.
Honneth, A. (1995) *The Struggle for Recognition: The Moral Grammar of Social Conflicts,* Cambridge: MIT Press.
Hooks, B. (1993) 'Postmodern blackness,' in P. Williams and L. Chrisman (eds), *Colonial Discourse and Post-Colonial Theory,* London: Harvester Wheatsheaf.
Hopf, T. (1991) 'Polarity, the offense-defense balance, and war,' *American Political Science Review* 85: 475–93.
—— (1998) 'The promise of constructivism in international relations theory,' *International Security* 23: 171–200.
Horkheimer, M. (1974) 'Schopenhauer today' in M. Horkheimer (ed.), *Critique of Instrumental Reason*, New York: Continuum.
—— (1976) 'Traditional and critical theory,' in P. Connerton (ed.), *Critical Sociology: Selected Readings*, Harmondsworth: Macmillan.
—— (1993) 'Materialism and morality,' in M. Horkheimer (ed.), *Between Philosophy and Social Science*, Cambridge, MA: MIT Press.
—— and Adorno, T. (1947) *Dialectic of Enlightenment*, Amsterdam: Verlag.
—— (1977) *Dialectic of Enlightenment: Philosophical Fragments*, New York: Stanford University Press.
Howard, M. (1981) *War and the Liberal Conscience*, Oxford: Oxford University Press.

Huntington, S. (1997) *The Clash of Civilisations and the Remaking of World Order*, New York: Simon and Schuster.

Hurrell, A. (2002) ' "There are no rules" (George W. Bush): international order after September 11,' *International Relations* 16: 185–203.

Hutchings, K. (1999) *International Political Theory: Rethinking Ethics in a Global Era*, London: Sage.

Huth, P.K. and Allee, T.D. (2002) *The Democratic Peace and Territorial Conflict in the Twentieth Century*, Cambridge: Cambridge University Press.

Ikenberry, G.J. (1986a) 'The state and strategies of international adjustment,' *World Politics* 39: 53–77.

—— (1986b) 'The irony of state strength: comparative responses to the oil shocks in the 1970s,' *International Organization* 40: 105–37.

—— (1995) 'Funk de Siècle: impasses of western industrial society at century's end,' *Millennium: Journal of International Studies* 24: 113–26.

—— (1996) 'The myth of post-Cold War chaos,' *Foreign Affairs* 76: 79–91.

International Commission on Intervention and State Sovereignty (2001) *The Responsibility to Protect*, Ottawa: International Development Research Centre.

Irigaray, L. (1985) *This Sex Which Is Not One*, trans. C. Porter with C. Burke, New York: Cornell University Press.

Jackson, R.H. (1990) *Quasi-States: Sovereignty, International Relations and the Third World*, Cambridge: Cambridge University Press.

—— (1993) 'The weight of ideas in decolonization: normative change in international relations,' in J. Goldstein and R.O. Keohane (eds), *Ideas and Foreign Policy: Beliefs, Institutions, and Political Change*, Ithaca: Cornell University Press.

—— (1995) 'The political theory of international society,' in K. Booth and S. Smith (eds), *International Relations Theory Today*, Cambridge: Polity Press.

Jacquard, R. (2002) *In the Name of Osama Bin Laden: Global Terrorism and the Bin Laden Brotherhood*, Durham: Duke University Press.

James, A. (1993) 'System or society?' *Review of International Studies* 19: 269–88.

Jeffrey, R. (2005) 'Tradition as invention: the "traditions tradition" and the history of ideas in international relations,' *Millennium: Journal of International Studies* 34: 57–84.

Jepperson, R.L., Wendt, A. and Katzenstein P. (1996) 'Norms, identity, and culture in national security,' in P. Katzenstein (ed.), *The Culture of National Security: Norms and Identity in World Politics*, New York: Columbia University Press.

Jervis, R. (1976) *Perception and Misperception in International Politics*, Princeton, NJ: Princeton University Press.

—— (1978) 'Cooperation under the security dilemma,' *World Politics* 40: 167–214.

—— (1997) *Systems Effects: Complexity in Political and Social Life*, Princeton, NJ: Princeton University Press.

—— (2002) 'Theories of war in an era of leading-power peace: presidential address, American Political Science Association,' *American Political Science Review* 96: 1–14.

—— and Snyder, J. (eds) (1991) *Dominoes and Bandwagons*, New York: Oxford University Press.

Johnston, A.I. (2001) 'Treating international institutions as social environments,' *International Studies Quarterly* 45: 487–515.

Jones, D.V. (1994) 'The League of Nations experiment in international protection,' *Ethics and International Affairs* 8: 77–95.

Jones, R.E. (1981) 'The English School of International Relations: a case for closure?,' *Review of International Studies* 7: 1–13.

Kahler, M. (1997) 'Inventing international relations: international relations theory after 1945,' in M.W. Doyle and G.J. Ikenberry (eds), *New Thinking in International Relations Theory*, Boulder, CO: Westview Press.

—— (1998) 'Rationality in international relations,' *International Organization* 52: 919–41.

Kampwirth, K. (2004) *Feminism and the Legacy of Revolution*, Athens, OH: Ohio University Press.

Kaplan, R.D. (1994) 'The coming anarchy: how Scarcity, crime, overpopulation and disease are rapidly destroying the social fabric of our planet,' *Atlantic Monthly* February: 4–76.

Katzenstein, P. (1995) 'The role of theory in comparative politics,' *World Politics* 48: 10–15.

—— (1998) 'International organization and the study of world politics,' *International Organization* 52: 645–85.

—— (2005) *A World Of Regions: Asia and Europe in the American Imperium*, Ithaca, NY: Cornell University Press.

—— and Sil, R. (2004) 'Rethinking Asian security: a case for analytical eclecticism,' in J.J. Suh, *et al.* (eds), *Rethinking Security in East Asia – Identity, Power, and Efficiency*, Stanford: Stanford University Press.

Katzenstein, P.J. and Okawara, N. (2001/02) 'Japan, Asian-Pacific security, and the case for analytical eclecticism,' *International Security* 26: 153–85.

Kaul, I. and Conceição, P. (eds) (2006) *New Public Finance: Responding to Global Challenges*, Oxford: Oxford University Press.

Keck, M.E. and Sikkink, K. (1998) *Activists Beyond Borders: Advocacy Networks in International Politics*, Ithaca, NY: Cornell University Press.

Kegley, C.W. (1993) 'The neoidealist moment in international studies? Realist myths and the new international realities,' *International Studies Quarterly* 37: 131–46.

Kennan, G.F. (1951) *American Diplomacy, 1900–1950*, Chicago: University of Chicago Press.

Kennedy, D. (2004) *The Dark Sides of Virtue: Reassessing International Humanitarianism*, Princeton, NJ: Princeton University Press.

Keohane, R.O. (1984) *After Hegemony: Cooperation and Discord in the World Political Economy*, Princeton, NJ: Princeton University Press.

—— (1986) *Neorealism and its Critics*, New York: Columbia University Press.

—— (2002) 'Governance in a partially globalized world,' in R.O. Keohane (ed.), *Power and Governance in a Partially Globalized World*, London and New York: Routledge.

—— and Martin, L. (2003) 'Institutional theory as a research program,' in C. Elman and M.F. Elman (eds), *Progress in International Relations Theory: Appraising the Field*, Cambridge: the MIT Press.

—— and Nye, J.S. (1977) *Power and Interdependence*, Boston, MA: Little and Brown.

Keynes, J. (1919) *The Economic Consequences of the Peace*, New York: Bibliobazaar.

Kim, W. (1991) 'Alliance transitions and great power war,' *American Journal of Political Science* 35: 833–50.

—— (1992) 'Power transitions and great power war from Westphalia to Waterloo,' *World Politics* 45: 153–72.

—— (1996) 'Power parity, alliances, and war from 1648 to 1975,' in J. Kulgler and D. Lemke (eds), *Parity and War: Evaluations and Extensions of the 'War Ledger'*, Ann Arbor, MI: University of Michigan Press.

—— (2002) 'Power parity, alliance, dissatisfaction, and wars in East Asia, 1860–1993,' *The Journal of Conflict Resolution* 46: 654–71.

King, A. (1975) 'Overload: problems of governing in the 1970s,' *Political Studies* 23: 284–95.

Knutson, T. L. (1992) *A History of International Relations Theory*, Manchester: Manchester University Press.

Kolakowski, L. (2005), *Main Currents of Marxism*, New York: Norton.

Kowert, P. and Legro, J.W. (1996) 'Norms, identity, and their limits: a theoretical reprise,' in P. Katzenstein (ed.), *The Culture of National Security – Norms and Identity in World Politics*, New York: Columbia University Press.

Kratochwil, F. (2003) 'The monologue of "science",' *International Studies Review* 5: 124–8.

Krishna, S. (1993) 'The importance of being ironic: a postcolonial view on critical international relations theory,' *Alternatives* 18: 385–417.

Kristeva, J. (1991) *Strangers to Ourselves*, trans. L.S. Roudiez, New York: Columbia University Press.

Kuehls, T. (1996) *Beyond Sovereign Territory*, Minneapolis, MN: University of Minnesota Press.

Kugler, J. and Lemke, D. (2000) 'The power transition research program: assessing theoretical and empirical advances,' in M. Midlarsky (ed.), *The Handbook of War Studies II*, Ann Arbor, MI: Michigan University Press.

—— and Organski, A.F.K. (1989) 'The power transition: a retrospective and prospective evaluation,' in M.I. Midlarsky (ed.), *Handbook of War Studies*, Boston: Unwin Hyman.

Kuhn, T. (1970) *The Structure of Scientific Revolutions*, Chicago, IL: Chicago University Press.

Kydd, A. (2001) 'Trust building, trust breaking: the dilemma of NATO enlargement,' *International Organization* 55: 801–28.

Kydd, A.H. (2005) *Trust and Mistrust in International Relations*, Princeton, NJ: Princeton University Press.

Labs, E.J. (1997) 'Beyond victory: offensive realism and the expansion of war aims,' *Security Studies* 6: 1–49.

Lacan, J. (1980) *Écrits: A Selection*, trans. A. Sheridan, London: Routledge.

Lacher, H. (2002) 'Making sense of the international system: the promises and pitfalls of the newest Marxist theories of international relations,' in M. Rupert and H. Smith (eds), *Historical Materialism and Globalization*, London: Routledge.

Lakatos, I. (1970) 'Falsification and the methodology of scientific research programmes,' in I. Lakatos and A. Musgrave (eds), *Criticism and the Growth of Knowledge*, New York: Cambridge University Press.

Langlois, A. J. (2001) *The Politics of Justice and Human Rights: Southeast Asia and Universalist Theory*, Cambridge: Cambridge University Press.

Lawson, S. (2002) *International Relations*, Cambridge: Polity Press.

Lebow, R.N. (2001) 'Thucydides the constructivist,' *American Political Science Review* 95: 547–60.

—— (2003) *The Tragic Vision of Politics: Ethics, Interests and Orders*, Cambridge: Cambridge University Press.

Lee Koo, K. (2002) 'Confronting a disciplinary blindness,' *Australian Journal of Political Science* 37: 525–36.

Legro, J.W. (1997) 'Which norms matter? Revisiting the "failure" of internationalism,' *International Organization* 51: 31–63.

—— and Moravcsik, A. (1999) 'Is anybody still a realist?,' *International Security* 24: 5–55.

Lemke, D. (1995) 'Toward a general understanding of parity and war,' *Conflict Management and Peace Science* 14: 143–62.

—— (1996) 'Small states and war: an expansion of power transition theory,' in J. Kugler and D. Lemke (eds), *Parity and War: Evaluations and Extensions of 'the war ledger'*, Ann Arbor, MI: University of Michigan Press.

Levy, J.S. (1985) 'Theories of general war,' *World Politics* 37: 344–74.

—— (1991) 'Long cycles, hegemonic transitions, and the long peace,' in C. Kegley (ed.), *The Long Postwar Peace*, New York: Harper-Collins.

Liberman, P. (1993) 'The spoils of conquest,' *International Security* 18: 125–53.

Lijphart, A. (1974) 'The structure of the theoretical revolution in international relations,' *International Studies Quarterly* 18: 41–74.

Lindblom, C. (1977) *Politics and Markets*, New York: Basic Books.

Linklater, A. (1990) 'The problem of community in international relations,' *Alternatives* 15: 135–53.

—— (1998) *The Transformation of Political Community*, Columbia, SC: University of South Carolina Press.

—— (2004) 'Norbert Elias, "the civilizing process" and international relations,' *International Politics* 41: 3–35.

—— (2005) 'Discourse ethics and the civilizing process,' *Review of International Studies* 31: 141–54.

—— (2007) 'Distant suffering and cosmopolitan obligation,' *International Politics* 44: 19–36.

Little, R. (2000) 'The English School's contribution to the study of international relations,' *European Journal of International Relations* 6: 395–422.

—— (2003) 'The English School vs. American realism: a meeting of minds or divided by a common language,' *Review of International Studies* 29: 443–60.

—— (2005) 'The English School and world history,' in A.J. Bellamy (ed.), *International Society and its Critics*, Oxford: Oxford University Press.

Long, D. and Wilson, P. (eds) (1995) *Thinkers of the Twenty Years Crisis: Inter-War Idealism Reassessed*, Oxford: Clarendon Press.

Loomba, A. (1996) *Colonialism/Postcolonialism*, London: Routledge.

Louriaux, M. (1992) 'The realists and Saint Augustine: skepticism, psychology, and moral action in international relations thought,' *International Studies Quarterly* 36: 401–20.

Lovin, R. (1995) *Reinhold Niebuhr and Christian Realism*, Cambridge: Cambridge University Press.

Luttwak, E.N. (1993) 'The coming global war for economic power: there are no nice guys on the battlefield of geo-economics,' *The International Economy* 7: 17–23.

Lynch, M. (2000) 'The dialogue of civilisations and international public spheres,' *Millennium: Journal of International Studies* 29: 307–30.

Lynn-Jones, S.M. (1995) 'Offense-defense theory and its critics,' *Security Studies* 4: 660–91.

—— (2001) 'Does offense-defense theory have a future?,' working paper, Research Group in International Security, Université de Montréal.

MacIntyre, A. (1990) *Three Rival Versions of Moral Enquiry: encyclopaedia, genealogy and tradition*, London: Duckworth.

MacMillan, J. (1998) *On Liberal Peace*, London: I.B. Tauris.

—— (1993) *The Sources of Social Power, Vol. 2, The Rise of Classes and Nation-States, 1760–1914*, Cambridge: Cambridge University Press.

Mann, M. (2003) *Incoherent Empire*, London: Verso.

Manning, C.A.W. (1962 [1975]) *The Nature of International Society*, 2nd edn, London: Macmillan for the LSE.

Mansfield, E.D. (1993) 'Concentration, polarity, and the distribution of power,' *International Studies Quarterly* 37: 105–28.

March, J.G. and Olsen, J.P. (1998) 'The institutional dynamics of international political orders,' *International Organization* 52: 943–69.

Marchand, M.H. and Runyan, A.S. (eds) (2000) *Gender and Global Restructuring*, London and New York: Routledge.

Marcuse, H. (1964) *One-Dimensional Man*, London: Routledge.

Marshall, A. (1890) *The Principles of Economics*, London: Macmillan and Co.

Marx, K. (1977) *Capital*, trans. Ben Fowkes, New York: Vintage.

—— (2000) *Selected Writings*, 2nd edn, David McLellan (ed.) Oxford: Oxford University Press.

Mastanduno, M (1991) 'Do relative gains matter? America's response to Japanese industrial policy,' *International Security* 16: 73–113.

Mbembe, A. (2001) *On the Postcolony*, Berkley: University of California Press.

McCarthy, T. (1993) 'The idea of critical theory and its relation to philosophy,' in S. Benhabib, *et al.* (eds), *On Max Horkheimer: New Perspectives*, Cambridge, MA: Cambridge University Press..

Mearsheimer, J. (1990a) 'Back to the Future: instability in Europe after the Cold War,' *International Security* 15: 5–56.

—— (1990b) 'Why we will soon miss the Cold War,' *The Atlantic Monthly* August: 35–50.

—— (1994/1995) 'The false promise of international institutions,' *International Security* 19: 5–49.

—— (2001) *The Tragedy of Great Power Politics*, New York: WW. Norton.

Memmi, A. (1990) *The Colonizer and the Colonized*, London: Earthscan Publications.

Mendelsohn, B. (2005) 'Sovereignty under attack: the international society meets the Al Qaeda network,' *Review of International Studies* 31: 45–68.

Midgeley, C. (1993) 'Anti-slavery and feminism in nineteenth century Britain,' *Gender and History* 5: 475–88.

Migdal, J.S. (2001) *State in Society: Studying How States and Societies Transform and Constititute One Another*, Cambridge: Cambridge University Press.

Milner, H. (1992) 'International theories of cooperation among nations,' *World Politics* 44: 466–96.

Mohanty, C.T. (1993) 'Under western eyes: feminist scholarship and colonial discourses,' in P. Williams and L. Chrisman (eds), *Colonial Discourse and Post-Colonial Theory*, London: Harvester Wheatsheaf.

Molloy, S. (2003) 'The realist logic of international society,' *Cooperation and Conflict* 38: 83–99.

Moon, K. (1993) *Sex Among Allies: Military Prostitution in U.S.–Korea Relations*, New York: Columbia University Press.

Moore, M. (ed.) (1998) *National Self-Determination and Secession*, United Kingdom: Oxford University Press.

Moravcsik, A. (1997) 'Taking preferences seriously: a liberal theory of international politics,' *International Organization* 51: 513–53.

—— (2003) 'Theory synthesis in international relations: real not metaphysical,' *International Studies Review* 5: 131–3.

Morgenthau, H.J. (2005 [1948]) *Politics Among Nations*, 7th edn, New York: McGraw-Hill.

Mosley, L. (2005) 'Globalisation and the state: still room to move,' *New Political Economy* 10: 355–62.

Nandy, A. (1983) *The Intimate Enemy*, Delhi: Oxford University Press.

Nardin, T. (1985) *Law, Morality and the Nature of States*, Princeton, NJ: Princeton University Press.

—— (2005) 'Justice and coercion,' in A.J. Bellamy (ed.), *International Society and its Critics*, Oxford: Oxford University Press.

Nicolson, H. (1939) *Diplomacy*, London: Oxford University Press.

Niebuhr, R. (1940) *Christianity and Power Politics*, New York: Scribner's.

—— (2002 [1932]) *Moral Man and Immoral Society*, Westminster: John Knox Press.

Niou, E.M.S. and Ordeshook, P.C. (1994) ' "Less filling, tastes great", the realist–neoliberal debate,' *World Politics* 46: 209–34.

Norris, P. and Inglehart, R. (2004) *Sacred and Secular*, Cambridge: Cambridge University Press.

North, D.C. and Thomas, R.P. (1973) *The Rise of the Western World*, Cambridge: Cambridge University Press.

Nye, J.S. (2004) *Soft Power: The Means to Success in World Politics*, New York: Perseus.

Oakeshott, M. (1962) *Rationalism in Politics*, New York: Basic Books.

O'Brien, R. (1992) *Global Financial Integration*, London: Pinter.

Ogata, S. (1993) *Financing an Effective United Nations*, New York: Ford Foundation.

Ohmae, K. (1995) *The End of the Nation State*, London: Harper Collins.

O'Neill, O. (2000) *Bounds of Justice*, Cambridge: Cambridge University Press.

Orford, A. (2003) *Reading Humanitarian Intervention*, Cambridge: Cambridge University Press.

Organski, A.F.K. (1968) *World Politics*, 2nd edn, New York: Knopf.

—— and Kugler, J. (1980) *The War Ledger*, Chicago: University of Chicago Press.

Paolini, A.J. (1999) *Navigating Modernity: Postcolonialism, Identity and International Relations*, Boulder, CO: Lynne Rienner.

Paterson, M. (2005) 'Global environmental governance,' in A.J. Bellamy (ed.), *International Society and its Critics*, Oxford: Oxford University Press.

Patton, P. and Smith, T. (eds) (2001) *Jacques Derrida: Deconstruction Engaged*, Sydney: Power Publications.

Pauly, L.W. (1995) 'Capital mobility, state autonomy and political legitimacy,' *Journal of International Affairs* 48: 373–85.

Peterson, V.S. (2003) *A Critical Rewriting of Global Political Economy*, London: Routledge.

Petito, F. and Hatzopolous, P. (eds) (2003) *Religion in International Relations*, New York: Palgrave Macmillan.

Pettman, J.J. (1996) *Worlding Women: A Feminist International Politics*, Sydney: Allen and Unwin.

Philips, N. (2005) *Globalizing International Political Economy*, Basingstoke: Palgrave Macmillan.

Phillips, W. and Brown, W. (1991) *Making Sense of Your World*, Chicago: Moody Press.

Philpott, D. (2001) *Revolutions in Sovereignty*, Princeton, NJ: Princeton University Press.

Poggi, G. (1978) *The Development of the Modern State*, Stanford, CA: Stanford University Press.

Pogge, T.W. (2002) *Human Rights and World Poverty*, Oxford: Polity Press.

—— (ed.) (2001) *Global Justice*, Oxford: Blackwell Publishing.

Polanyi, K. (1957[1944]) *The Great Transformation*, Boston: Beacon Press.

Powell, R. (1991) 'Absolute and relative gains in international relations theory,' *American Political Science Review* 85: 1303–20.

—— (1994) 'Anarchy in international relations theory: the neorealist-neoliberal debate,' *International Organization* 48: 313–44.

Prakash, G. (1990) 'Writing post-orientalist histories of the third world,' *Comparative Studies in Society and History* 32: 383–408.

—— (1996) 'Who's afraid of postcoloniality?' *Social Text* 49: 187–203.

Price, R. and Reus-Smit, C. (1998) 'Dangerous liaisons? Critical international theory and constructivism,' *European Journal of International Relations* 4: 259–94.

Rae, H. (2002) *State Identities and the Homogenisation of Peoples*, Cambridge: Cambridge University Press.

Ralph, J. (2006) *America and the International Criminal Court*, Oxford: Oxford University Press.

Rasler, K. and Thompson, W.R. (2001) 'Malign autocracies and major power warfare: evil, tragedy, and international relations theory,' *Security Studies* 10: 46–79.

Rasmussen, D. (ed.) (1999) *The Handbook of Critical Theory*, Oxford: Blackwell Publishing.

Rawls, J. (1993) *Political Liberalism*, New York: Columbia University Press.

Ray, J.L. (2003) 'A Lakatosian view of the democratic peace research program,' in C. Elman and M.F. Elman (eds), *Progress in International Relations Theory*, Cambridge: the MIT Press.

Reus-Smit, C. (1996) 'Constructivism,' in S. Burchill (ed.), *Theories of International Relations*, Basingstoke: Palgrave.

—— (1999) *The Moral Purpose of the State*, Princeton, NJ: Princeton University Press.

—— (2001a) 'Human rights and the social construction of sovereignty,' *Review of International Studies* 27: 519–38.

—— (2001b) 'The strange death of liberal international theory,' *European Journal of International Law* 12: 573–94.

—— (2001c) 'Constructivism,' in S. Burchill, *et al.*, *Theories of International Relations*, 2nd edn, London: Palgrave.

—— (2002) 'Imagining society: constructivism and the English school,' *British Journal of Politics and International Relations* 4: 487–509.

—— (2004) *American Power and World Order*, Cambridge: Polity.

—— (2005) 'The constructivist challenge after September 11,' in A.J. Bellamy (ed.), *International Society and its Critics*, Oxford: Oxford University Press.

Richardson, J.L. (2001) *Contending Liberalisms in World Politics*, Boulder, CO: Lynne Rienner.

Ricks, T. (2006) *Fiasco: The American Military Adventure in Iraq*, New York: Penguin.

Robinson, W. (2004) *A Theory of Global Capitalism*, Baltimore: Johns Hopkins University Press.

Rorty, R. (1996) 'Who are we? Moral universalism and economic triage,' *Diogenes* 173: 5–15.

Rosamond, B. (2003) 'Babylon and on? Globalization and international political economy,' *Review of International Political Economy* 10: 661–71.

Rose, G. (1998) 'Review: neoclassical realism and theories of foreign policy,' *World Politics* 51: 144–72.

Rosecrance, R. (1982) 'Comments: reply to Waltz,' *International Organization* 36: 682–5.

Rosenau, J.N. (ed.) (1993) *Global Voices*, Boulder: Westview Press.

Rosenberg, J. (1994) *Empire of Civil Society*, London: Verso.

Rosow, S.J. (1994) 'On the political theory of political economy: conceptual ambiguity and the global economy,' *Review of International Political Economy* 1: 465–88.

Rotberg, R. (2002) 'Failed states in a world of terror,' *Foreign Affairs* 81: 127–40.

—— (ed.) (2004) *When States Fail: Causes and Consequences*, Princeton, NJ: Princeton University Press.

Rousseau, D.L. (2002) 'Motivations for choice: the salience of relative gains in international politics,' *Journal of Conflict Resolution* 46: 394–426.

Ruggie, J.G. (1993) 'Territoriality and beyond: problematizing modernity in international relations,' *International Organization* 47 (1): 139–74.

—— (1998) 'What makes the world hang together? Neoutilitarianism and the social constructivist challenge,' in J.G. Ruggie (ed.), *Constructing the World Polity: Essays on International Institutionalization*, London, Routledge.

Rupert, M. (1995) *Producing Hegemony*, Cambridge: Cambridge University Press

Russett, B. and O'Neal, J. (2001) *Triangulating Peace: Democracy, Interdependence, and International Organizations*, New York: Norton.

Sabrosky, Alan (ed.) (1985) *Polarity and War*, Boulder, CO: Westview Press.

Said, E. (1979) *Orientalism*, London: Penguin.

—— (1993) *Culture and Imperialism*, London: Vintage.

Sassen, S. (1996) 'The spatial organization of information industries: implications for the role of the state,' in J.H. Mittelman (ed.), *Globalization: Critical Reflections*, Boulder, CO: Lynne Rienner.

Sayer, D. (1991) *Capitalism and Modernity*, London: Routledge.

Schlesinger, A.M. (1974) *The Imperial Presidency*, London: Andre Deutsch.

Schmidt, B. (2002) 'On the history and historiography of international relations,' in W. Carlsnaes, T. Risse, and B. Simmons (eds), *Handbook of International Relations*, London: Sage.

Schwartz, H. (1994) *States versus Markets*, London: Macmillan Press.

Schwarzenberger, G. (1941) *Power Politics*, New York: Praeger.

Schweller, R.L. (1992) 'Domestic structure and preventive war: are democracies more Pacific?' *World Politics* 44: 235–69.

—— (1993) 'Tripolarity and the Second World War,' *International Studies Quarterly* 37: 73–103.

—— (1994) 'Bandwagoning for profit: bringing the revisionist state back in,' *International Security* 19: 72–107.

—— (1996) 'Neorealism's status-quo bias: what security dilemma?' *Security Studies* 5: 90–121.

—— (1998) *Deadly Imbalances: Tripolarity and Hitler's Strategy of World Conquest*, New York: Columbia University Press.

—— (2003) 'The progressiveness of neoclassical realism,' in C. Elman and M.F. Elman (eds), *Progress in International Relations Theory*, Cambridge, MA: MIT Press.

—— (2004) 'Unanswered threats – a neoclassical realist theory of underbalancing,' *International Security* 29: 159–201.

—— (2006) *Unanswered Threats: Political Constraints on the Balance of Power*, Princeton, NJ: Princeton University Press.

Scott, D. (1999) *Refashioning Futures: Criticism after Postcoloniality*, Princeton, NJ: Princeton University Press.

Scott, J. (1985) *Weapons of the Weak*, New Haven, CT: Yale University Press.

—— (1990) *Domination and the Art of Resistance*, New Haven, CT: Yale University Press.

Seabury, P. (1965) *Balance of Power*, San Francisco, CA: Chandler Publishing Co.

Seager, J. (2003) *The Penguin Atlas of Women in the World*, New York: Penguin Books.

Sellers, M. (ed.) (1996) *The New World Order: Sovereignty, Human Rights and the Self-Determination of Peoples*, Oxford: Berg.

Seth, S. (2000) 'A "postcolonial world"?' in G. Fry and J. O'Hagan (eds), *Contending Images of World Politics*, London: Macmillan.

Shapcott, R. (2001) *Justice, Community and Dialogue in International Relations*, Cambridge: Cambridge University Press.

—— (2004) 'Defining a classical approach: IR as practical philosophy,' *British Journal of Politics and International Relations* 6: 271–91.

Shapiro, M.J. (1997) *Violent Cartographies: Mapping Cultures of War*, Minneapolis, MN: University of Minnesota Press.

—— (2004) *Methods and Nations*, New York: Routledge.

—— and Alker, H.R. (eds) (1996) *Challenging Boundaries*, Minneapolis, MN: University of Minnesota Press.

Sheridan, A. (1980) *Michel Foucault: The Will to Truth*, London: Tavistock.

Shue, H. (1980) *Basic Rights: Subsistence, Affluence and US Foreign Policy*, Princeton, NJ: Princeton University Press.

Shuman, F. (1933) *International Politics*, New York: McGraw-Hill.

Simpson, G. (2004) *Great Powers and Outlaw States*, Cambridge: Cambridge University Press.

Singer, P. (1985) 'Famine, affluence and morality,' in C. Bietz, *et al.* (eds) *International Ethics*, Princeton, NJ: Princeton University Press.

—— (2002) *One World*, New Haven, CT: Yale University Press.

Smith, M.J. (1986) *Realist Thought from Weber to Kissinger*, Baton Rouge, LA: Louisiana State University Press.

Smith, S. (1995) 'The self-images of a discipline: a genealogy of international relations theory,' in K. Booth and S. Smith (eds), *International Relations Theory Today*, Cambridge: Polity.

——, Booth, K. and Zalewski, M. (eds) (1996) *International Theory: Positivism and Beyond*, Cambridge: Cambridge University Press.

Snidal, D. (1991a) 'International cooperation among relative gains maximizers,' *International Studies Quarterly* 35: 387–402.

—— (1991b) 'Relative gains and the pattern of international cooperation,' *American Political Science Review* 85: 701–26.

Snyder, J.L. (1985) 'Perceptions of the security dilemma in 1914,' in R. Jervis, *et al.* (eds), *Psychology and Deterrence*, Baltimore, NJ: Johns Hopkins University Press.

—— (1991) *Myths of Empire: Domestic Politics and International Ambition*, Ithaca, NY: Cornell University Press.

Soguk, N. (1999) *States and Strangers*, Minneapolis, MN: University of Minnesota Press.

Sørenson, G. (1997) 'An analysis of contemporary statehood: consequences for conflict and cooperation,' *Review of International Studies* 23: 253–69.

—— (2004) *The Transformation of the State*, Basingstoke: Palgrave Macmillan.

Spirtas, M. (1996) 'A house divided: tragedy and evil in realist theory,' *Security Studies* 5: 385–423.

Spivak, G.C. (1985) 'Subaltern studies: deconstructing historiography,' in R. Guha and G. Spivak (eds), *Subaltern Studies IV: Writing on South Asian History and Society*, Delhi: Oxford University Press.

—— (1988) 'Can the subaltern speak?' in C. Nelson and L. Grossberg (eds), *Marxism and the Interpretation of Culture*, Basingstoke: Macmillan.

—— (1990) 'The political economy of women as seen by a literary critic,' in E. Weed (ed.), *Coming to Terms*, London: Routledge.

—— (1999) *A Critique of Postcolonial Reason*, Cambridge, MA: Harvard University Press.

Spruyt, H. (1994) *The Sovereign State and Its Competitors*, Princeton, NJ: Princeton University Press.

—— (2002) 'The origins, development, and possible decline of the modern state,' *Annual Review of Political Science* 5: 127–49.

Steans, J. and Pettiford L. (2005) *Introduction to International Relations: Perspectives and Themes*, 2nd edn, Harlow: Pearson.

—— (2005) *Introduction to International Relations: Perspectives and Themes*, Harlow: Pearson.

Sterling-Folker, J. (ed.) (2006) *Making Sense of International Relations Theory*, Boulder, CO: Lynne Rienner.

Stern, M. (2005) *Naming Security, Constructing Identity*, Manchester: Manchester University Press.

Stilwell, F. (2002) *Political Economy: The Contest of Economic Ideas*, Melbourne: Oxford University Press.

Stirk, P.M.R. (1992) *Max Horkheimer: A New Interpretation*, Hemel Hempstead: Harvester Wheatsheaf.

Stoler, A.L. (1995) *Race and the Education of Desire*, Durham: Duke University Press.

Strange, S. (1970) 'International economics and international relations: a case of mutual neglect,' *International Affairs* 46: 304–15.

—— (1987) 'The persistent myth of lost hegemony,' *International Organization* 41: 551–74.

—— (1991) 'An eclectic approach,' in Craig Murphy and Roger Tooze (eds), *The New International Political Economy*, Boulder, CO: Lynne Rienner.

—— (1994) 'Wake up, Krasner! The world *has* changed,' *Review of International Political Economy* 1: 209–19.

—— (1995a) 'Political economy and international relations,' in K Booth and S. Smith (eds), *International Relations Theory Today*, Cambridge: Polity Press.

—— (1995b) 'The limits of politics,' *Government and Opposition* 30: 291–311.

—— (1996) *The Retreat of the State*, Cambridge: Cambridge University Press.

—— (2003) *States and Markets*, 2nd edn, London: Continuum.

Strassler, R.B. (ed.) (1996) *The Landmark Thucydides*, New York: The Free Press.

Straw, J. (2002) 'Failed and failing states,' speech to the European Research Institute, Birmingham, 6 September.

Suganami, H. (2005) 'The English School and international theory,' in A.J. Bellamy (ed.), *International Society and its Critics*, Oxford: Oxford University Press.

Tan, K.-C. (2000) *Toleration, Diversity and Global Justice*, Princeton, NJ: Princeton University Press.

—— (2004) *Justice Without Borders*, Cambridge: Cambridge University Press.

Tannenwald, N. (2005) 'Ideas and explanation: advancing the theoretical agenda,' *Journal of Cold War Studies* 7: 13–42.

Taylor, C. (1971) 'Interpretation and the sciences of man,' *Review of Metaphysics* 25: 3–51.

Teschke, B. (2003) *The Myth of 1648*, London: Verso.

Tesón, F. (2003) 'The liberal case for humanitarian intervention,' in J.L. Holzgrefe, and R.O. Keohane (eds), *Humanitarian Intervention: Ethical, Legal and Political Dilemmas*, Cambridge: Cambridge University Press.

Thucydides (1954) *History of the Peloponnesian War*, Harmondsworth: Penguin.

Tickner, J. (1997) 'You just don't understand: trouble engagements between feminists and IR theorists,' *International Studies Quarterly* 41: 611–32.

Tickner, J.A. (1992) *Gender in International Relations*, New York: Columbia University Press.

—— (2001) *Gendering World Politics*, New York: Columbia University Press.

Tilly, C. (1985) 'War making and state-making as organized crime,' in P.B. Evans *et al.* (eds), *Bringing the State Back In*, Cambridge: Cambridge University Press.

—— (1990) *Coercion, Capital and European States, AD 990–1990*, Oxford: Basil Blackwell.

Tormey, S. (2004) *Anticapitalism*, Oxford: Oneworld.

Torpey, J. (1998) 'Coming and going: on the state monopolization of the legitimate "means of movement",' *Sociological Theory* 16: 39–259.

True, J. (2005) 'Feminism,' in A.J. Bellamy (ed.), *International Society and its Critics*, Oxford: Oxford University Press.

Turner, B.S. (1996) *The Body and Society*, London: Sage.

Underhill, G.R.D. (1994) 'Conceptualising the changing global order,' in G.R.D. Underhill and R. Stubbs (eds), *Political Economy and the Changing Global Order*, London: Macmillan.

—— (2000) 'State, market, and global political economy: genealogy of an (inter-?) discipline,' *International Affairs* 76: 805–24.

US Government (2001) *The National Security Strategy of the United States of America*, Washington, DC: The White House.

Van Creveld, M. (1999) *The Rise and Decline of the State*, New York: Cambridge University Press.

Van Evera, S. (1999) *Causes of War: The Structure of Power and the Roots of War*, Ithaca, NY: Cornell University Press.

Vasquez, J.A. (1997) 'The realist paradigm and degenerative versus progressive research programs,' *American Political Science Review* 91: 899–912.

—— and Elman, C. (eds) (2003) *Realism and the Balancing of Power: A New Debate*, Upper Saddle River, NJ: Prentice Hall.

Vincent, R.J. (1974) *Nonintervention and International Order*, Princeton, NJ: Princeton University Press.

—— (1981) 'The Hobbesian tradition in twentieth century international thought,' *Millennium: Journal of International Studies* 10: 91–101.

—— (1983) 'Change in international relations,' *Review of International Studies* 9: 63–70.

—— (1986) *Human Rights and International Relations*, Cambridge: Cambridge University Press.

Waever, O. (1996) 'The rise and fall of the inter-paradigm debate,' in S. Smith, K. Booth and M. Zalewski (eds), *International Theory: Positivism and Beyond*, Cambridge: Cambridge University Press.

Walker, R.B.J. (1993) *Inside/Outside: International Relations as Political Theory*, Cambridge: Cambridge University Press.

Wallerstein, I. (1974) *The Modern World-System* (Volume One), San Diego, CA: Academic Press.

Waltz, S.M. (1954) *Man, the State and War*, New York: Columbia University Press.

—— (1979) *Theory of International Politics*, Reading, MA: Addison-Wesley.

—— (1987) *The Origins of Alliances*, Ithaca, NY: Cornell University Press.

—— (1988) 'Testing theories of alliance formation: the case of southwest Asia,' *International Organization* 42: 275–316.

—— (1991) 'Alliance formation in southwest Asia: balancing and bandwagoning in Cold War competition,' in R. Jervis and J. Snyder (eds), *Dominoes and Bandwagons*, New York: Oxford University Press.

—— (1992a) 'Revolution and war,' *World Politics* 44: 321–68.

—— (1992b) 'Alliances, threats, and US grand strategy: a reply to Kaufman and Labs,' *Security Studies* 1: 448–82.

—— (1996) *Revolution and War*, Ithaca, NY: Cornell University Press.

—— (1996) 'International politics is not foreign policy,' *Security Studies* 6: 54–7.

—— (1999) 'Globalization and governance,' *Political Science and Politics* 32:

—— (2000) 'Containing rogues and renegades: coalition strategies and counterproliferation,' in V.A. Utgoff (ed.), *The Coming Crisis: Nuclear Proliferation, U.S. Interests and World Order*, Cambridge, MA: Cambridge University Press.

—— (2002) 'The enduring relevance of the realist tradition,' in I. Katznelson and H.V. Milner (eds), *Political Science: State of the Discipline*, New York: Norton.

Walzer, M. (1994) *Thick and Thin – Moral Argument at Home and Abroad*, Notre Dame: University of Notre Dame Press.

—— (2000) *Just and Unjust Wars*, 2nd edn, New York: Basic Books.

—— (2004) *Arguing about War*, New Haven: Yale University Press.

Watson, A. (1984) *Diplomacy: The Dialogue Between States*, London: Routledge.

—— (1992) *The Evolution of International Society*, London: Routledge.

Wayman, F. (1984) 'Bipolarity and war: the role of capability concentration and alliance patterns among major powers 1816–1965,' *Journal of Peace Research* 21: 25–42.

Weber, M. (1919) 'Science as a vocation,' in H. Gerth and C. Wright Mills (eds), *From Max Weber: Studies in Sociology*, New York: Oxford University Press.

Weiss, L. (ed.) (2003) *States in the Global Economy*, Cambridge: Cambridge University Press.

Welch, D.A. (2003) 'Why international relations theorists should stop reading Thucydides,' *Review of International Studies* 29: 301–20.

Weldes, J. (1999) Cultures of Insecurity, Minneapolis, MN: University of Minnesota Press.

Welsh, J. (2003) 'I is for ideology: conservatism in international affairs,' *Global Society*. 17: 165–85.

Wendt, A. (1987) 'The agent-structure problem in international relations,' *International Organization* 41: 335–70.

—— (1992) 'Anarchy is what states make of it: the social construction of power politics,' *International Organization* 46: 391–425.

—— (1994) 'Collective identity formation and the international state,' *American Political Science Review* 88: 395–421.

—— (1999) *Social Theory of International Politics*, Cambridge: Cambridge University Press.

—— (2000) 'On the via media: a response to the critics,' *Review of International Studies* 26: 165–80.

Wheeler, N.J. (1992) 'Pluralist or solidarist conceptions of international society: Bull and Vincent on humanitarian intervention,' *Millennium: Journal of International Studies* 21: 463–87.

—— (2000) *Saving Strangers*, Oxford: Oxford University Press.

—— (2003) 'The Bush doctrine: the dangers of American exceptionalism in a revolutionary age,' *Asian Perspective* 27: 183–216.

Whitworth, S. (2004) *Men, Militarism and UN Peacekeeping*, Boulder: Lynne Rienner.

Wiggershaus, R. (1994) *The Frankfurt School*, Cambridge: Cambridge University Press.

Wight, M. (1946) *Power Politics*, London: Royal Institute of International Affairs.

—— (1966) 'Why is there no international theory?' in H. Butterfield and M. Wight (eds), *Diplomatic Investigations*, London: Allen and Unwin.

—— (1977) *Systems of States*, edited and introduced by H. Bull, Leicester: Leicester University Press.

—— (1979) *Power Politics*, 2nd edn, London: Penguin.

—— (1987) 'An anatomy of international thought,' *Review of International Studies* 13: 221–7.

—— (1991) *International Theory: The Three Traditions*, London: Leicester University Press.

Williams, A. (1997) 'The postcolonial flaneur and other fellow travellers: conceits for a narrative of redemption,' *Third World Quarterly* 18: 821–41.

Williams, M.C. (1996) 'Hobbes and international relations: a reconsideration,' *International Organization* 50: 213–36.

—— (2005) *The Realist Tradition and the Limits of International Relations*, Cambridge: Cambridge University Press.

—— and Neumann, I.B. (2000) 'From alliance to security community: NATO, Russia, and the power of identity,' *Millennium: Journal of International Studies* 29: 357–87.

Williams, P.D. (2005) 'Critical security studies,' in A.J. Bellamy (ed.), *International Society and its Critics*, Oxford: Oxford University Press.

Wilson, P. (1989) 'The English School of International Relations: a reply to Sheila Grader,' *Review of International Studies* 15: 49–58.

Wivel, A. (2005) 'Explaining why state x made a certain move last Tuesday: the promise and limitations of realist foreign policy analysis,' *Journal of International Relations and Development* 8: 355–80.

Wohlforth, W.C. (1993) *The Elusive Balance: Power and Perceptions During the Cold War*, Ithaca: Cornell University Press.

Wolf, E. (1982) *Europe and the People Without History*, Berkeley, CA: University of California Press.

Wolfers, A. (1962) *Discord and Collaboration: Essays on International Politics*, Baltimore, MD: Johns Hopkins Press.

Wollstonecraft, M. (1792) *A Vindication of the Rights of Women*, Boston: Peter Edes.

Wood, E. (2003) *Empire of Capital*, London: Verso.

Wright, S. (2002) *Storming Heaven*, London: Pluto.

Wriston, W. (1992) *The Twilight of Sovereignty*, New York: Scribner.

Wyn Jones, R. (1999) *Security, Strategy and Critical Theory*, Boulder, CO: Lynne Rienner.

—— (ed.) (2001) *Critical Theory and World Politics*, Boulder, CO: Lynne Rienner.

Young, R. (2001) *Postcolonialism: An Historical Introduction*, Oxford: Basil Blackwell.

Youngs, G. (2004) 'Feminist international relations,' *International Affairs* 80: 75–88.

Zakaria, F. (1998) *From Wealth to Power*, Princeton, NJ: Princeton University Press.

Zalewski, M. and Parpart, J. (eds) (1998) *The 'Man' Question in International Relations*, Boulder, CO: Westview Press.

Zehfuss, M. (2002) *Constructivism in International Relations: The Politics of Reality*, Cambridge: Cambridge University Press.

Zizek, S. (1991) *Looking Awry*, Cambridge, MA: MIT Press.

—— (1992) *Enjoy Your Symptom: Jacques Lacan in Hollywood and Out*, New York: Routledge.

Zolberg, A. (1981) 'Origins of the modern world-system: a missing link,' *World Politics* 33: 253–81.

Index

International Relations: The Key Concepts

Routledge Key Guides

Martin Griffiths, Griffith University, Australia, **Terry O'Callaghan**, University of South Australia and **Steven C. Roach**, University of South Florida, USA

International Relations: The Key Concepts is certain to be a considerable success.
Michael Banks, London School of Economics, UK

This is an excellent volume. Students in an introductory course are likely to find it an invaluable resource; more advanced students are likely to find it a worthwhile reference to have handy.
David Edelstein, Georgetown University, USA

Featuring over twenty new entries, *International Relations: The Key Concepts*, now in its second edition, is the essential guide for anyone interested in international affairs. Comprehensive and up-to-date, it introduces the most important themes in international relations in the post 9/11 era.

Key areas cover international criminal law, human rights, the developing world (the Arab League, African Union), globalization and strategic studies. New entries include:

- The English School
- The Digital Divide
- The War on Terror
- The Bush Doctrine
- The International Criminal Court
- Legitimacy
- Global warming
- Unilateralism
- The Organization of Petroleum-Exporting Countries (OPEC).

Featuring suggestions for further reading as well as a unique guide to web sites on international relations, this accessible guide is an invaluable aid to an understanding of this expanding field and is ideal for the student and non-specialist alike.

October 2007: 216x138: 424pp
Hb: 978-0-415-77436-9: **£60.00 / $120.00**
Pb: 978-0-415-77437-6: **£14.95 / $26.95**

Routledge
Taylor & Francis Group

www.routledge.com/politics